The Psychology of Genocide

Genocide has tragically claimed the lives of over 262 million victims in the last century. Jews, Armenians, Cambodians, Darfurians, Kosovars, Rwandans, the list seems endless. Clinical psychologist Steven K. Baum sets out to examine the psychological patterns to these atrocities. Building on trait theory as well as social psychology, he reanalyzes key conformity studies (including the famous experiments of Ash, Milgram, and Zimbardo) to bring forth a new understanding of identity and emotional development during genocide. Baum presents a model that demonstrates how people's actions during genocide actually mirror their behavior in everyday life: there are those who destroy (perpetrators), those who help (rescuers), and those who remain uninvolved, positioning themselves between the two extremes (bystanders). Combining eyewitness accounts with Baum's own analysis, this book reveals the common mental and emotional traits among perpetrators, bystanders, and rescuers, and how a war between personal and social identity accounts for these divisions.

STEVEN K. BAUM is a Lecturer in the Department of Psychology at the University of New Mexico. He is the book review editor for the *Journal of Hate Studies* and author of *When Fairy Tales Kill?: Origins and Transmission of Antisemitic Beliefs* (2008).

The Psychology of Genocide

Perpetrators, Bystanders, and Rescuers

STEVEN K. BAUM

CAMBRIDGE
UNIVERSITY PRESS

CAMBRIDGE UNIVERSITY PRESS
Cambridge, New York, Melbourne, Madrid, Cape Town, Singapore, São Paulo, Delhi

Cambridge University Press
The Edinburgh Building, Cambridge CB2 8RU, UK

Published in the United States of America by Cambridge University Press, New York

www.cambridge.org
Information on this title: www.cambridge.org/9780521713924

First published 2008

Printed in the United Kingdom at the University Press, Cambridge

A catalogue record for this publication is available from the British Library

Library of Congress Cataloguing in Publication data
Baum, Steven K., 1953–
    The psychology of genocide: perpetrators, bystanders, and rescuers /
Steven K. Baum.
        p.   cm.
    Includes bibliographical references and index.
    ISBN 978-0-521-88631-4 (hardback) – ISBN 978-0-521-71392-4 (pbk.)
    1. Genocide.   I. Title.
    HV6322.7.B378 2008
    304.6'63–dc22   2007052914

ISBN 978-0-521-88631-4 hardback
ISBN 978-0-521-71392-4 paperback

For Audrey Hummelen to honor Bert Hummelen,
And to the rescuers, *alles goeie mensen* – those good people
who live above hate.

To be human is to recognize the cultural perspectives that bind us to a tribe, sect, religion, or nation and to rise above them.

David Krieger, Nuclear Age Peace Foundation

Contents

Figures

Tables

Acknowledgments

This book could not have been written without the professional guidance of Gail Stanger, Franklin and Marcia Littell of Holocaust and the Churches. Thanks to James Waller of Whitworth College and Joanie Eppinga for her masterful editing of earlier drafts, Gonazaga University's George Critchlow, Jeri Shepard and the staff at the *Journal of Hate Studies*. Additional thanks to Steven L. Jacobs for his encouragement via the International Association of Genocide Scholars. I am also appreciative of Frederick Schweitzer, Seth Schwartz, Jeff Rudski, Israel Charny, Robert Carom, Amer Menkara, Paddy Rawal, Dennis Jackson, Saul Nosenchuk, Ryan Eastwood, John Emory Bush, Martin Gilbert, Shimon Samules, and Hubert Locke for reading drafts, and for data from Peter Fleissner of the European Monitoring Centre on Racism and Xenophobia, Vienna, and for interviews with Pieter Broersma, Marion Pritchard, Rudy Florian, as well as the librarian Sara Grosveld at the Vidal Sassoon International Center for the Study of Antisemitism, Hebrew University, Jerusalem; Mary Vergowven at the Dorsch Branch of the Monroe County Library; and Denine Parker at the Juan Tabo branch of the Albuquerque Public Library.

This book could not have been published without the foresight of Andrew Peart, Carrie Cheek, and Elizabeth Davey at Cambridge University Press, and the reviewers' helpful suggestions.

This book could not have been written without the unflagging support of Kawagamites, Chathamites, and Windsorites Stephen Winbaum, Dan & Ruth Winbaum, Karen Tabachnick, Jimmy Heller, Ron "R. J." Barb and Silver, Patty and Muriam Muroff, Bonnie L. Croll, Lampie/Cuddles; Lisa Taylor, Paul Nesseth, Jim Seltz, Joel Sekely, Joe Hindin, Karen Petersen, Alex McKee, Rose Burko, Jordan, Shaina and Josh, Elizabeth Isack,

Henry & Rita Muroff, Herb Willis, Jack Kahn, Eve Kahn, Ken Carte, and Jan Williams, Harvey Kessler, Sandi Malowitz, Mark and Randi Biederman, Paul Adams, George Bernstein, Mark and Melinda Harris, Mary Linda Murphy, Gay, Drs. John, Nick, and Bill Pignanelli, Robert Glanz, Carmine Marotta and Mazel, Diane "DeDe" Lampe, Helen Sharpe, and Betty Baum, Sylvia Baum, Ginette Baum, Jack Baum, and Alice Nemeth, Lisa Isack, Lauree Pasquilito, John Pasquilito, Pat Duronio, Morris Paulson, Joel Barkoff, Julianna Lerner, Annette Pont-Gwire, Diana Trivax, Ruth & Irwin Kahn, Beth Greenbaum, Madie Weingarten, Neal Rosenberg, Darlene Kopke, Sue Bellino, Bonnie Frederick, Annette Sherry, coach Laury Dworet, and spiritual supporters Vince Vanlimbeek and Lois Liedel. *Hartelijk bedankt* to Audrey's *familie inzonderheid* Mary Hummelen, Andrew, Tena, Greg, Robert, Rebecca and Michael Hummelen, Oom Koos and Tante Anya Hummelen, Bert and Judith Hummelen, Heleen and Henk Van Zuiden, Tante Rennie Hummelen, Oom Hittjo and Tante Ria Hummelen, Jacob and Adriana Bax and the whole Bax family, Uncle Jake and Tante Rennie Hulzebos. Back in Southwestern Ontario – the usual Theatre Kent suspects Norm McLeod, Bill Shaw, Dennis O'Neil, Ruthie Baleka, Sharon and Leonard Jubenville and other friends, Robert Fox, Jack Carroll, Rick and Annette Birmingham, Cheryl Crawford, Cammie Mathers, Lu-Ann Cowell, Penny Harper, Chisanga Puta-Chekwe, Evelyn Dodds, Terry Torrence and Bryan Chambers, Bryan and Shannon Prince and, of course, Richard Howard and Audrey who live this from Les Mis:

To love another person is to see the face of God.

Introduction

As I walked into the Los Angeles Museum of Tolerance at the Simon Wiesenthal Center, I was confronted with a choice of two doors: one was marked *Prejudiced,* while the second door was marked *Not Prejudiced.* With the best of intentions, all visitors try to enter through the second door and cannot, as that door remains permanently locked. Consequently all must pass through the prejudiced door. Initial perplexed looks soon subside giving way to the realization that all of us harbor prejudiced and hateful beliefs. Visitors are left to explore more of their assumptions as they move through a maze of photographs and exhibitions.

Meandering through the gallery of inhumane indignity, I saw something else – a look in the eyes of those in the photographs. Several of the photos seemed to capture a feeling state that appeared quite distinct and quite different from others. The eyes of the perpetrators had a mocking and gleeful quality to them. By contrast, the eyes of others who were helping the victims held an alertness, alacrity, and kindness. And a third group's eyes remained a mystery; they appeared to be staring into space as if they were watching the whole thing on television.

The victim's eyes were all the same – sad and scared. I did not know any of them but through an austere museum's exhibit sixty years later our eyes locked and they asked me a question – why? Why was it that in the hell called the Holocaust, some people rescued and others maimed and the majority remained immobilized?

Note: I have all but avoided the term "evil" since it carries religious and philosophical overtones. Instead I would offer the idea that in a population there will be some who will be perpetrators, and they will harm innocents.

"It is easier to denature plutonium than to denature the evil spirit of man," said Albert Einstein. I didn't think so. For several years in Canada I worked for the Ministry of Corrections, often noting that the dark side of people had more to do with pedestrian psychological processes than an ethereal "evil." By the same token, when one looks towards traditional psychiatry and psychology for answers regarding genocide, one finds none. Even Sigmund Freud once wrote to a colleague regarding antisemitism and threw in his hat: "mankind on the average and taken by and large are a wretched lot." Several months later he was proven right as he and his daughter Anna narrowly escaped his beloved Vienna for London, never to return or to speak about it again.[1]

Before it had a name, Holocaust research by the mid-1960s was the interest of a select few historians who believed something major had occurred and began to document the event. While the first wave of researchers had searched for flaws in the German character and culture, this next wave of researchers looked more towards situational determinants. About that time, psychologists' attentions began turning towards the social psychological forces involved in prejudice.

The search for a German national character, as with all national character research, proved futile. It was not until psychology began to focus on ordinary people that an understanding of such horrors shifted from character to cultural setting, though it would take another decade or two to fully integrate the research on ordinary people into a comprehensive understanding of genocide.

Conformity was key to understanding how people were seduced by the power of the situation. Yet, the social psychological approach had its limitations as well. For instance, social psychologists often gave short shrift when findings contained anything that

---

[1] Freud never spoke about genocide though, through a series of letters to Einstein in 1931–1932, he tried to explain the purpose of war in "Why War?" See O. Nathan & H. Norden (1960) *Einstein on peace.* New York: Schocken Books, pp. 186–203.

resembled a "trait" component. Like an allergy, the researchers interpreted their findings to avoid, downplay, or explain away that which would have anything to do with the personality.

Let me provide an example. In the often-cited Milgram study, most (65 percent) subjects were prepared to shock one another into unprecedented levels of danger and alleged death. A small group even forced the resisting victim's hand down onto a shock plate. According to social psychology, the fate of humankind was sealed. We are all genocidalists. Put the average person in a similar situation and they will "just follow orders."

While it is frightening to think that most (65 percent) people will comply with a legitimate authority's request to injure another, that was not the whole story. Downplayed were the findings that *one third of the subjects*, and another third in other key conformity experiments, *defied* the researcher's demands to harm one another. In fact, some delayed or sabotaged or went out of their way to help those they thought would be victims. While not a formal cover-up, an important finding received subsequent attention – those who defied Dr. Milgram's orders had a constellation of personality traits that revealed a bigger story. These *defiant traits* appear as polar opposite to the *obedients* – those who followed orders and continued to shock another to a lethal level. "I am certain," concluded lead researcher Stanley Milgram, "that there is a complex personality basis to obedience and disobedience. But I know we have not found it."[2]

What Milgram had yet to discover was that those who defied authority, those who questioned him and chose to stop, those who were not as vulnerable to the social forces were more *emotionally developed*. The converse was equally as true. Those who were

---

[2] S. Milgram (1974) *Obedience to authority*. New York: Harper & Row, p. 205. Also see A. C. Elms & S. Milgram (1966) Personality characteristics associated with obedience and defiance toward authoritative command. *Journal of Experimental Research in Personality*, 1, 282–289; L. Kohlberg (1969) Stage and sequence: The cognitive-developmental approach to socialization. In D. A. Goslin (ed.), *Handbook of socialization theory and research* (347–480). Chicago: Rand-McNally.

compliant and conformed to the experimenter's orders and "just followed orders" were less emotionally developed. Between both those extremes lay a middle group who were moderately developed and ranged between the two extremes. Milgram's elusive "complex personality basis" of conformity appeared to be linked directly to emotional development. But what is emotional development?

As Stanley Milgram was lamenting the complexity of obedience findings, a research psychologist named Jane Loevinger and her colleagues at St. Louis's Washington University were developing a separate line of research called ego development. Ego development theory suggested that people complied and conformed based on how mature they were.

Maturity for the average person is generally defined socially. For developmentalists, maturity has to do with nuances of cultural conformity, ideas that were a bit ahead of their time. Even today there is more evidence and budding data, but mainstream psychology rarely mentions the name Jane Loevinger. Part of the problem is that the instrument she developed to measure maturity, the Sentence Completion Test (WUSCT) was cumbersome, unwieldy and difficult to score, making it an unlikely tool for dissertation work and related scientific use.

Yet, at the same time, there was plenty of related research data to back up Loevinger's theory and findings, especially in development, e.g. adult development, lifespan development, moral development, cognitive development, and religious development.

Loevinger's theory and research findings are actually quite simple and can be understood as follows – in terms of development, we are not all equal. Regarding maturity, some of us grow, some of us flounder, and in others growth remains stunted. In a general population, Loevinger said the vast majority of adults are somewhere in between the middle and lowest echelons of maturation.

While Loevinger's research did not address genocide per se, her research pointed towards the same psychological processes I had observed at the genocide exhibition. People who were emotionally developed were more independent minded – they conformed less to their social group and surrounding culture. People who were emotionally developed functioned at the highest levels of living. In civilian life, they helped others much more than the average person. In genocide, they rescued.

Conversely, the opposite was true of those in the least emotionally developed group. The least evolved people were the ones who were most likely to adhere to social standards and tradition. These were the ones who most closely identified with their social group and were more susceptible to the culture's norms. The less emotionally developed people were the ones who would comply with orders. In daily life, they ranged from misfits to true believers. In genocide, such persons would turn in Jews, round up the Gypsies and shoot Tutsis on sight. Like Milgram had suggested, all that was required was an authority (state, church, popular opinion) to deem the killing legitimate or, in the case of copycat killing, just the perception of permission.

While the proportions of each of these groups in a population can be debated, there is usually little debate on those who are midpoint between the two extremes. Bystanders constitute the majority of any population and are characterized by their moderate stance between the highly conforming perpetrators and the independently minded rescuers. Bystanders appear to play it safe by alternating between the two extremes.[3] Yet they are wrong. There is no stance that is safe.

Disparities of all sorts (e.g. economic, educational) exist in life, but such disparities do not account for hate, terrorism, and genocide. While prejudice seems to decrease with education and income, only emotional development can explain the following exceptions – some very educated and wealthy people hate and prepare for jihads and genocides. By contrast, some very poor and uneducated people know to "do the right thing," helping where they can and rescuing. The

---

[3] S. K. Baum (2004) A bell curve of hate. *Journal of Genocide Research*, 6, 118–132.

great spiritual teachers have suggested the same thing – life's inequalities were never so much about racial, economic, religious, or cultural differences, as about levels of conscious awareness.

I ask the reader's indulgence with some aspects of my model as levels of emotional development are difficult to see and even harder to prove. At the time of writing, Jane Loevinger has emeritus status from Washington University and though her ideas are esteemed, outside of adult development her work is largely unknown. Hampered by small numbers of subjects and unpublished doctoral dissertations, her work is yet to be introduced into those disciplines that currently dominate genocide studies. Many of the ideas that appear in this book are based on other nascent survey research studies as well.

Genocide experts write about the causes of genocide from a top-down approach, e.g. utopia or authoritarian regimes. By contrast, this study is a bottom-up perspective of genocide that has to do with what the average person thinks and how they act when the rules change or in the absence of rules.

The top-down genocide theorists would tell you that manipulative elites orchestrate genocide from the get-go and they may be correct in that genocides seem to be led by demagogues, some charismatic and others not so charming: Stalin (Russia), Mao/Chiang Kai-shek (China/Taiwan), Tojo (Japan), Agha Mohammed Yahya Khan (East Pakistan now Bangladesh), Pol Pot (Cambodia), Milosevic (Yugoslavia), Hitler (Germany), to name a few. But from a bottom-up analysis, by the time a demagogue has emerged on the scene, he is preaching to the converted. From this perspective, Hitler and his ilk said nothing new, nothing that the *volk* hadn't heard before. For years, people had retained all the social myths about Jews in the back of their minds. Such myths were reflected in fairy tales (the Grimms' *Jew in the Bush*), children's rhymes, state-sponsored statues (such as the Judensau) and church-sanctioned pilgrimage sites that honored sainthood for children martyred by "The Jews." Like a good populist, Hitler echoed what everyone "knew." It was as if God had read their minds.

Manipulative leaders will always exist, but they cannot succeed without the support of a following. Without the masses, without the support of ordinary people, a demagogue's diatribe would be dismissed as the rantings of a madman on his soapbox. Whether the soapbox is in Central Park, Hyde Park, or Dam Square matters not. "What really matters," observes Bard College's Ian Buruma, "is that the seductive quality of hate appeals to the average person's irrational fears, their vanities, their greed and their blood lust."[4]

This book focuses exclusively on identity formation and membership in each of three groups: perpetrators, bystanders, and rescuers. Chapter 1 presents an overview of the current state of research and pleads a case for an adult developmental perspective. Chapter 2 begins to fashion an answer by proposing a normal population or bell curve of hate and rescue and linking it to perpetrators, bystanders, and rescuers. To better understand how each of these categories form, the psychological makeup of perpetrators, bystanders, and rescuers is delineated in the next three chapters. Chapter 3 explores the genocidal proclivities inherent in ethnic fundamentalists, religious fanatics and political ideologues – those that have become known in and out of genocide research as the perpetrators. Chapter 4 extends the inquiry into an examination of bystander psychology and the ease of transition into provisional perpetrator or rescuing mode. Chapter 5 highlights those who function at the highest levels of psychological health, examining why rescuers function as they do. The final chapter summarizes the material and invites the reader to ponder whether it is the individual or culture (or both) that needs to develop beyond the fray of social forces.

Like all other genocide scholars, I am trying to find a cure for the malignacy of hate. Often the evening news reminds us of the pervasiveness of jihadi terrorism and the genocidal mindset it

---

[4] I. Buruma: see *New York Times Book Review* 12/10/2000, p. 13. For an interesting parallel between 9/11 and World War II Japanese rationale of war against the West see Ian Buruma and Avishai Margalit (2002) Occidentalism. In *New York Review of Books* 1/17/02, pp. 4–7.

engenders. Usually we just shake our heads and resign ourselves to the notion that this oldest and most primitive form of relating is here to stay. What has changed is that the scientific inquiry into hate and genocide has come of age. Perhaps, this time, a developmental approach can lead us to do something about it. From such a perspective – the only way out is up.

Prologue

The history of the world is a history of hate and genocide. At one level, it is difficult to deny this reality. In the 1980s, anthropologists in Belgium found more than 30 wounded, battered, and perforated skulls, of men, women, and children, believed to be at least 7,000 years old.[1] And while ethnic conflict and group hatred may not be the only motives for war, such enmity seems to play a large part in most armed conflicts around the world. Only 16 of the world's 193 countries currently remain untouched by war. At any given time, an average of 50 nations are engaged in armed conflict, with some employing children as young as 6 years of age in combat.[2]

But the actual investigation, cataloguing, and defining of genocide is very recent. Following attorney/survivor Raphael Lemkin's (1900–1959) lead, Article 2 of the United Nation's *Convention on the Prevention and Punishment of the Crime of Genocide* defines genocide as:

> any of the following acts committed with intent to destroy, in whole or in part, a national, ethnic, racial or religious group, as such: Killing members of the group; Causing serious bodily or mental harm to members of the group; Deliberately inflicting on the group conditions of life calculated to bring about its physical destruction in whole or in part; Imposing measures intended to prevent births within the group; and forcibly transferring children of the group to another group.[3]

At this time, Lemkin's United Nations definition remains the most widely accepted, even with its limitations. Definitional limits notwithstanding, we can see that the cost of genocide over the past century is particularly high. While the victims' only "crime" was their identity as members of the "wrong" social group, e.g. in religion, race, culture or politics, the effects are particularly lethal. With fifteen major genocides, and non-combat victims estimated at more than a quarter billion, the twentieth century has the dubious honor of being the bloodiest.

Experts remain uncertain about how to acknowledge unrecognized genocides, e.g. South American colonization death rates (13–30 million), and what to make of the more recent state governments' La Violencia (1970–1990s) campaigns, which made an estimated 3,000 Chileans, 30,000 Argentinians, 180,000 Colombians, and 200,000 Guatemalans simply "disappear."

Then there are the estimated third of Armenians (2.5 million) who marched their way to death in the Syrian Desert. Should you speak to a Turk national, you would be told that the claims of genocide are exaggerated or wholly fabricated. Armenians understandably, had a different experience.

What is to be made of the various colonizations which took an estimated 10,000 Sudanese, 64,000 of 80,000 Namibian Herero, and 4 million Congolese? What of the lesser known South African Dutch (25,000 Boer) who died in what may have been the first concentration camps by the English? What of Cambodia's Tonle Sap and other massacres not well known? At one point, the US government offered bounties on the heads of Native Americans, and Central and South Americans.

"Many of the problems we have today are because of hatred," observed the Dalai Lama, in exile in northern India since his own nation of Tibet was occupied in 1959. A little over a decade ago, cards identifying people as White, Black, Indian or Colored (mixed race) reduced the civil rights for South Africans, Coloreds and Asians. Such apartheid notions were believed to be natural, and ordained by God. Such thinking paved the way for assimilation efforts by their Commonwealth cousins. In Australia, from 1910 to 1970, 55,000 Aboriginal children were adopted out to white Christian citizens; these children are now known as the stolen generations. Public policy dictated that "half caste children should be taken from their kin and land in order to be made white."

Canada fared no better with church-managed efforts to meet government mandates of "getting the Indian out." By the 1970s, assimilation efforts ground to a halt due to widespread physical, sexual, and emotional abuse. The government and several church officials, including the Pope and Archbishop of Canterbury, quickly issued apologies. Part-Mohawk and part-Potawatomi Mona Stonefish Jacobs, age 54, recounts her experience.

> I grew up on a reservation where the residential school tried to rape our minds by giving us a different language and culture. The missionaries told us we were savages. "Be Christian," they said and "act like Europeans." They told us to be passive and accept it and if we didn't we would go to Hell and burn. That we should intermarry. They even went so far as to tell us that our skin would become White and our eyes blue and we would be better for it. It was all bullshit – psychological warfare to keep us docile. My grandfather said one day there will be people with no eyes and no ears and he meant the selfish Europeans. There are only the aboriginal and the visitor. If we step into their ship, we lose our canoe.

Currently, India's 160 million Dalits (untouchables) remain without civil rights, unable to attend university or hold government positions because of the crime of having been born into the wrong caste. Civil rights have yet to be granted to many of Europe's Roma/ Gypsies. There are over a hundred UN resolutions for the Palestinian people and none for the 750,000 Jews ejected from Arab lands when Israel declared independence.[4] Misogynist practices that undermine dignity as well as life are widespread, for example as in honor deaths (family killing of a daughter for bringing a dishonor, usually sexual); stoning for female infidelity; female genital mutilation (FGM) of 100–140 million women; unenforced dowry laws (torturing new wives); sati (immolation due to family dishonor); and acid thrown in women's faces in Asia, Africa, and the Middle East.

Table 1 *Partial list of twentieth-century genocides*

77 million Mao communists (35 million (PRC) 1949–1987+ famine 38
  million + 3.5 million Sino–Japanese Civil War (1923–1949))
60–70 million Stalinized Russians (includes 0.4 million Chechen-Ingush
  + 0.2 million Tartar + 3 million Ukrainians +10.5 million Slavs)
  (1917–1987)
6.0 million Jews (one in three) (Nazi Germany)
4.0 million Belgium colonized Congolese. 3 million multinational
  Congolese (current)
3.0 million Bangladeshis during secession from Pakistan (1971)
3.0 million Poles (Nazi Germany)
2.5 million Ethnic German expulsion in Poland and Czechoslovakia
  (Nazi Germany)
2.0 million North Koreans
1.5 million Afghans
1.5–2.0 million Sudanese (Islamic–Christian conflict)
1–2 million Cambodians via Khmer Rouge (one in three)(1975–1979)
1.4 million Armenians (1915) (excludes 100,000 (1895) and
  30,000 (1909))
1.0 million Tibetans (one in five)
1.0 million Nigerian Ibos
850,000 Tutsis/Hutus (1990s)
0.5–1 million Sinti Romani (Nazi Germany)
0.5–1 million Indonesian communists (1966)/200,000 E. Timorese (one in
  three)(1980s–1990s)
500,000 Angolans (Civil War)
300,000 Darfur Sudanese Black non-Muslims (2003–)
250,000 Chinese (Nanking, 1937)
250,000 Yugoslavs and 100,000 former Bosnians (1990s)
250,000 Burundians
200,000–500,000 Ugandans (Idi Amin critics)
200,000 Ethiopians (Dergue Red Terror, 1974–1991)
200,000 Vietnamese (1975–1987)

Table 1 (cont.)

200,000 Spanish (Civil War, Republicans, 1936)
200,000 Guatemalans (Disappearances, 1981–1983)
150,000 Liberians
70–100,000 "useless eaters" /handicapped (Nazi Germany)
75,000 Ukrainian Jews (1917–1920)
70,000 Algerians (ongoing, Islamic fundamentalists)
50,000 Eritreans (separation from Ethiopia, 1990s)
50,000 Sierra Leoneans (ongoing)
30,000 Argentinians (dirty war, 1976–1983)
20,000 Dominican Haitians (1937)
20,000 Azerbaijanis and Armenians (Karabakh, USSR,1988)
10,000 homosexuals (Nazi Germany)
10,000 ethnic Albanians (Serbia, 1995)

Total: 262 million murdered by governments via genocide, massacres, mass murder, extrajudicial executions, assassinations, atrocities, intentional famines. The range of 174–262 million includes colonial genocides (of 50 million) since 1900. See updates by Rudy Rummel: http://freedomspeace.blogspot.com/2005/12/new-estimate-of-20th-century-democide.html

About two thirds of the world's 15 million international refugees flee from ethnopolitical violence each year. In the past decade, ethnic/religious strife has also exacted the following death tolls: Sikhs (4,000); Kurds (100,000/PKK retaliation of 35,000); Algerians (70,000 Muslims/Fundamentalist Muslims); Colombians (45,000); Indonesians (4,000 Christians/Muslims); Northern Irish (3,500 Catholics/Protestants); Sri Lankans (2,000 Hindus/Buddhists); Peruvians (69,000 Shining Path/Government); Algerians (100,000 Islamists/Government); Kashmir (1,283 Indians/Pakistanis); and many more in the ongoing conflict between Israeli Jews and surrounding Arab

Muslim nations since 1948. These numbers pale in comparison to other numbers, such as the current Sudanese genocide in Darfur (300,000 +).

Historian Lord Acton once observed that power tends to corrupt and "absolute power corrupts absolutely." University of Hawaii political scientist Rudolph J. Rummel agrees. In reviewing the past century, he estimates civilian genocide by non-democratic regimes at 262 million (see Table 1). This number excludes untold relocations, maimings, and the psychological aftermath that invariably follows – a figure that is likely to be at least four times greater than that describing those who have perished in war.[5]

NOTES ON THE PROLOGUE

1. Excavations in Northeast Belgium revealed a mass grave of 30 men, women, and children where the skeleton skulls had holes probably from blunt objects. The settlement is thought to date to 7,000 years ago. See J. Shreeve (1995) *The Neandertal enigma*. New York: Avon.

2. C.P. Scherrer (2002) *Structural prevention of ethnic violence*. Chicago: Palgrave Macmillan, states that in 1998 there were 27 armed conflicts. The Carnegie Commission on Preventing Deadly Conflict count is slightly higher, with 38 conflicts reported, resulting in at least 100,000 deaths per annum. This includes island states like Tonga, as well as third-world nations such as Botswana, and some modern industrial nations like Sweden and Switzerland. See Stockholm International Peace Research Institute (1997) *Preventing deadly conflict*. New York: Carnegie. In W. Durant & A. Durant (1968). *The Lessons of history*. New York: Simon and Schuster, Will and Ariel Durant point out that in 3,421 years of recorded history, only 268 years are without war. Self-interest/ideology, sadism, and tribalism are the reasons cited, from a moral historical perspective. See M. Davis (2001) *Late Victorian holocausts*. New York: Verso, but death tolls from the Irish potato famine (1 million) and African Middle Passage (4 million) are not included; and see R. Conquest (1999) *Reflections on a ravaged century*. New York: W. W. Norton. For Guatemala see V. Sanford (2003) *Buried secrets*. New York: Palgrave Macmillan. Casualties for both World Wars total approximately 70 million. Scottish sociologist Gil Elliot ((1972) *Twentieth century book of*

the dead. New York: Scribners) estimates that 110 million people have been killed by others between 1900 and 1972. See R. J. Rummel (1994) *Death by government.* New Brunswick, NJ: Transaction, and his update to 262 million on his website http://freedomspeace.blogspot.com/2005/12/new-estimate-of-20th-century-democide.html

3. UN Definition currently adopted by International Association of Genocide Scholars (see www.iasg-iags.org).

4. M. Shaw (2007) *What is genocide?* Malden, MA: Polity Press. For Armenians and Jews see www.theforgottenrefugees.org

5. Also see C. Simpson (1993) *The splendid blond beast.* New York: Grove.

1   Charlotte's question

Man's inhumanity to man makes countless thousands mourn.

Robert Burns, *Man Was Made to Mourn*

On a warm summer evening in 1941, the Christians in Jedwabne, Poland, herded their Jewish neighbors into a barn, closed the door, and set it on fire. On a rainy day in April 1994 the Catholic Rwandan Hutu parishioners and clergy macheted to death their fellow Catholic Rwandan Tutsi parishioners and clergy. In 1920s America, while White girls were flapping and drinking champagne, the Black girls of Rosewood Florida, Elaine Arkansas, and Tulsa Oklahoma were fleeing for their lives as their homes were torched by angry mobs.

Why? What would possess the perpetrators in Laramie Wyoming to kill a 5'2" 105 lb. homosexual named Matthew Shepard?

Experts are just beginning to understand the extent and nature of such a mindset. It sounds very strange to most of us because such a mindset wants to kill not only Matt Shepard, but also all homosexuals. Then, under the right conditions, the same mindset would search for those who were sympathetic to gays and kill them as well. In genocide, such mindedness would seek out those with ideas that are too liberal, too effete or artistic – all would be game for the genocidal mind. And when the entire population of homosexuals and their lackeys have been killed, those with the mindset would not rest. New enemies would be created, sought, and destroyed. For them, there is no end to the hate and even a joy in hating.

"The sight of bodies blown apart are some of the happiest moments of their lives – comparable to peak sexual experience," notes English historian Joanna Bourke in her examination of frontline letters from American, British, and Australian soldiers. "They had a ball! ... nobody failed to turn up," observed a Krakow police official. He later testified that his border police were "quite happy" to take part in the shooting of Jews.[1] Like the Roman coliseum crowds, "an uncomfortably large number of soldiers ... delighted in death as spectators or as perpetrators."[2] During the Nanking massacre, Japanese soldiers were known to compete with one another, tallying up their killings, tortures, and rapes of Chinese victims.[3] Photos of gleeful American soldiers torturing Iraqi Abu Ghraib prisoners reveal the latest but not last entry into humankind's schadenfreude. Former war correspondent Chris Hedges reminds us of the:

> excitement, exoticism, power, and chances to rise above our small stations in life, and in a bizarre and fantastic universe that has a grotesque and dark beauty. It dominates culture, distorts memory, corrupts language and infects everything around it, even humor which becomes preoccupied with the grim perversions of smut or death. Fundamental questions about the meaning or meaninglessness of our place on the planet are laid bare when we watch those round us sink to the lowest depths.[4]

Hedges is speaking of war, but one does not need a war to feel alive. Hate can be equally exciting and its taboo status makes it all the more alluring. So, the Royal Family's bad boy Prince Harry dons a swastika armband at a party. And players of the SIMS computer game trade torture secrets of their imagined creations over the Internet. Newly released photos of the spectacle of Southern White lynch mobs reveal several men who are beaming as they hang an immobilized African-American man out to dry. They look drugged but the narcotic of hate is more powerful than any street drug and much more freely available. Teacher Charlotte Opfermann observed the same enchantment with evil in her Texas high school.

> I was helping direct a play about the life of Pastor Dietrich Bonhoeffer [Douglas Anderson's *The Beams Are Creaking*]. Our performance was enormously successful on the artistic level; it

won first regional and national prizes. It was, however, a total flop educationally: The students were completely involved, absorbed, and fascinated with the jack boots, the flags, the display of unlimited power, and cruelty. They thoroughly disliked Bonhoeffer (played by the school's intellectually and academically most gifted student). The other actors loved the strutting and heel clicking and thunderous Sieg Heil demonstrations.[5]

For the kids, it was exciting. For the teacher it was frightening – all too reminiscent of her schoolmates' fascination which she witnessed before she and her sister escaped from Nazi Germany. She later apologized for their behavior. "They are young and do not understand," said Charlotte, "I guess I still don't understand – where does all the hate come from?"[6]

What Charlotte was implying is that the students lacked the maturity and the wherewithal to appreciate the nature and extent of their enamor. That notion assumes we know those ingredients that constitute maturation. It also assumes that we understand the link between maturation and prejudice. But as is often the case with understanding the nature of prejudice, there are more assumptions than answers.

The purpose of this book is to examine the psychology of hate and the genocidal mind with regard to maturation. Its premise is simple. People are psychologically built the same, but mature at different rates. Some may mature a lot and some not at all. And it is the immature and somewhat ill mind that hates. The remainder of this book will try to fashion an answer to Charlotte's question as to where all the hate comes from, why maturation differences occur, and what can be done about it.

ANIMAL ROOTS

We begin to answer Charlotte's question with exploring the naturalness of prejudice in social groups. The parallels to animal groups are striking. For instance, mobbing is observed when outsiders approach groups of birds or mammals. The same processes occur among rival gang members.

So does ostracism. In one study, twelve cats became pariahs and when they ventured from their private drainpipe, the other cats attacked them. Unless a researcher stood guard, the alienated cats did not eat. Social ostracism is even more virulent among wolves. A wolf cub may be not only ousted from the pack, but also viciously attacked and even killed by peers. Group outing has been documented in baboons toward other baboons with injured legs, in herring gulls toward distressed gulls, in lizards toward lizards with deformed tails, and in gorillas toward ill gorillas.

Jealousy may not be of the kind that dominates television soap operas but several primate versions exist. While dog and cat owners have multiple anecdotes to tell, observers of the Great Apes and elephants have their stories too. In one case, a gorilla uncle continually swatted and threw branches at his nephew and had to be separated from him. In a similar example, a young male elephant caught the eye of an older female. After delivering their offspring, the female lost interest in her paramour and shifted her attentions to the newborn calf. The young male elephant had to be separated from them, as he would dig the calf with his tusks when the opportunity arose.

In humans, it seems to have anger as a base, but rape and other forms of sexual violence occur regularly in orangutans, dolphins, seals, goats, bighorn sheep, wild horses, dogs, and several species of birds. After killing an infant, the langur (monkey) male mates with the bereaved mother. The killing of her offspring and siring of his own cub is theorized as that which may enhance his genes and minimize future competition. Killing offspring is not unknown in cats, certain breeds of dogs, and chimps. The killing of competitors is also documented in langur, bears, deer, prairie dogs, bumblebees, dung beetles, mice, squirrels, lions, and gorillas. The animal war-rape phenomena may not be so different from the human ones that occurred in Nanking or Bosnia, or the one in Bengal that in 1971 produced 25,000 births.[7]

Both physical and psychological torture have been observed in cats with mice and other animals. Killer whales appear to "play" with unfortunate seals before tearing them apart. One chimp, raised by humans, began soliciting cigarettes from zoo visitors. He would then chase other chimps, trying to burn them.

Ant wars are legendary. Some ants take slaves and others, acting as suicide bombers, literally blow themselves up in front of enemies. Bees buzz with attack dances, eager to alert the forces of impending battles. Bands of dwarf mongoose injure each other and some die in battle. English primatologist Jane Goodall has stated that chimpanzees would use weapons such as rifles if they could. Aside of humans, Gombe chimps have been known to shame other chimps in both their in- and outside group, lethally invade other bands of chimps, and at times gang up and plot retributive murder in ways that would make Shakespeare jealous. While allusions to civil war may be a bit over the top, there is no question about what happened when primatologists took one group of Gombe chimps and separated them. For years some were raised in the northern region and the others were raised in the south. Irrespective of earlier bonds, the former friends killed each other en masse.

Though rare, cannibalism has been documented in chimps as well as humans. Barbara Ehrenreich suggests that war ritualizes such cannibalization themes. Never too far from our animal counterparts, sports crowds taunt the competition with chants of "We'll eat you for breakfast." The Asmat of Irian Jaya, Indonesia, are more to the point. They consider all outsiders (manowe) as "the edible ones."

But even among chimps, some groups are non-aggressive and the conduct of their cousins, the bonobos is exemplary. You will not hear much about the bonobos, because their peaceful ways do not make exciting reading or go with the notion of people as natural killer apes. Whereas chimpanzees hunt, fight and compete for social status, bonobos make love, not war. They are ambisexual and matriarchal. The little-mentioned bonobos may be just as much a role model for insight into human nature as the chimp, suggests primatologist Frans de Waal.[8]

So our true "nature" may not be the Hobbesian nightmare that chimp researchers have previously suggested any more than our nature is the bonobo way: playful, sexual, and peaceful. It depends where we look and how we aspire to be. At times, nurture clearly overrules nature. There are cases of "natural enemies" such as cats and mice remaining close companions over their lifespan. And dolphins, hyenas, and bonobo apes have been documented gesturing and making consolation efforts.

Maturity seems to be part of the equation. Male chimps become less violent when a strong maternal or paternal bond is in place. To thwart attacks on endangered white rhinos in Kenya, rangers introduced older bull elephants. The presence of the elder statesmen elephants stopped the teen bull elephants from further killings. Even in animals, maturation makes a difference.[9]

BENEATH THE SURFACE

Where all the animal tendencies lead is uncertain. Humans possess a neocortex with the capacity to delay impulse. Along with the opposable thumb, this makes us unique among most of the earth's creatures. Yet there is plenty of evidence to suggest that we do not employ higher functioning thinking, at least not regularly enough. In our quest to find an answer to the genocidal mind, there are two ways of proceeding. From one perspective, we can form a theory and then go about the business of searching for confirmatory evidence. Or, from a different perspective, we can collect the evidence, and propose a theory. Either way, without the evidence and sufficient data, a theory is no good. In a sense, understanding genocide is a bit like detective work in that we have arrived at the scene and have found the body and now must reconstruct the crime. Except over the course of the last century the crime scene contains 262 million bodies spread over the entire planet.

Let us begin the examination of hate and the genocidal mind with a working definition. According to social psychologist Gordon

Allport, hate is a particularly stubborn structure, an "ending organization of aggressive impulses toward a person or class of persons."[10] Allport offered up the concept as on a continuum where initial stages built up until they were acted upon. He addressed briefly the extent of the problem in an American adult population (see Chapter 2) and noted that it was difficult for people to admit that they were prejudiced. Even before political correctness came of age, the difficulty with admitting to hate beliefs was largely ascribed to the unconscious.

Scientists have long known that when thoughts and feelings are socially unacceptable, such processes may become unconscious. These unconscious or implicit thoughts rarely surface unless alcohol, stress, or lack of sleep has loosened the tongue, as some politicians or actors periodically can attest. What slips from the inside out may surprise many of us. Such thoughts may reside in a state of suspended animation, waiting for alcohol or the right challenge.

Today, much of the challenging is performed in computer laboratories on college campuses. In these labs, the students complete something called the Implicit Association Test (IAT). The IAT consists of a series of names that, when flashed onto a computer screen very quickly, are thought to bypass the perceptual threshold or just-noticeable differences. As the African-American or Jewish or Hispanic name appears on the screen, the subject presses a key indicating whether a word was good or bad before they can reflect on the social consequences.[11] A computer then tracks the speed of response and level of emotionality.

Most experiment subjects, including about half African-Americans, respond positively to the word when a White-sounding name appears, suggesting among other things, we conform much more to the dominant culture than previously believed. Just reading word lists of stereotypical African-American words (e.g. jazz, basketball) produced more hostility (see Table 1.1).[12]

Images of disdained ethnic groups are easily paired with unpleasant words, while famous people, men, the wealthy, Whites and heterosexuals are consistently favored over their opposites. The

Table 1.1 *Implicit association tests (IATs)*

Native American ("Native – White American" IAT).	This IAT requires the ability to recognize White and Native American faces in either classic or modern dress, and the names of places that are either American or foreign in origin.
Weapons ("Weapons – Harmless Objects" IAT).	This IAT requires the ability to recognize White and Black faces, and images of weapons or harmless objects.
Sexuality ("Gay–Straight" IAT).	This IAT requires the ability to distinguish words and symbols representing gay and straight people. It often reveals an automatic preference for straight relative to gay people.
Age ("Young–Old" IAT).	This IAT requires the ability to distinguish old from young faces. This test indicates that Americans have automatic preference for young over old.
Asian-American ("Asian–European American" IAT).	This IAT requires the ability to recognize White and Asian-American faces, and images of places that are either American or foreign in origin.
Disability ("Disabled–Abled" IAT).	This IAT requires the ability to recognize symbols representing able and disabled individuals.
Weight ("Fat–Thin" IAT).	This IAT requires the ability to distinguish faces of people who are obese and people who are thin. It often reveals an automatic preference for thin people relative to fat people.
Gender–Career.	This IAT often reveals a relative link between family and females and between career and males.

Table 1.1 (cont.)

Race **("Black–White" IAT).**	This IAT requires the ability to distinguish faces of European and African origin. It indicates that most Americans have an automatic preference for White over Black.
Arab-Muslim **("Arab-Muslim–Other People" IAT).**	This IAT requires the ability to distinguish names that are likely to belong to Arab-Muslims versus people of other nationalities or religions.
Religion **("Judaism–Other Religions" IAT).**	This IAT requires the ability to recognize religious symbols from various world religions, especially Judaism.

Harvard's Project Implicit: see http://implicit.harvard.edu/implicit/index.html

same results occur for all minorities. Unconscious and automatic bias can also get to us on the inside. Research psychologists Claude Steele and John Dovidio found heightened blood pressure and negative test performance among African-American students who were merely present in a classroom with Whites.

Troubling as well are the findings that automatic bias may involve police action. Testing showed a tendency for police to shoot unarmed Blacks more than unarmed Whites, whether in fact the police are African-American or White.[13] It seems unlikely that people will voluntarily rid themselves of automatic reactions to race.

Automaticity may be natural but the associations are learned in the family social group and culture at large. Psychoanalyst Mort Ostow and his colleagues observed that almost all of their patients recalled early antisemitic teachings, such as coloring in pictures of Jews crucifying Christ in Sunday school. The same patients later deplored anything Jewish and did not know why. In his study, mental health problems explain some of the more extreme anti-semitic views but in general there seemed to be a mental health pattern with the more disturbed patients harboring more anti-semitic beliefs.[14]

So, if everyone gets mentally healthy does hate fly away? Probably – especially if maturation is part of mental health. Yet this is unlikely to occur since only a handful of people are truly interested in becoming mentally healthy. Until then, we would have to dry up the wellsprings of hate belief. And such beliefs reside wherever there are social groups that form insiders and outsiders.

In Christian-based cultures, the outsiders are the Jews. In Islamic nations, the outsiders are Christians, Jews and other non-Muslims. Elsewhere it is darker skinned or indigenous people and so on. Comments from apartheid South Africa are telling. "In South Africa, few thought about hate – it was so much a part of the air. 'We were taught to hate,' states one apartheid supporter. 'The Blacks were satanic and godless, uncivilized in their impulses. And they were going to swamp us.'"[15]

Where does all the hate come from? Some experts maintain that a combination of certain traits and world views creates prejudice.[16] Some experts focus on personal and social-group threat[17] while others pinpoint feeling states and key emotions.[18] But how much we hate and whom we hate does seem to vary between cultures.

At the same time, it is certain that some people are more prone to hate. Certain personality traits and authoritarian attitudes suggest that some of us are just more prone to prejudice, fundamentalism, and fascism.[19]

One study's findings are particularly telling. Prejudice was so highly correlated with social and group approval that individual attitudes and personal identity almost didn't matter.[20] In this battle for hearts and minds, it is all about the mind and the lack of emotional development. But to fully appreciate this process, we must first appreciate the tension between personal and social identity.

HATE AND GENOCIDE – WHAT THE EXPERTS SAY

The influence of social group identity as a key component to hate and genocidal mindedness is a concept repeated throughout this work. Not everyone agrees, though much of the disagreement depends on one's vantage point. In genocide research there are two types of people – those who view genocide as induced by ruling elites from above and those who see genocide as more endemic, with deep roots of hatred that are boiling up from below.

There has been plenty of research from the top-down perspective. To a degree, this top-down approach to understanding genocide makes sense in that genocide cannot exist without a manipulative elite who do what they can to magnify all social differences. For instance, after the collapse of the Soviet Union (1987–1991) researchers observed that Armenia and Azerbaijan were contesting the historic status of Nagorno-Karabakh. In government campaigns, Armenian heroes were quickly constructed and previously established facts were "revised" while others were simply "forgotten." Previously uncontroversial memories and territorial claims were made controversial – it worked.[21]

Political scientist Chip Gagnon's analysis of the Yugoslav war suggested that (pre-war) intermarriage rates and the percentage of draft-resisters indicate less ethnic enmity and manipulation from elites of "ancient blood hatreds." Similar conclusions were reached by other experts examining evidence in Rwanda and elsewhere. Such arguments indicate that the ancient tribal hatreds currently involved in Darfur might not be what they seem. Genocide, they argue, had not occurred until the non-Arab tribes organized and posed a threat in 2003.

But does manipulation of ethnicity by elites assume an ethnic "blank slate"? Hardly. A review of Table 1 in the Prologue suggests that all major genocides employed social myths to exploit and maximize ethnic conflicts. This notion is consistent with Mark Howard Ross's analysis of ninety cultures, concluding that group conflict was based on "assumptions, perceptions and images about the world that are widely shared with others."

And while it is true that an elite's use of propaganda amplifies these differences, ongoing ethnic, religious, and racial myths seem to succeed without much help from elites. Consider the ongoing nature of hate crimes, many of which go unreported, and the bottom-up perspective.

From a bottom-up perspective, the Nazis were masters at socially constructing enemies, but could not have succeeded without a base of everyday antisemitism from which to launch their campaigns. From this perspective, antisemitism and all forms of hate feed the masses' hunger for blood. When saturation or tipping point is reached and "everybody knows" "The Jews/The Blacks/The - " are the problem, then pogroms or lynchings become the social justice meted out to even the imaginary score (see Table 1.2). In nations where law does not prohibit antisemitism and instead is supported by the mosque, state, and media, polls conducted by the Pew Research Center reveal antisemitism rates ranging between 89 and 98 percent, roughly double or triple what they are in Western democracies.

Daniel J. Goldhagen[22] speaks of the pervasiveness of antisemitism in European culture. And, while he is not without his critics, the base of his argument makes sense. As historian Ian Kershaw reminds us, the road to Auschwitz was indeed built by hate.

In terms of criticism, Goldhagen held the German people accountable for the Holocaust when he should also have included those willing executioners in Austria, Hungary, Czechoslovakia, Romania, Poland, the Baltics, France, Spain, and so on. He just wasn't expansive enough. Critics also point out that other "inferior" groups like the Gypsies were sanctioned for genocide. Certainly true. Yet only Jews merited a separate Wannsee Conference to answer the Jewish question with the final solution. (It may be an academic exercise to regard the intention to kill 14 million others as a spillover effect, since it is unlikely the victims would care, but that indeed is how it appears.) Thanks to the laudable efforts of Christopher Browning, Ervin Staub, and James Waller, we know that primary social psychological forces of conformity, peer pressure, and careerism played a key role. Those forces, operating in

Table 1.2 *Top antisemitic pogroms in Christendom*

Pogrom	year	numberkilled
The Deluge or Cossack Rebellion of Chmielnicki, Russia	1648–1656	100,000–300,000
The Russian Revolution and Civil War	1917–1922	100,000–200,000
includes 1,700+ Proskurov, Vilna, Lvov	1919	
Antonescu-led purge in Odessa	1941	30,000
Host Desecration myth in Rindfleisch/Armleder Germany	1298/1336	20,000–100,000
Seville/Cordova Spain	1391	10,000–50,000
PreNazi pogrom Iasi, Romania	1941	13,000–15,000
Crusades, Europe	1096–1254	10,000+
Easter pogrom, Prague	1389;1744	3000, n/a
Bloody Sunday Pogrom St. Petersburg	1905	3000
Hungary White Terror	1919	3000
Strasbourg	1349	2,000 burned
Lisbon	1506	2,000 mobs
Black Death Accusation Europe	1348–1350	1,000s + burned
Inquisition Europe	1288–1739	1,000s
Inquisition Toledo, Spain	1355	1,200 riots
Kiev	1113; 1736; 1768	100s–1000s

concert with a mass propaganda campaign that focused almost exclusively on Jews, are not in question.

Yet none of those factors can explain the zeal people felt as they turned in their Jewish neighbors or the feeling of elation that had a millennium-long precedent of prior discrimination and murders. None of those factors take into account that one could send antisemitic postcards to friends, drink from a beer stein that lampoons Jews, publicly make anti-Jewish jokes, pray (until 1966) to St. Simon, the Patron Saint of Antisemitism, or make pilgrimage to any number of holy sites depicting children martyred by Jews for their pure blood to be used in their secret rituals, e.g. Passover dinner. That Jewish people were routinely beaten up at and around Easter is never mentioned. That Jewish homes were torched when the Passion Play was performed at Oberammergau, Germany, is omitted. That Jews were not permitted the same legal rights as other citizens throughout Europe until the 1800s – none of this seems to be contextually something for critics to consider.

By the same token, key evidence for the antisemitic customs of European Christendom is glossed over, including the precedent of 300–400,000 Jews killed in thousands of pogroms. The critics are equally quiet when it comes to explaining sociologist Helen Fein's statistical correlations linking popular antisemitism and the number of Jews killed in the Holocaust.[23] The critics are simply wrong in negating the impact of public opinion, collective fantasy, and genocidal intent.

In Nazi Germany, antisemitism as part of one's social identity became reinvented as "us–them" Aryanism. Hitler, the master populist that he was, knew that in order to control the masses, he had to stop people from thinking personally and independently. So after the burning of books and stifling of dissent, he continued to appeal to the volk's lowest common denominator – the social mind.

> It is thus writes Hitler that the individual should finally come to realize that his own ego is of no importance in comparison with the existence of the nation, that the position of the individual is conditioned solely by the interests of the nation as a whole.[24]

The same psychological processes occur elsewhere. During the Serbian–Croatian conflict, Croatian psychologist Ed Klain observed a similar process operating. Klain recalls that during the war, all sense of individuality was superseded by the collective or social group. The elites perpetuated that process by creating an ongoing enemy list.

They helped by orchestrating calls for vengeance, and obedience to authority – but the basic prejudices had been there for years.[25]

Reporting from the front lines of the Serbian–Croatian conflict, political scientist Michael Ignatieff captures a wonderful moment that speaks to the heart of ethnic group hate. At one point, a Bosnian Serb is trying to explain to Ignatieff his motivations to kill his Croat enemy. He then offers several fairly lame explanations. Further explanation of Serbian–Croatian ethnic differences proves too exasperating. The soldier eventually declares: "We're all just Balkan shit."[26]

Social psychologist Dan Bar-Tal affirms that ethnic, religious, and political conflicts are all part of human experience and that group members simply act on that. "Prejudice is a normal human tendency," UCLA psychiatrist Daniel Borenstein reminds us.[27] Members of one group act toward other groups on the basis of shared beliefs, attitudes, and stereotypes. The sharing occurs most within a specific culture, subculture, and group.[28]

But if prejudice is normal, how is it that genocides do not evolve more frequently? And why is genocide much less common in democracies? There is no one answer. Some experts have focused on the self-centered component of groups[29] or the power of group ideology[30] and others have focused on multiple factors including fears, e.g. fear of enemies, fear of polluting genes (degrading the essence), revenge for alleged abuses.[31]

Historian Ben Valentino[32] returns to the ruling-elite argument citing that only a few at the top found key perpetrators from below. Voila. In Rwanda, less than 9 percent of the Hutus killed 750,000. In the Soviet Gulag, 135,000 Stalinists killed 1.5 million. Estimates in Cambodia suggest 70,000 Khmer Rouge killed 1.5 million. And in the World War II genocide, 100,000 murdered 6 million Jews, 3 million Catholic Poles, and others.

Some experts have even argued that hate is not even involved and argue that group dehumanization is all that is needed. It turns out that devaluing others as morally inferior and dehumanizing them to animals is a key part to any genocide.[33] From a bottom-up perspective one is hard pressed to come up with examples of dehumanization that do not involve hatred of outsiders. There is, of course, no shortage of either and dehumanization often takes the form of name calling and dysphemism: usually animal or disease titles.

Sikh separatists and Hutu leaders aimed at the "weak, effeminate" Hindus and Tutsi "cockroaches" respectively. The Khmer Rouge killed all those who possessed "cabbage minds" or were "intellectuals," the "city-dwelling" Chinese and "ugly microbes." Burmese and Chinese governments cast a wider net, repressing all ideological enemies of the state. Christian Ethiopians killed Jewish Ethiopians because they were "hyena people," believed to transform at night and steal. Sudan's Janjaweed Arab militias killed the Zurga whom they deemed subjugated slaves.

At the same time, the experts are not wrong regarding additional motives for genocide, such as ideology, career advancement, or financial incentive. Treblinka commandant Franz Stangl believed greed was the primary motive. "They wanted the Jews' money," observed Stangl:

> "That racial business" said Stangl "was just secondary. Otherwise how could they have had all those 'honorary Aryans'? They used to say General Milch was a Jew you know" ... [Q: Why hate propaganda?] "To condition those who actually had to carry out these policies to make it possible for them to do what they did." [Jews were cargo, not hate?] It has nothing to do with hate.
> They were so weak; they allowed everything to happen to be done to them. They were people with whom there was no common ground, no possibility of communication and that is how contempt is born.

It seems likely that no one condition creates genocide, but how we view it as from above or below may affect our understanding. When we examine the predictors of genocide, we can see that a perfect storm of events from both the top and below are necessary.[34]

PREDICTING GENOCIDE

In the past few years genocide warning signs have been addressed while others have attempted to construct computer models that predict risk. Along with her researcher husband Ted Robert Gurr, Barbara Harff has proposed an ongoing "Minorities at Risk" project. The computer model correctly identifies seventy-three high-risk groups and predicts three out of four trouble spots globally. Like the current experience with North Korea, isolation from the rest of the international community was one prerequisite. Other predictors include political upheaval, elite fragmentation, and pre-specified accelerators.[35]

Along similar lines, Genocide Watch's Glenn Stannard[36] has created a brief listing of the stages of genocide formation. These eight stages of genocide are given in Table 1.3.

While there may be multiple motives for genocide, hating another's group is the perennial rallying point. That notion is particularly troubling since for most of us, the group is "we" and "we" are not about to give it up without a good fight.

GROUPS ARE US

"We always stay in a group, otherwise we're vulnerable," reports James, age 17, an African asylum seeker in Dyes, Germany. From roaming hominid hunting bands 12,000 years ago to membership in the automobile club, we know, as did our ancestors, that there is safety in numbers. Most of us belong to multiple organizations, civic clubs, and places of worship as part of a community of like-minded citizens. Drivers wink, nod, and even honk their horns to each other when driving the same model automobiles as if to say: "You and I – we are part of a group that has the same cool taste in cars."

"The communal mind may be more than that," observes Howard Bloom.[37] He believes that many aspects of group cohesiveness are life-sustaining.

The best evidence for groups being helpful seems to be in the face of tragedy. In the aftermath of 9/11, people came to New York

Table 1.3 *The eight stages of genocide formation*

1. Classification: All cultures have categories to distinguish people into "us and them" by ethnicity, race, religion, or nationality: German and Jew, Hutu and Tutsi. Bipolar societies that lack mixed categories, such as Rwanda and Burundi, are the most likely to have genocide. The main preventive measure at this early stage is to develop universalistic institutions that transcend ethnic or racial divisions, that actively promote tolerance and understanding, and that promote classifications that transcend the divisions. The Catholic church could have played this role in Rwanda, had it not been riven by the same ethnic cleavages as Rwandan society. Promotion of a common language in countries like Tanzania or Cote d'Ivoire has also promoted transcendent national identity. This search for common ground is vital to early prevention of genocide.

2. Symbolization: We give names or other symbols to the classifications. We name people "Jews" or "Gypsies," or distinguish them by color or dress; and apply them to members of groups. Classification and symbolization are universally human and do not necessarily result in genocide unless they lead to the next stage, dehumanization. When combined with hatred, symbols may be forced upon unwilling members of pariah groups: The yellow star for Jews under Nazi rule, the blue scarf for people from the Eastern Zone in Khmer Rouge Cambodia. To combat symbolization, hate symbols can be legally forbidden (swastikas) as can hate speech. Group marking like gang clothing or tribal scarring can be outlawed, as well. The problem is that legal limitations will fail if unsupported by popular cultural enforcement. Though Hutu and Tutsi were forbidden words in Burundi until the 1980s, code-words replaced them. If widely supported, however, denial of symbolization can be powerful, as it was in Denmark, when many Danes chose to wear the yellow star, depriving it of its significance as a Nazi symbol for Jews.

3. Dehumanization: One group denies the humanity of the other group. Members of it are equated with animals, vermin, insects, or diseases. Dehumanization overcomes the normal human revulsion against murder. At this stage, hate propaganda in print and on hate radios is used to vilify the victim group. In combating this dehumanization, incitement to genocide should not be confused with protected speech. Genocidal societies lack constitutional protection for countervailing

Table 1.3 (cont.)

---

speech, and should be treated differently than in democracies. Hate radio stations should be shut down, and hate propaganda banned. Hate crimes and atrocities should be promptly punished.

4. Organization: Genocide is always organized, usually by the state, though sometimes informally (Hindu mobs led by local RSS militants) or by terrorist groups. Special army units or militias are often trained and armed. Plans are made for genocidal killings. To combat this stage, membership in these militias should be outlawed. Their leaders should be denied visas for foreign travel. The UN should impose arms embargoes on governments and citizens of countries involved in genocidal massacres, and create commissions to investigate violations.

5. Polarization: Extremists drive the groups apart. Hate groups broadcast polarizing propaganda. Laws may forbid intermarriage or social interaction. Extremist terrorism targets moderates, intimidating and silencing the center. Prevention may mean security protection for moderate leaders or assistance to human rights groups. Assets of extremists may be seized, and visas denied to them. Coups d'etat by extremists should be opposed by international sanctions.

6. Identification: Victims are identified and separated out because of their ethnic or religious identity. Death lists are drawn up. Members of victim groups are forced to wear identifying symbols. They are often segregated into ghettoes, forced into concentration camps, or confined to a famine-struck region and starved. At this stage, a Genocide Alert must be called. If the political will of the US Government, NATO, and the UN Security Council can be mobilized, armed international intervention should be prepared, or heavy assistance to the victim group in preparing for its self-defense. Otherwise, at least humanitarian assistance should be organized by the UN and private relief groups for the inevitable tide of refugees.

7. Extermination begins, and quickly becomes the mass killing legally called "genocide." It is "extermination" to the killers because they do not believe their victims to be fully human. When it is sponsored by the state, the armed forces often work with militias to do the killing. Sometimes the genocide results in revenge killings by groups against each other, creating the downward whirlpool-like cycle of bilateral genocide (as in Burundi). At this stage, only rapid and overwhelming armed intervention can stop genocide. Real safe areas or refugee

Table 1.3 (cont.)

escape corridors should be established with heavily armed international protection. The UN Standing High Readiness Brigade – 5500 heavy infantry – should be mobilized by the UN Security Council if the genocide is small. For larger interventions, a multilateral force authorized by the UN should intervene. It is time for nations to recognize that the international law of humanitarian intervention transcends the narrow interests of individual nation states. If NATO will not intervene directly, it should provide the airlift, equipment, and financial means necessary for regional states to intervene with UN authorization.

8. Denial is the eighth stage that always follows a genocide. It is among the surest indicators of further genocidal massacres. The perpetrators of genocide dig up the mass graves, burn the bodies, try to cover up the evidence, and intimidate the witnesses. They deny that they committed any crimes, and often blame what happened on the victims. They block investigations of the crimes, and continue to govern until driven from power by force, when they flee into exile. There they remain with impunity, like Pol Pot or Idi Amin, unless they are captured and a tribunal is established to try them. The response to denial is punishment by an international tribunal or national courts. There the evidence is heard, and the perpetrators punished. Tribunals like the Yugoslav or Rwanda Tribunals, a tribunal to try the Khmer Rouge in Cambodia, or the International Criminal Court may not deter the worst killers. But with the political will to arrest and prosecute them, some may be brought to justice. And such courts may deter future potential genocidists who can never again share Hitler's expectation of impunity when he sneered, "Who, after all, remembers the Armenians?"

Reprinted, with permission, from the Genocide Watch website at: www. genocidewatch.org/aboutgenocide/8stages.htm

City to see if they could help from as far away as California and Canada. School shootings strike a similar chord. Within minutes there are groups of mourners huddling together and within hours candlelight vigils are being held. The rows of flowers when Diana died were among other things a testament to an adoring public and group support. The heartbreaking images of hundreds of stuffed dolls lined up along the elementary school fences in Dunblane, Scotland (1996), or Erfurt, Germany (2002), or Beslan, Russia (2004), or the high schools at Columbine (1999), or the university gates in Montreal (1989, 2006), and West Virginia (2007) all attest to our collective caring.

By definition, those from collectivist cultures in Asia, Africa and Latin America are more family-oriented and better caretakers of family. There is even some research to suggest that they are kinder to strangers. Few Thai families would not care for a loved one who has been taken ill. In group-conscious nations, a redistribution of family resources to take care is the norm.

Genocide expert James Waller reminds us that groups are incredibly helpful to those who are in need of support and organizational efforts have improved people's lives from weight loss to overcoming addictions. Groups have created democracies and freedom, he points out. "Groups amplify whatever is there – good or bad," notes Waller.[38] But amplification at times can be problematic. In groups, people do many things they would never do alone. For instance, decision-making goes awry as social forces take over logic, e.g. "group think" and confirmation bias, and create errors such as those that occurred in the Watergate scandal.

Moreover, when it comes to group loyalties and politics, we try not to let the facts get in our way – literally. Recently, cognitive scientists observed activity in the brain's regions for those who favored George Bush (Republican) or John Kerry (Democrat). When the subjects were told that their candidates flip-flopped on key issues, they still supported them. Not surprisingly, only the reward centers lit up and not the parts of the brain involved in logic and fact finding. Lead researcher Drew Westen concluded,

> None of the circuits involved in conscious reasoning were
> particularly engaged ... Essentially, it appears as if partisans twirl
> the cognitive kaleidoscope until they get the conclusions they

want ... Everyone ... may reason to emotionally biased judgments when they have a vested interest in how to interpret the facts.[39]

French sociologist Gustave Le Bon suggests that anonymity, suggestibility, and contagion combine in such a way that the individual is reduced to an "inferior form of evolution."[40] Submerged in the crowd, an individual loses self-control and becomes a puppet violating all personal or social norms. "Whoever supplies it with safety wins, those that threaten are bad/menacing and often the victim group," wrote Le Bon. The crowd's actions reflect a collective "racial unconscious," which allow primitive, and antisocial, instincts to take hold.

Anonymity is key – what writer Elias Canetti calls "the discharge" from individual identity and responsibilities. "This is the moment when all who belong to the crowd get rid of their differences and feel equal." Freud, also, wrote that in a crowd, individuals lose their personal opinions and focus in a specific direction and where there is a tendency to carry out the group's will, all the while diffusing anonymity and responsibility. Continuing Gustave Le Bon's work, Freud believed that when individuals join a crowd, they cease repressing their instincts, and become primitive. It is an "idealist transformation of the conditions existing in the primitive horde."[41] The "will of the people" is to motivate them towards the lowest common denominator. For instance, if the group is violent, we may act violently.

This "group mind," said British psychologist William McDougall[42] produces certain properties that cannot be well understood by focusing on individuals. But some have made compelling arguments that mobs and crowds are very focused and quite specific – they start, and stop once their goals are achieved.[43]

Even within the group, divisions form, especially when whole cultural systems support group differences such as India's caste system and Japan's approach to Korean immigrants, the Burakumin.[44]

The Burakumin are a fairly large outcast group constituting approximately two million people. They speak a dialect separate from the mainstream Japanese language. They are poor, and less educated. The mainstream Japanese perceives the Burakumin as innately inferior though no racial or inherited physical differences have ever been detected. The Burakumin face more job discrimination, which leads to the circle of poverty and diminished educational opportunities.

A fascinating portrayal of group identity could be glimpsed in Tim Blake Nelson's outstanding film, *The Grey Zone*. In this film, as in real life, those in the death camps are viewed as individuals trying to survive. Since all were Jewish prisoners facing death you would think they would have plenty in common. Instead, new group differences emerge and divide them, e.g. new arrivals vs. lifers, prisoners who bought time by helping the Nazis vs. prisoners who did not, esteemed Western European vs. less esteemed Eastern European.

Divide and conquer occurred among the socially constructed divisions among 1930s African-Americans. In the Southern US, it was not unusual for African-American bouncers to hold up a brown paper bag and admit only light-skinned African-Americans to a club. Patrons who were too dark just did not cut it. Admission was prohibited based on skin color.

But it is not just religion and skin color. Among dwarfs distinctions are made as well. Little People with pseudoachondroplasia dwarfism (rare normal-sized head and facial features) are more esteemed than those with achondroplasia (large foreheads and smaller mid-faces).

There seems to be a strange pattern here in that we manufacture group differences and then are intimidated by those differences – whether it is young as opposed to aged, old as opposed to new money, Harvard over Yale, Cambridge over Oxford – it seems all part of a natural process of identity formation – even if at times the consequences are somewhat lethal.

"I am no racist. I've never been a racist!" pleaded Vincent Chin's murderer, who in 1992 bludgeoned the 27-year old Chinese-American automotive engineer to death with a baseball bat outside of a Detroit bar. Witnesses at the bar testified that they heard Japanese racial slurs regarding the loss of American jobs. "There isn't a single racist bone in his body," his friends testified. After three trials, a Michigan judge believed them and let the plant supervisor go free.[45]

At the time, I was attending a concert of pop singer Randy Newman and witnessed the seedlings of group mind in action. Newman is known for his sardonic lyrics mocking Vonnegut-like characters and his song "Rednecks" lampoons Southern rednecks. Everyone in the audience was keeping beat and singing aloud. But when the chorus aping rednecks came, the predominantly White, middle-class, college-educated audience gleefully repeated the "N" word refrain loudly. After a minute, they were louder. A minute later, they shouted even louder. For anyone who has seen music concert crowds and thought for a moment of the Nuremberg rallies, it was clear that the audience had wholly identified with the Southern redneck group and for a brief moment its members were transported through time.

Membership may indeed have its privileges, but there is a dark side as well. While groups make us feel protected, and offer us an identity, we surrender our individuality and the group may not have our personal best interests at heart. Witness the lives lost through Japanese kamikaze, suicide bombers, and Jonestown/Heaven's Gate cultists. Witness the 4,000 Okinawan soldiers committing suicide in underground naval headquarters or the 33,000 soldiers and civilians who threw themselves off a surrounding cliff rather than face capture in Japan at the end of World War II. Group mindset can be life destroying.

GROUP NATURE

Our tribalism, [and] our tendency to go beyond a natural pride in our group, whether it's a racial or ethnic or religious group or whatever. [This results in] fear and distrust and dehumanization and violence against "the other."

President Bill Clinton to film critic Roger Ebert, discussing *The Three Kings*.

"Racial intolerance finds stronger expression strange to say in regard to small differences than to fundamental ones," observed Freud in what he called the narcissism of minor differences. But he did not really say why it existed. He never really said it had to do with how we adapt to the family, identified group, and culture. He never really said it was natural. He never really said that in the absence of any real differences, we would create new differences because we see and think in social groups.

Research years later proved what Freud did not know. People create social categories even on the basis of the most trivial differences. People will favor their in-group over outsiders even when the groups are minimally defined.[46] It may be a separate phenomenon,[47] but group loyalty occurs naturally as part of our social nature.

Perhaps driven by primal forces of herd protection, all groups are constitutionally ethnocentric, xenophobic, and prone to social dominance.[48] No matter what the size or shape of the group, all group members remain perpetually threatened and stand vigilant pending attacks from outsiders. Here is the most frightening part. It is all in our heads: ready for battle at the slightest provocation – like a teacher's direction.

Jane Elliott[49] discovered the powder key of social identity among school children. The setting was 1968, the day after Martin Luther King had been shot. In the White, Protestant enclave of Riceville, Iowa, Elliot's demonstration was soon to become a classic experiment on manufactured groups and prejudice.

Elliott knew that none of her students had met a Black person. She subsequently queried the kids on what they knew about Black people. Their responses: "They're dirty." "They don't smell good." "They riot." "They steal." "You can't trust them." "My dad says they better not try to move in next door to us."

Next, she divided the class into two groups – those with brown eyes and those with blue eyes. Anyone outside these categories, such as those with green or hazel eyes, were outsiders, not actively participating in the exercise. Elliott told her children that brown-eyed people were superior to blue-eyed, due to the amount of a color-causing chemical, melanin, in their blood. Elliott said that blue-eyed people were stupid and lazy and not to be trusted. To ensure that the eye-color difference could be made quickly, she distributed strips of cloth to be fastened around the neck.

The "brown eyes" gleefully affixed the cloth-made shackles on their blue-eyed counterparts. She withdrew the classroom rights of blue-eyed students, such as drinking from the water fountain or taking a second helping at lunch. Brown-eyed kids received preferential treatment. They bossed around the blues and were given an extended recess. Elliott recalls, "It was just horrifying how quickly they became what I told them they were." Within thirty minutes, a blue-eyed girl named Carol had regressed from a "brilliant, self-confident carefree, excited little girl to a frightened, timid, uncertain little almost-person."

The brown-eyed children excelled under their newfound superiority. Elliott had seven students with dyslexia in her class and four of them had brown eyes. On the day the browns were "on top," those four brown-eyed boys with dyslexia read words that Elliott "knew they couldn't read" and spelled words that she "knew they couldn't spell." Prior to that day, her students hadn't expressed any thoughts about each other based on eye color.

Elliott soon saw her brown-eyed students act like "arrogant, ugly, domineering, overbearing White Americans" with no instructions to do so. She understood that racism is learned – carefully or not. She then reversed it. "I made a mistake" she informed the class. "It was the blue-eyed children who are better!" Within minutes the blue-eyed children began acting like their brown-eyed superiors and the brown-eyed children assumed depressed attitudes. Elliott had taught them it was okay to judge one another based on eye color, but she did not teach them how to oppress. "They already knew how to be racist because every one of them knew, without my telling them, how to treat those who were on the bottom," says Elliott.

For years, when Elliott repeated the experiment, parents would call the school principal with invariably the same complaints: "I don't want my kid in that nigger-lover's classroom!" Her own children were beaten by other school children and she received death threats. She has since retired from teaching and now acts as a business consultant where she still continues a variation of the same experiment, on adults.

Workplace and school cliques and elites are based on those same principles. People want to think well of their group. When group members are equally exposed to both honest and flattering versions of the past, they remember and repeat only the flattering ones. As we have said, groups polarize and amplify preexisting ideas and perceptions. Those of the in-group are viewed individually, while outsiders are viewed homogeneously and as less trustworthy. People also hear, see, and remember that which reaffirms their own special attitudes toward their group. And, all groups like to feel superior to others.

The social mind prepares our perceptions and mindsets. I recall watching a television show one day with a colleague of Lebanese descent. The episode included a scene with a Jewish supervising psychoanalyst. My colleague made a crack about the Jews. There it was in terms of prepared narrative and perceptions. I saw a doctor that happened to be Jewish, while my colleague saw a Jew who happened to be a doctor.

Group belonging is everything and ostracism is often the price for group disloyalty. In some cultures, infanticide, nose amputations, and ice flow drifts are punishment for not fitting into the group. In psychology, the laboratory may offer sufficient proof of group fit. Recall the IAT – the test where reaction times are measured on each subject. Researchers found that if you identify yourself in one group, it's easier to pair images of that group with pleasant words and easier to pair the out-group with negative ones.

In God we trust, but groups are a close second. We tend to think more highly of those in our group, prefer our group members' company, and believe them to be similar to us. Once we trust them, we listen to them and the surrounding narratives, and follow the social norms.

SOCIAL NORMS

Suspended in time and space for a moment, your introduction to Miss Janet Tyler, who lives in a very private world of darkness – a universe whose dimensions are the size, thickness, length of a swath of bandages that cover her face. In a moment, we'll go back into this room – and also in a moment we'll look under those bandages ... keeping in mind, of course, that we're not to be surprised by what we see. Because this isn't just a hospital and this patient 307 is not just a woman. This happens to be the Twilight Zone – and Miss Janet Tyler, with you, is about to enter it.[50]

For most of us, commentator Rod Serling's stark appearance and stern voice-over is alarming enough though the subject matter of cultural conformity is arguably more frightening. In the above episode, Janet Tyler (Donna Douglas) is a young woman believed to be ugly. We see everything from the patient's point of view and all hospital staff faces are oddly shadowed. Patient Tyler has undergone eleven facial plastic surgeries designed to make her appear normal. The doctor tries to explain to her that everyone is given as much opportunity as possible to fit into society. Should this procedure fail, she could move to a special area that has been set aside where people of her kind have been congregated. "People of my kind congregated? she says sobbing through her bandages. "You mean segregated! You mean imprisoned, don't you Doctor? You're talking about a ghetto, aren't you? A ghetto designed for freaks!" In a later scene the doctor is speaking to the nurse and musing his ethics. "Why shouldn't people be allowed to be different?" When the last bandages are removed the medical team balks at their failure. "No change! No change at all," screams the doctor, and the nurses recoil in horror.

The *Twilight Zone* twist is that when the last bandages are removed, the patient's face is beautiful while the hospital staff surrounding her have distorted pig faces. Ugliness on this planet is the prevailing norm that everyone accepts at "face" value.

NORMS OF HATE

Every group and culture has shared beliefs and codes of conduct called norms. Some norms are conscious and obvious, such as customs and language, roles, history, literature, and folklore. Other norms are unconscious, such as communication styles and social perceptions. Certain norms are literally a given. Traditionally, dolls are given to girls, not boys. Tips are given to restaurant waiters and waitresses. And while many norms may be in transition, e.g. women tending to marry up – older and wealthier, norms not only guide us to appropriate social behavior – they fill us with our social beliefs and guide our behavior.[51]

Can norms dictate who and how much to hate? For the most part the answer seems to be yes and we seem to feel okay about it. Those who conform to group standards have more positive emotions than those who violate group norms.[52]

For Pakistani students who have spent several years in one of the 10,000 registered (or 25,000 unregistered) madrassas or religious seminaries, they feel okay learning that Western values are Satanic. Perhaps we shouldn't be surprised by one student's remarks: "All things come from Allah – the atomic bomb comes from Allah, so it should be used."[53]

Much of the early research was based on group-norm theory[54] but more sophisticated work[55] has been able to statistically separate the wheat from the chaff concluding that when it comes to prejudice, group norms trump an individual's perspective. In a series of seven studies utilizing a large sample of 1,504 people, Chris Crandall and his research team at the University of Kansas looked at prejudice towards 105 social groups. Whether subjects were evaluating discrimination scenes or reacting to ethnic jokes, that which was prejudiced was highly correlated with social approval and social norms.

It is often the case in social psychology that personality traits are downplayed and to find anything that looks like personality components, you have to read between the lines. As Crandall delved deeper to examine which research subjects were most at risk for following group norms and being prejudiced, here is what they found: There were two distinct groupings of subjects – high and low suppressors. Suppressors quickly gave up their connections to their old identified group and then they worked to become a member of a new group. The most marginal group members liked the idea of gaining more social status.

In an atmosphere and culture that dislikes prejudice, the exact opposite occurs as well. "To fit in, and adjust their beliefs and values to match the group norm, they must suppress their prejudices. In this case, they are trying to be good citizens," notes Crandall.[56]

Dr. Crandall did not investigate to see if traits were correlated to high and low suppressors, but if he did, here is what he would have found:

> *High suppressors were more prejudiced and had poorer mental health and believed in the social norms more than others.*
> *By contrast, low suppressors were less prejudiced, had better mental health and were less susceptible to social norms.*

Perhaps another way of understanding this is to think about the results as suggesting that those without emotional backbone cave in to social forces all too easily, tend to believe social prejudices and, in a genocide these are the ones who are more likely to "just follow orders." So the larger question is – who are these guys?

WHO COMPLIES?

Is it the case that less emotionally evolved people are more susceptible to the prevailing cultural prejudices? Yes. And by contrast, those who are more emotionally developed are less prone to social influence.

Psychoanalyst Erich Fromm cautioned that in lieu of living emotionally authentic lives, fascism and materialism would develop. Fifty years later, there is plenty of research to back him up. Concerning Fromm's concept of materialism and emptiness, here are some fascinating findings. Irrespective of the number of goods surrounding them, materialistic people are more insecure, are more superficial and self-centered, and are more impulsive. Materialistic people are more conforming and less giving to others as well.[57]

Table 1.4 *Personal and cultural differences*

	Social identity	Personal identity
Percentage	70	20–30
Mode	intellectual	emotional
Theme	status role	awareness, needs
Values	conservative	liberal
Motives	fear	openness to experience
Rewards	external/cultural	emotionally confirmed
Social	superficial	deep
Language	power, status, security	needs, feeling states
Material	high	low
Enemy	others	inauthenticity
Goals	cultural success	meaningful
Relation	stereotypes	personal experience

From S. K. Baum (1994) *Growing up at any age*. Deerfield Beach, FL: Health Communications.

Shalom Schwartz's cross-cultural research continued in the same vein. He found that people clustered around two quite separate values on opposite ends of the emotional continuum – a self that values cultural and social success and achievement, and a self that values benevolence and universalistic principles.[58]

A Dutch uncle of mine once said that there are only two kinds of people – Dutch and those who wish they were. But in terms of identity, he was correct in that there are only two kinds of people, those who are living emotionally (personally identified) and those who are living via their social group (socially identified). Elsewhere I have suggested that those differences did not arise until an individual was well into their thirties and were often mistakenly identified as a midlife crisis. Table 1.4 highlights several of the differences between the two groups.[59]

Table 1.5 *Personal and social identification theories*

Theory	Social/Group	Individual/Personal
Freudian	other	self
NeoFreudian	authoritarian	nonauthoritarian
Charny	fascist	democratic
Identity	foreclosed/moratorium	achieved
Lakoff	paternal father	nurturing parent
Block/Jost	republican conservative	liberal democrat
Nationhood	collective	individualist
Kasser	materialist	nonmaterialist

Researchers have suggested that the differences between personal and social identities may account for political differences. Long-suspected differences between conservatives and liberals were vindicated when people identified themselves as either one or the other and then were given a battery of psychological tests. Not surprisingly, the two groups were polarized down the line in terms of the following dimensions: stability vs. change, order vs. complexity, familiarity vs. novelty, conformity vs. creativity, and loyalty vs. rebellion – suggesting among other things that conservatives are more emotionally cautious and social-group bound.[60]

The split between personal and social identification has a long history, some of which is highlighted by theories summarized in Table 1.5.

There is related work to suggest that personal and social differences may have nation-based wellsprings. University of Illinois Harry Triandis suggests that we think and feel as a function of the culture in which we live. For Triandis people from individualistic cultures are more independent of cultural norms. Conversely, collective-based persons, e.g. those from family-based agrarian nations, are prone to group-mindedness.

According to Triandis, the tendencies toward individualism and collectivism exist within every individual. In collectivist cultures, the detachment appears as minimal; people think of themselves as parts of their collectives and subordinate their personal goals to those of their group. Social behavior becomes a consequence of norms. Collectivist types rarely leave their collectives; when they get married, they link with another collective and their children are brought up to be good members of the collective. By contrast, those in individualistic cultures are more detached, more autonomous, and when the goal of the collective does not match their personal goals, the personal goals take precedence.

Individualists change relationships more often and marriage is decided on the basis of personal emotions. Children are raised to be less dependent on their collectives. Freedom from the influence of the collective is a very important value. Triandis adds,

> Within any culture, there are people who act more like collectivists or like individualists. In collectivist cultures people act like collectivists in most situations in which they are dealing with the in-group but they act like individualists maximizing their benefits and outcomes in most situations where they deal with out-groups ... In individualist cultures, people deal with each other as individuals and pay little attention to the group membership of others. However there are conventional ways of making group memberships salient. For example, race, religion, politics or belief systems can function to create in-groups and out-groups and then people can act like collectivists.[61]

Dutch colleague Geert Hofstede's work is particularly germane. Like Triandis, Hofstede found that cultures can be divided into individualist and collectivist, but emphasized three other dimensions as well: masculinity/machismo, uncertainty avoidance (open, flexible vs. rigid, controlled) and power distance (equality/inequality of power and wealth). People from collective cultures are more prone to machismo, more authoritarian and more prone to unequal power distribution. They are vulnerable to group prejudices and always at odds with emotional development.

Of course Madison Avenue has not let the work on individualism and collectivism get by. Here are statements with contrasting individualistic and collectivistic sentiments, taken from American and Korean advertisements:[62]

American Ads

She's got a style all her own.

You – only better

How to protect the most personal part of the environment – your skin

Making your way through the crowd.

Korean Ads

A more exhilarating way to provide for your family.

We have a way of bringing people closer together.

Celebrating a half-century of partnership.

Our family agrees with this selection of home furnishings.

In sum, most of us follow group norms but there are always some who do not. There are those who are more autonomous and independent, more internally driven, are not so quick to follow the leaders, rules, and culture when told to do so. And, as we shall see, such persons have a greater sense of maturity and are less prejudiced.

GROUP FEELINGS AND PREJUDICE

There seem to be individual and group differences in our thoughts, attitudes, and feelings as well. Depending on how much we feel part of the group, can we incorporate group feelings and beliefs?

The short answer is a resounding yes. A team of researchers in Holland has recently found that those from collectivist nations and, by implication, those with more social identity are likely to experience key group emotions, e.g. guilt. And related work by researcher

Peter Glick[63] found that grudging admiration of certain minorities produced group envy. Glick added that the admiration was quickly tinged with other attitudes including resentment, shrewdness, and fears of planetary takeover targeting Americans, East Indians, Asians, Jews, the Dutch, and Germans.

Such grudging admiration often includes calls for retaliation, where genocide is in the offing. It matters not if the retaliation is orchestrated by rumor or reality. A case in point is the anti-Israeli sentiment that has pervaded so much of the news lately. The results of a BBC poll ranked Israel as the world's most hated nation.

How did that occur? Such disdain cannot be based on civil rights violations of Palestinians as Amnesty International cites a multitude of other nations far outranking Israel. It cannot be based on a long history of disdain since for years Israel was popular in the Western media – a David among Goliaths of Arab neighbors trying to destroy it. What has changed in the past decade? In a word, the media – the Internet, satellite tv and, with it, the dissemination of the Arab perspective that, with a few exceptions, is uncritically adopted by Western media.[64]

What remains is a social movement dedicated to delegitimize anything Israeli and, by association, that which is Jewish. Suicide bombings, missiles fired into Israeli cities, intimidation of Jewish students on college campuses, intimidation against teaching the Holocaust, rises in antisemitic hate crimes – all is justice meted out for alleged abuses complete with the universal call for genocide – "they deserve it."

The same process occurs with other groups and the familiar refrain can be heard throughout the world. "The Ibo had it coming to them," was said after the killings in Nigeria of 1996. The 1969 anti-Muslim riot in Ahmedabad, India was deemed "very necessary" as reported by a Hindu mill owner. Yale law professor Amy Chua[65] has documented that the introduction of a free-market economy led to free-for-all ethnic rioting in Indonesia where a 3 percent Chinese minority control 70 percent of the private economy. In 1998, the

Indonesian backlash of 150 rapes, 5,000 homes and businesses looted, and 2,000 deaths were the price of group-felt envy.

Collective shame and retaliatory anger are common as well. The retaliatory anger for the shamed Muslim youth was apparent, resulting in the French riots of 2005 and 2006 and the Danish cartoon riots of 2006.

Social science researchers are beginning to incorporate the bifurcation in thinking and experience of the personal and social realms. There is even evidence of separate retrieval cues for personal and collective memories[66] so that we can perceive others and ourselves as individuals and as part of a group, simultaneously.[67]

Infant development researchers and theorists focus on the me/ not me phase of the mother–child bond. As an infant's self develops, he/she maintains the sense of "mother and I as one" (precursor to social identity) and "mother and I are separate" (precursor to personal identity). This rudimentary social self may evolve from the bonding and feeding and soothing of one ("my group") in contrast to the over and underfeeding and dependence when needs are not met (threatening or persecutory other). The initial mother–child bond may extend to a family bond and later include surrounding family members and others within the family, tribe, or social group. The larger social group (ethnic/racial/religious) transfers family pride (ethnocentrism), family trust (xenophobia), and family/clan dominance to the social group.

Children emotionally wear their ethnic group or nation as an identity badge, a primordial practice that may have been used at one point to ward off marauding tribes (see Figure 1.1). Parents reinforce cultural identification, especially in the formation of early friendships and dating practices. "You should stick with your own kind" and "I just want the best (same ethnic/religious/racial group) for you," are common variations of this theme. Years later, such advertisements as "single, White, Christian nonsmoker looking for same" need little justification. Eventually, the group and tribe and collective self form a social identity.

Group tribal mind
    ethnocentric   social identity
    xenophobic   → (associations)
    social dominance

Individual mind
    ego   personal identity
    narcissism   → (emotional development)

FIGURE 1.1 Identity model: A tale of two minds

SOCIAL IDENTITY

Mass movements can rise and spread without a belief in God, but never without belief in a devil.

Eric Hoffer, *The True Believer*

In any society people possess not only individual, but multiple, self-concepts. Their societal self-concepts include shared evaluations of their group, myths that transmit the self-concepts and ideal self, goals that a people set for themselves and shared beliefs.[68] Collective identity consists of many shared group experiences, e.g. values as well as group shared grievances, adversarial attributions, and involvement of society at large.[69]

A recent example of social identity is that of Jane. She is a 56-year-old, single, White, female clinic patient from rural Kentucky.

PT: That Dr. Ravi over there is nice looking, but I'd never go out with him.

–: Why?

PT: Well he's Indian or something and I'm from the South. That's just not right.

–: How do you know it's not right?

PT: Everybody knows. I just wouldn't. I wouldn't even sleep with someone who slept with a Black one – you could catch something ... AIDS maybe.

–: What if you were attracted to someone Arabic or Asian or Latino?

PT: I just wouldn't let myself. I couldn't explain it to my mother.

–: What about Jews or Muslims or Hindus?

PT: Don't know any.

–: I think you have an illness – one that is culturally accepted, but nevertheless an illness.

PT: Look, I don't have to explain it. More people agree with me than you!

It is true. Most people will agree with much of what Jane says and not see it as racist but rather as protective of herself and the culture to which she's accustomed. When pressed she invokes what social psychologists call false consensus. She now has the imaginary backing of the larger social group behind her. In her mind, she is protected by the group's sheer numbers and size and does not have to change her racist attitude. It is a numbers game and she wins.

French journalist Amin Maalouf says:

> Identity is in the first place a matter of symbols, even of
> appearances. When, in any gathering, I see people with names that
> seem like mine with the same color of skin, with the same
> affinities, even the same infirmities, it is possible for me to feel
> that that gathering represents me. A "thread of affiliation" links
> me to the crowd: the thread may be thick or thin, strong or weak
> but it is easily recognizable by all those who are sensitive on the
> subject of identity.[70]

"The more strongly you feel the bonds of belonging to your own group, the more hostile, the more violent will your feelings be to outsiders," observes former Harvard political scientist Michael Ignatieff. Each group also "ends up demonizing and dehumanizing the other group," notes psychiatrist Aaron Beck: Ethnocentrism and xenophobia are not the only parts of group belonging, so is social dominance.

> You see evidence in football and team sports as allegiance for one
> team exists over the other. When placed in opposition to another

group, the rating of one group goes up, and the rating of the other group goes down. In intergroup conflict there is ... a bias, and ... a misinterpretation of the other group's behavior in a negative way.[71]

Sometimes the results are disastrous, especially in sport. Bard College's Ian Buruma witnessed that when Dutch football fans dislike another team, they hiss, reminiscent of gassing Jews at Auschwitz.[72] When Argentina played Nigeria in the 1996 gold medal soccer match in Atlanta, a front-page headline in the Buenos Aires sport tabloid declared, "The monkeys are coming."[73]

Social identification never sleeps. A young Asian-Canadian woman reports the following experience.

> I had a child with an African man and the baby is dark skinned. People regularly come up to me and ask, "Is that your baby? " or state "Your baby is Black." I feel like telling them "This is a baby. He doesn't know what he is. He doesn't care. Why do you?"

Perhaps they shouldn't, but they do.

Historian Robert Wistrich rightly ponders the question of where social group beliefs end and extremist thinking begins.

> At what point does "normal" ethnocentrism turn into xenophobia, racism and antisemitism? When does family or group egoism, the tendency to exclude or distrust the other, turn into hatred, aggressive hostility, deliberate persecution, even massacre? When does ethnocentrism become a xenophobic security belt around a specific cultural identity or, worse still, a racist paranoia directed against the dangers of "pollution" and contamination from without or within? Or, as in the case of Nazism, how do racist fantasies acquire a genocidal dynamic that attributes intrinsically evil qualities to the identity and being of the mythical enemy, whose existence is so threatening that he must be totally destroyed?[74]

To many people, group differences are everything and the noticing of such differences begins very young.

"The surprising thing is how quickly these attitudes start to be expressed almost as soon as the children can talk" observed University of Ulster sociologist Paul Connolly.[75] In his study he found that children learned as early as age three to be intolerant of either Catholics or Protestants. "Our results frankly condemn the overall structure of Northern Ireland society," Connolly concluded. Northern Ireland is hardly alone in this matter. More than half to two thirds of the world's violent conflicts are ethnic based.

Social identification is so pervasive that the media routinely reports it alongside an individual's name and age. A review of MIT neurophysiologist Steven Pinker's books provides a typical example. A national Canadian magazine[76] notes Pinker's professorship and two-decade Boston residency, but concludes with the following: Pinker is endearingly Canadian: polite, soft-spoken, attentive to what others say.

Apparently, Pinker's manner has nothing to do with genes, family background or the score of developmental steps that make Steven Pinker style. According to the magazine, his personality and the best parts of his mind developed as a result of his formative years in Canada. Canadians are expected to be mild-mannered; consequently the cultural narrative of mild manners is maintained.

Social identity is our calling card. "What's your background?" inquire those who are stumped by the ethnically ambiguous. Like inspectors at immigration border crossings, checks determine friend-or-foe status before any other boundaries are crossed. How well the border is patrolled depends not only on the vigilance of the examiner, but also on the reputation of the pending ethnic intruder. The methodology employed begins with observations of racial difference, followed by those of cultural and religious deviation and culminating in a ubiquitous surname search: Smith is okay, Schmidt, maybe not; Farley is good, Ferraro is suspect; Wallace yes, Waheed no.

Facial features also are used for ethnic security screening. Eyebrows too thick, foreheads too low, big noses and thick lips, faces too wide or too thin, skin color too light or dark, as well as coarse or kinky hair, qualify one immediately for the dangerous persons list. Body type may arouse ethnic radar. Short and squat remains more questionable than long and slender. The disabled and homely are always suspect. Those who are too thin or too fat may rouse equal concern.

As fashion models and plastic surgeons know, symmetry and beauty often soften the ethnic lines of distinction. Fame and fortune similarly blur the ethnic identity lines. The hint of an accent remains another telltale sign of cultural indiscretion, though certain accents, like Oxford English, remain esteemed. When ethnic detection doesn't follow these rules, one can always resort to the time-honored: "What's your background?" and allow for the whole range of ethnic fantasy.

Automobile bumper stickers and apparel display are used to foster national-origin identification. Flags, T-shirts, badges, license plates, and decorative stickers identify our religious and national affiliations. GER, NDL, I, the Christian cross and fish, Muslim crescents and Catholic saints, Buddhist statues and Hindu dashboard gods announce our social identity faster than any conversation.

At times we employ vehicles and libations to announce our collective cause. Advertisements capitalize on it to a degree. A beer's social identity reminds us that it (Molsons) is proudly Canadian. Mercedes prides itself by being German-engineered. There are playful variations on these declarations as in the bumper stickers "Kiss me, I'm Polish," and "Irishmen do it drunk." Even born-again Christians announce, "This is a God squad car," reminding us to watch our moral ps and qs by asking "Where will you be on Judgment Day?"

The more visible the ethnic difference (e.g., darker skin, specific cultural apparel) the more inclined we are to attribute stereotypes. We like to know who the enemy is and where we stand. Conversely, those who are from mixed backgrounds or ethnically vague make us feel unsettled. *Brown* author Richard Rodriguez identifies himself as a "queer, Catholic, Indian, Spaniard at home in a temperate Chinese city in a fading blond state in a post-Protestant nation."[77] Social identity's racial schizophrenia was constant for television sitcom writer Angela Nissel as well.

> When I'm with my family, I'm a Black girl shouting at racist news coverage, fanning people down in my mother and stepfather's church when they get the Holy Ghost. At home, in my predominately White neighborhood, I choose to be racially neutral at times, flaunting my exoticness when people ask me what I am. I'm everything or I'm American, I say, enjoying the looks on their faces when they're caught between being politically correct and just dying to ask me to be more concrete, so they can put me in some kind of box.

Filmmaker Spike Lee also captures the schism of personal and social identities in *Bamboozled*,[78] the story of a young, African-American, Harvard-educated writer who joins the comedy team of a failing television show. Under pressure from the network, he promotes a farce based on black-faced minstrels. Caught between the split of personal and cultural loyalties, he is reduced to an overwhelming state of no identity and simply cannot function. Being bright, motivated and successful is no match for the complexities and politics of social identity.

THE PROBLEM OF SOCIAL IDENTITY

> *I felt like shouting aloud that this is how murders are made*
> *– it's [identity] a recipe for genocide.*
> > –A. Maalouf from *In the name of identity*

While the limits of social identity should be clear, the pathology behind it is not as obvious. Such identities are prone to the sway of the crowd, they are prone to hate, they are prone to kill.[79] The following news item attests to the pathology inherent in social identity:

> Retired Toronto police officer Scott picked up a hunting rifle and took aim through his living room window and pumped four fatal

bullets into a neighbor. Officer Scott believed the man down the street with the Italian sounding surname had Mafia connections. It was a preemptive act and based on what Scott had heard about a group called Italians. "I was in fear of my life. I shot that I may live," he later informed authorities.[80]

Social group members engage in intergroup discrimination in order to achieve, maintain, or enhance the positive distinctiveness of their social identity. In other words, group members are motivated to manage their social self-esteem: the esteem in which they hold the shared self-image that constitutes their social psychological in-group.

Psychologically, there is no growth for the social identified, there are only associations made to the larger, more powerful group. As with the clinic patient Jane, their racism remains intact, protected by the larger group – in Jane's case Southerners. Arabs link up with the larger group of Muslims, African-Americans to the motherland Africa and a generalized people of color, and so on.

Social identification associations enhance the individual via collective or group esteem. "I found myself attaching to the power and success of famous White Europeans," says one skinhead member.[81]

The problem with social identity is that it co-opts emotional life discounting all that lives on the inside. By contrast, everything social remains on the surface, operating at a sound-bite and stereotype level. No surprisingly, politics enters quickly and vying for position occurs. Writer Amin Maalouf echoes a similar concern:

> It presupposes that deep down inside everyone is just one
> affiliation that really matters, a kind of fundamental truth about
> each individual, an essence that is determined once and for all at
> birth never to change thereafter. As if the rest, all the rest ...
> counted for nothing.[82]

He continues,

> Grasping for one's identity in a world that threatens to reduce
> everyone [who is not part of the elite to a low-paid worker or a

consumer of cheap mass-produced commodities] creates a hunger for meaning and a sense of self-worth that can most easily be satisfied by a consciousness of race or religion.[83]

Though not everyone agrees that strong group identities produce prejudice,[84] for the most part the research is consistent. Strong forms of identity are least affected by context and social situation.[85] The more people are socially identified, the more they incorporate the culture's and social group's values, feelings, and attitudes including prejudices.

When social identity is the only identity, as is often the case when religions fuse with culture and politics, assimilation problems are not far off. Currently, assimilation crises in Europe and elsewhere include a large influx of Arab and non-Arab Muslims. Studies in Belgium are just now beginning to find that, in tests, immigrants from Muslim nations are more religious, and less open to considering adopting the identity of Belgians in their newly adopted country.[86] Islamicist expert David Pryce-Jones has observed "above all, they [Muslims] owe it to themselves to have no other identity than Islam." He continues,

> It is as though the Arabs have trapped themselves inside a closed circle from which they sense that they must break out for their own good, but within which identity and its supportive values paralyze endeavors of rescue.[87]

But it is not just Arabs. To the extent that ethnicity, religion or politics is the only source of identity, we can all become identity fundamentalists or, as writer Ian Buruma aptly called them, identity warriors.[88]

"It is a nationalist delusion," observes political scientist Michael Ignatieff, "that the identities of individuals are or should be subsumed into their national [cultural] identities." Traveling throughout war-torn former Yugoslavia, Ignatieff made the following observations:

> In the fear and panic, which swept the ruins of the communist states, people began to ask: So who will protect me now? The

culture provides an answer: trust those of your own blood. The best weapon against pluralism is a single good/common enemy. Without made solid identity, so the mythology goes, the disintegration of states will occur and the Hobbesian fear (inter ethnic war) results in ethnic fragmentation and war. Ethnicity and national sentiment create the feel of safety.[89]

In times of turmoil, people become polarized and cling to their social identity as a lifeline. For the socially identified, killing off an aspect of culture is killing part of them personally – a precursor to self-annihilation. It is this locked-in cultural/tribal identity that acts as hate's springboard. "It's not you personally," a Nazi guard once confided to his prisoner "– as a person I like you – it is your group."

We long for that which social identity can never provide. Nationalism's glue cannot hold together a sense of self for any length of time. All that is solid will melt into air taking with it all of social identity's old allies – materialism, racism, nationalism, fundamentalism, sexism, and chauvinism.

TOWARDS DEVELOPING PERSONAL IDENTITY

By contrast, human connection, personal meaning, emotional attunement, and authenticity are the way of personal identity. Personal identity is a set of unique traits and attributes that differentiate the person from others. This part of the identity is experienced as key values by individuals, as "core" or "unique" to themselves in ways that Social Identity (group, category membership and role identities) are not. Personal identity development is not chronological, but emotional. Progression from one stage to another appears to be subject to developmental delays and arrests from ego-based injury or narcissistic tragedies.[90]

Burnaby, British Columbia, is home to Simon Fraser University and its emeritus professor James Marcia. Continuing the work of developmentalist Erik Erikson, Marcia has proposed personal identity status which incorporates the inevitable twists, turns, and arrests and delays one experiences over the course of a lifespan. Marcia focuses on four types:

Diffusion
>This person has not made a commitment, and may or may not have experienced an identity crisis. He or she appears to have given up any attempt to make the commitments needed for developing a clear sense of identity as Marcia defines the term (not explored, not invested).

Foreclosure
>Foreclosed people have made commitments to an occupational future, but have not experienced an identity crisis. They have conformed to the expectations of others concerning their future. For example, an individual may have allowed a parent to decide what career they will pursue (no crisis – so adopts parent's perspective).

Moratorium
>Individuals in moratorium are actively exploring alternative commitments, but have not yet made a decision. They are experiencing an identity crisis, but appear to be moving forward toward identity formation, making commitments (in crisis, but no commitment).

Achieved Identities
>These are committed to identity exploration and have attained a solid sense of self. Researchers have demonstrated that achieved identities are more mature and adapt better.

It seems to fit a pattern. For instance, in Milgram-style experiments, developmentally foreclosed individuals shock more frequently and intensely and their more open counterparts were less apt to hit the lever.[91]

Throughout the lifespan, there has always been a tension between social and individual emotional development. The social mind, so essential to whom we are and how we adapt, becomes a liability later if not developed. When development does not occur, people remain, as Fromm suggested, terribly destructive things.[92]

It is a little premature to answer Charlotte's question though we have the seedlings of an answer. There is so much hate because of an allegiance to group beliefs and overidentification with a social self. But why some move beyond the social fray requires a new understanding of an old idea – maturity.

NOTES ON CHAPTER I

1. J. Bourke (1999) *An intimate history of killing*. New York: Basic.
2. R. Hilberg (1992) *Perpetrators, victims and bystanders*. New York: Harper.
3. I. Chang (1997) *Rape of Nanking*. New York: Basic. To view lynch mobs smiling see P Dray (2001) *At the hand of persons unknown*. New York: Random House.
4. C. Hedges (2002) *War is a force that gives us meaning*. New York: Public Affairs.
5. C. Opfermann H-Genocide 5/21/04.
6. Personal communication 7/12/04.
7. M. Ghiglieri (2000) *The dark side of man*. Reading: Perseus. Also D. Peterson & R. Wrangham (1996) *Demonic males*. New York: Houghton Mifflin. Stepchild infanticide rates are sixty times higher than biologic infanticides. For disability intolerance see H. K. Bloom (2000) *The global brain*. New York: John Wiley & Sons. Also R. J. Rummel (1997) *Death by government*. New Brunswick, NJ: Transaction Publishers.
8. B. Ehrenreich (1998) *Blood rites*. New York: Owl; J. Waller (2002) *Becoming evil*. New York: Oxford University Press; F. de Waal (2007) *Primates and philosophers*. Princeton, NJ: Princeton University Press, and the tongue-in-cheek F. de Waal (2006) *Our inner ape*. New York: Riverhead.
9. See www.save-the-elephants.org/Elephant%20News%20Items/Adult%20elephants%20 keep%20 adolescents%20 in%20check.html
10. G. Allport (1954) *The nature of prejudice*. Garden City, NY: Doubleday, p. 363.
11. For Harvard's Project Implicit see http://implicit.harvard.edu/implicit/index.html. Just reading word lists can evoke prejudice, see M. Banaji, K. M. Lemm, & S. J. Carpenter (2000) The social unconscious. In

M. B. Brewer & M. Hewstone (eds.) (2004) *Social cognition*. Malden, MA: Blackwell.

12. S. L. Gaertner & J. F. Dovidio (2000) *Reducing intergroup bias*. Philadelphia: Psychology Press; and C. M. Steele & J. Aronson (1995) Stereotyped threat and the intellectual test performance of African-Americans. In C. Stangor (ed.)(2000) *Stereotypes and prejudice*. Philadelphia: Psychology Press. C. M. Steele (1997). A threat in the air: How stereotypes shape intellectual identity and performance. *American Psychologist*, 52, 613–629. C. M. Steele & J. Aronson (1995). Stereotype threat and the intellectual test performance of African-Americans. *Journal of Personality and Social Psychology*, 69, 797–811. When several emotional states were tested, not surprisingly, anger created automatic prejudice. D. DeSteno, N. Dasgupta, M. Y. Bartlett & A. Cajdric (2004) Prejudice from thin air: The effect of emotion on automatic intergroup attitudes. *Psychological Science*, 15, 319–324.

13. J.Correll, B. Park, C. M. Judd & B. Wittenbrink (2002).The police officer's dilemma: Using ethnicity to disambiguate potentially threatening individuals. *Journal of Personality & Social Psychology*, 83, 1314–1329.

14. M. Ostow (1996) Myth and madness: A report of a psychoanalytic study of antisemitism. *International Journal of Psychoanalysis*, 77, 15–31.

15. "Blacks will swamp us": Paul Erasmus, see p. 263 in Erna Paris (2001) *Long shadows*. New York: Bloomsbury.

16. J. Duckitt (1992) Psychology and prejudice. *American Psychologist*, 47, 1182–1193; also S. Feldman (2003). Enforcing social conformity: A theory of authoritarianism. *Political Psychology*, 24, 41–74.

17. R. I. Eidelson & J. I. Eidelson (2003) Dangerous ideas. *American Psychologist*, 58, 182–192.

18. S. T. Fiske, A. J. C. Cuddy, P. Glick & J. Xu (2002) A model of (often mixed) stereotype content: Competence and warmth respectively follow from perceived status and competition. *Journal of Personality and Social Psychology*, 82, 878–902. Also see S. T. Fiske (2004). *Social beings*. New York: Wiley.

19. B. Altemeyer (1996) *The authoritarian specter*. Cambridge, MA: Harvard University Press.

20. C. Crandall, A. Eshleman & L. O'Brien (2002) Social norms and the expression and suppression of prejudice: The struggle for internalization. *Journal of Personality & Social Psychology*, 82, 359–378.

21. N. C. Dudwick (1994) Memory, identity and politics in Armenia. Unpublished doctoral dissertation. University of Pennsylvania. DAI, 55 (05A) p. 1303.

22. S. Straus (2006) *The order of genocide*. Ithaca, NY: Cornell University Press and B. A. Valentino (2004) *Final solutions*. Ithaca: Cornell University Press. For a good overview see D. G. Dutton (2007) *The psychology of genocide*. Westport, CT: Praeger Security International. Also see C. Gagnon (2004) *The myth of ethnic war*. Ithaca: Cornell University Press; M. H. Ross (1993) *The Culture of Conflict*. New Haven: Yale University Press, p. 10. For Pew, see Pew Global Attitudes (2006) at http://pewglobal.org/reports/display.php?ReportID=206; D. J. Goldhagen (1996) *Hitler's willing executioners*. New York: Knopf.

23. H. Fein (1979) *Accounting for genocide*. New York: Free Press. See J. Semelin (2007) *Purify and destroy*. New York: Columbia University Press, and related work in social myths by M. H. Ross (1993) *The culture of conflict*. New Haven: Yale University Press.

24. Hitler quote from www.hkweaponsystems.com/cgi-bin/quote.pl?adolf_hitler

25. E. Klain (1998) Intergenerational aspects of the conflict in the former Yugoslavia. In Y. Danieli (ed.) *International Handbook of multi-generational legacies of trauma*. New York: Plenum.

26. M. Ignatieff (1998) *The warriors' honor*. New York: Metropolitan/Holt.

27. Borenstein quoted with Alvin Poussaint www.abcnews.go.com/sections/living/InYourHead/allinyourhead_58 hmtl.

28. D. Bar-Tal & Y. Teichman (2005) *Stereotypes and prejudice in conflict*. New York: Cambridge University Press; D. Kelner & R. J. Robinson (1996) Extremism, power and the imagined basis of social conflict. *Current Directions in Psychological Science*, 5, 101–105; E. S. Kunnen (2006) Are conflicts the motor in identity change? *Identity*, 6, 169–186; M. Lucas (1997) Identity development, career development and psychological separation from similarities and differences between men and women. *Journal of Counselling Psychology*, 44, 123–132.

29. A. Jones (2006) *Genocide: A comprehensive introduction*. New York: Routledge.

30. E. A. Weitz (2005) *A century of genocide*. Princeton, NJ: Princeton University Press.

31. D. Chirot & C. McCauly (2006) *Why not kill them all?* Princeton, NJ: Princeton University Press.

32. B. A. Valentino (2004) *Final solutions.* Ithaca: Cornell University Press.

33. D. Moshman (2004) Genocidal hatred: Now you see it now you don't. In R. J. Sternberg (ed.) *The psychology of hate.* Washington, DC: APA; also S. Straus (2006) *The order of genocide.* Ithaca, NY: Cornell University Press; www.genocidewatch.com

34. G. Sereny (1983) *Into that darkness.* New York: Vintage, pp. 232–233.

35. T. Gurr (2000) *People vs. States.* Washington, DC: US Institute of Peace Press. Also see earlier work by Franklin Littell (1988) Essay: Early warning. *Holocaust and Genocide Studies*, 3, 483–490.

36. www.genocidewatch.org/

37. H. Bloom (2000) *The global brain.* New York: John Wiley.

38. J. Waller, personal communication, "Becoming evil" Lecture on genocide at Calvin College, Grand Rapids MI 2006.

39. D. Westen, P. S. Blagov, K. Harenski, C. Kilts & S. Hamann (2006) Neural bases of motivated reasoning: An fMRI study of emotional constraints on partisan political judgment in the 2004 US presidential election. *Journal of Cognitive Neuroscience*, 18, 1947–1959. Also see I. L. Janis (1972) *Victims of groupthink.* New York: Houghton Mifflin.

40. G. Le Bon (1896/1960) *The crowd: A study of the popular mind.* London: Ernest Benn, p. 40. Also see C. Mackay (1841/1980) *Extraordinary popular delusions and the madness of crowds.* New York: Harmony.

41. S. Freud (1955) *Moses and monotheism.* New York: Vintage. Also see S. Freud *The future of an illusion;* E. Canetti (1984) *Crowds and Power.* Farrar, Straus & Giroux, p. 17.

42. W. McDougall (1921) *The group mind.* New York: G. P. Putnam & Sons.

43. D. Horowitz (2003) *Deadly ethnic riot.* Berkeley: University of California Press; see also Tim Blake Nelson's film *The Grey Zone* (New York: Lions Gate 2001).

44. The Burakumin, Japan's Invisible Outcasts – *UNESCO Courier*, Sept, 2001.

45. Vincent Chin, cited in http://en.wikipedia.org/wiki/Vincent_Chin A similar news story from Anchorage, Alaska, describing a violent assault is all too familiar: "But while Afoula, who was 17 at the time, was hitting victim Katsura Matsui, he repeated several times that he 'hated Japanese.' The defendant was Samoan."

46. H. Tajfel (1981) *Human groups and social categories*. Cambridge: Cambridge University Press.

47. M. B. Brewer (1999) The psychology of prejudice: Ingroup love or outgroup hate? *Journal of Social Issues*, 55, 429–444. Also M. B. Brewer & W. Gardner (1996) Who is this we? Levels of collective identity and self representations. *Journal of Personality and Social Psychology*, 71, 83–93.

48. Evolutionary theorists suggest that our social need for dominance, hierarchy, and obedience has paved the way for such thinking. As social primates, humans share this evolutionary legacy, one that carries with it considerable political baggage. This genetic heritage, we submit, constitutes a (probably even the) major obstacle to the emergence and survival of democratic government. Dominance and hierarchy do not easily accord, history testifies, with basic democratic ideals of political equality, majority rule, and equality before the law.

49. Jane Elliott, cited online, see www. janeelliott.com

50. *Twilight Zone* see Episode 42–The Eye of the Beholder (original air date November 11, 1960).

51. R. B. Cialdini (1984) *Influence*. New York: William Morrow.

52. P. N. Christensen, H. Rothgerber, W. Wood, & D. Matz (2004) Social norms and identity relevance: A motivational approach to normative behavior. *Personality and Social Psychology Bulletin*, 30, 1295–1309; also see B. Dietz-Uhler & A. Murrell (1998) Effects of social identity and threat on self esteem and group attributions. *Group Dynamics*, 2, 24–35.

53. Hate school (2002) *Readers Digest*, April, p. 104.

54. M. Sherif & C. W. Sherif (1953) *Groups in harmony and tension*. New York: Harper.

55. C. Crandall, A. Eshleman & L. O'Brien (2002) Social norms and the expression and suppression of prejudice: The struggle for internalization. *Journal of Personality and Social Psychology*, 82, 359–378. Also see R. Luhtanen & J. Crocker (1992) A collective self-esteem scale: Self-evaluation of one's social identity. *Personality and Social Psychology Bulletin*, 18, 302–318.

56. Crandall, personal communication, 4/12/07.

57. L. Chan & R. Arkin (2002) Materialism as an attempt to cope with uncertainty. *Psychology and Marketing*, 19, 389–406. See T. Kasser (2002) *The high price of materialism*. Cambridge, MA: MIT Press.

58. S. H. Schwartz (1994) Are there universal aspects in the content and structure of values? *Journal of Social Issues*, 50, 19–45. Also see S. H. Schwartz (1994) Beyond individualism/collectivism: New cultural dimensions of values. In U. Kim, H. C. Triandis, C. Kagitcibasi, S. C. Choi & G. Yoon (eds.) *Individualism and collectivism*. Newbury Park, CA: Sage.

59. S. K. Baum (1994) *Growing up at any age*. Deerfield Beach, FL: Health Communications.

60. J. T. Jost (2006) The end of ideology. *American Psychologist*, 61, 651–670. Researchers have shown that the concept of political conservatism has more to do with being cautious, than anything else. A meta-analysis (22,818 persons from 12 countries) revealed several psychological traits but of the same themes. When you add up all the factors – death anxiety, system instability, dogmaticism, intolerance of ambiguity, openness to experience, uncertainty tolerance, need for order, structure, closure, integrative complexity, fear of threat and loss, and poor esteem – the core components suggest a rigidity (resistance to change), justification of inequality, and threat vigilance. J. T. Jost, J. Glaser, A. W. Kruglanski & F. J. Sulloway (2003) Political conservatism as motivated social cognition. *Psychological Bulletin*, 129, 339–375.

61. H. C. Triandis (1994) *Individualism and collectivism*. Boulder: Westview Press, pp. xiii–xiv. A speculative fifth dimension called long-term orientation was recently added. G. Hofstede (2001) *Culture's consequences*. Thousand Oaks: Sage.

62. S. Han & S. Shavitt (1994) Persuasion and culture: Advertising appeals in individualistic and collectivistic societies. *Journal of Experimental Social Psychology*, 30, 325–350.

63. B. Doojse, N. R. Branscombe, R. Spears & A. S. R. Manstead (1998) Guilt by association: When one's group has a negative history. *Journal of Personality and Social Psychology*, 75, 872–886. Peter Glick, see www.apa.org/monitor/oct04/prejudice. 64 honestreporting.com; P. Glick (2002) Sacrificial lambs dressed in wolves' clothing. In L. S. Newman & R. Eber (eds.) *Understanding genocide*. New York: Oxford University.

64. www.nctimes.com/articles/2007/05/04/science/9_35_195_2_07.txt. Also see www.honestreporting.com and www.bbcwatch.com. Media Tenor, a Bonn-based independent research group conducted a study in 2003 which found BBC Middle East coverage was 85 percent negative, 15 percent neutral and 0 percent positive toward Israel.

65. A. Chua (2004) *World on fire*. New York: Arrow.
66. D. Trafimow, H. C. Triandis & S. C. Goto (1991) Some tests of the distinction between the private self and the collective self. *Journal of Personality and Social Psychology*, 60, 649–655.
67. R. I. Eidelson & J. I. Eidelson (2003) Dangerous ideas. *American Psychologist*, 58, 182–192.
68. E. Staub (1989) *Roots of evil*. New York: Cambridge University Press, p. 104.
69. B. Simon & B. Klandermans (2001) Politicized collective identity. *American Psychologist*, 56, 319–331.
70. A. Maalouf (2003) *In the name of identity*. New York: Penguin, p. 120; L. Huddy (2001) From social to political identity: A critical examination of social identity theory. *Political Psychology*, 22, 127–156. Also see M. Rubin & M. Hewstone (1998) Social identity theory self-esteem hypothesis: A review and some suggestions for clarification. *Personality and Social Psychology Review*, 2, 40–62.
71. Beck interview; see Brown, *Daily Herald*, 12/07/99 and his Prisoners of Hate.
72. *New York Times Book Review*, 12/10/2000, p. 13. For an interesting parallel between 9/11 and World War II Japanese rationale of war against the West see Ian Buruma and Avishai Margalit's article "Occidentalism" in *New York Review of Books*, 1/17/02, pp. 4–7.
73. Racial insults inflame soccer rivalry. *Seattle Times*, 4/17/05, p. A21.
74. R. S. Wistrich (1999) The devil, the Jews and hatred of the "other." In R. S. Wistrich (ed.) *Demonizing the other*. Amsterdam: Harwood Academic, p. 2.
75. See multiple studies on stereotyping in children. e.g. D. Bar-Tal & Y. Teichman (2005). *Stereotypes and prejudice in conflict: Representations of Arabs in Israeli Jewish society*. Cambridge: Cambridge University Press. Also see P. Connolly & M. Keenan (2002) Racist harassment in the white hinterlands: the experiences of minority ethnic children and parents in schools in Northern Ireland. *British Journal of Sociology of Education*, 23(3), 341–356.
76. Steven Pinker in *Macleans* (2000) May 1, p. 43. How different the article would have read had it addressed his ethnicity and Jewish religion as contributing to his esteemed Canadian traits.
77. Rodriguez (2002) *Brown*. New York: Viking.
78. A. Nissel (2006) *Mixed*. New York: Villiard, p. 223; Spike Lee (2000) *Bamboozled*. New Line.

79. D. Moshman (2004) In C. Lightfoot, C. E. Lalonde & M. J. Chandler (eds.) *Changing conceptions of psychological life*. Mahwah, NJ: Lawrence Erlbaum. Also see D. Moshman (2004) Genocidal hatred: Now you see it now you don't. In R. J. Sternberg (ed.) *The psychology of hate*. Washington, DC: APA; see also A. Maalouf (2003) *In the name of identity*. New York: Penguin.

80. Officer Scott, cited from *Toronto Sun*, 1/21/2000, p. 1.

81. "I found myself attached" I. Hasselbach (1996) *Fuhrer-Ex*. New York: Random House.

82. A. Maalouf (2003) *In the name of identity*. New York: Penguin.

83. M. Mann (2005) *The dark side of democracy*. New York: Cambridge University Press. Also see P. Herriot (2007) *Religious fundamentalism and social identity*. London: Routledge. Also see J. Semelin (2007) *Purify and destroy*. New York: Columbia University Press; and Scott Straus (2006) *The order of genocide*. Ithaca, NY: Cornell University Press.

84. J. Gibson (2006) Do strong group identities fuel intolerance? Evidence from the South African case. *Political Psychology*, 27, 665–705.

85. B. Kinket & M. Verkuyten (1997) Levels of ethnic self-identification and social contact. *Social Psychological Quarterly*, 60, 338–354.

86. V. Saroglou & P. Galand (2004) Identities, values and religion: A study among Muslims, other immigrants, and native Belgian young adults after the 9/11 attacks. *Identity*, 4, 97–132.

87. D. Pryce-Jones (2002) *The closed circle*. Chicago: Ivan R. Dee. "Muslims have religious endorsement to live in the West so long as they do not integrate," he notes in D. Pryce-Jones (2006) Among the cicadas. *Commentary*, June, 121 No.6, p. 76. See also E. Staub (2001) Ethnopolitical and other group violence: Origins and prevention. In D. Chirot & M. E. Seligman (eds.) *Ethnopolitical warfare*. Washington, DC: APA, pp. 289–304, and E. Staub (2001) Individual and group killings in genocide and mass killing. In R. D. Ashmore, L. Jussim & D. Wilder (eds.) *Social identity, intergroup conflict and conflict reduction*. New York: Oxford University Press.

88. Buruma, reviewing for *The New York Review of Books*, April 11, 2002.

89. M. Ignatieff (1994) *Blood and belonging*. London: Vintage, p. 6.

90. J. E. Marcia (1966) Development and validation of ego identity status. *Journal of Personality and Social Psychology*, 3, 551–558; J. E. Marcia (1967) Ego identity status: Relationship to change in self-esteem,

"general maladjustment," and authoritarianism. *Journal of Personality*, 35, 118–133; J. E. Marcia, A. S. Waterman, D. R. Matteson, S. L. Archer & J. L. Orlofsky (1993) *Ego identity: A handbook for psychosocial research.* New York: Springer-Verlag; S. Hitlin (2003) Values as the core of personal identity: Drawing links between two theories of self. *Social Psychology Quarterly*, 66, 118–137; S. H. Schwartz (1994) Are there universal aspects in the content and structure of values? *Journal of Social Issues*, 50, 19–45.

91. M. H. Podd (1972) Ego identity status and morality: The relationship between two developmental constructs. *Developmental Psychology*, 6, 197–207. For the related work in personal identity see J. E. Marcia (2002) Identity and psychosocial development. *Identity*, 2, 7–28. Also see J. E. Marcia, A. S. Waterman, D. R. Matteson, S. L. Archer & J. L. Orlofsky (1993) (eds.) *Ego identity.* New York: Springer-Verlag.

92. For a good overview of Fromm and pathology see S. J. Bartlett (2005) *The pathology of man.* Springfield, IL: Charles C Thomas.

2 A bell curve of hate?

People know more about their automobiles than they do their minds.

E. O. Wilson from *Consilience*

"I feel badly about some of the things I did when I was young," says retired farmer Vern. "We didn't know what we were doing back then," he adds, recalling the time he and some friends toppled over headstones in an African-American cemetery. Farm life in St. Paul, Minnesota, during the early 1960s was difficult. "Short days, long winter nights and plenty of boredom," replies Vern when asked about the reasons for his actions. His friends had never known any minorities; they know they had heard of such groups. Vern's social world was saturated with ethnic stereotypes, ignorance and young males seeking out mischief.

Vern later came to realize that his actions were racist, but larger questions loom. What of those who never regret their actions? Where do naiveté and social faux pas end and where does hate begin? How much were Vern's antics influenced by his cronies? What if there were countless Verns and they were state sanctioned? Vern at age 16 and never in trouble with the law may have something in common with Buford Furrow Jr. at age 66.

While most people grow out of adolescent antics, some do not. These same individuals may commit similar acts throughout their lifespan. Buford Furrow Jr. was one such individual. Furrow made national news for one brief moment several years ago. On August 10, 1999, 66-year-old Buford Furrow Jr. drove from Seattle to Los Angeles for a "wake up call to America to kill Jews," wounding five at a Jewish Community Center and killing nearby mailman Joseph Ileto, because he was a Philippino and a good "target of opportunity." Furrow had just left a Washington state psychiatric facility after serving a six-month jail sentence for a hate crime. He had made a prior suicide attempt but was arrested after threatening psychiatric hospital staff with a knife. They are fifty years apart in age but they may have shared the same level of development.

The field of psychiatry has mixed feelings on the matter. "It would be wonderful," notes UCLA's Daniel Borenstein, "if we could somehow decrease racism by making it a diagnosis but the diagnostic nomenclature isn't set up to cure social problems; it's set up to diagnose and treat mental illness." By contrast Harvard colleague Alvin Poussaint remarked, "This is my peeve, if we want to do any kind of prevention, psychiatrists have to know and believe themselves that this [hate] is a serious mental disorder."[1]

As we will see, the traditional approaches that examine phenomena, such as hate crimes and genocidal mindset, are limited. Another method and approach is needed and emotional development may provide a clearer understanding.

Over the course of the past decade, genocide studies have emerged as a separate discipline designed in part to explain the workings of hate and mass murder. There have been several debates within the field, trying to explain what is normal and reasonable to expect in a genocide and if the concept exonerates the perpetrators of such horrific crimes.[2]

The concept of perpetrators as abnormal seems to have evolved from Freudian-based clinicians who found merit in the Frankfurt School's original analysis of postwar Nazis. Among their conclusions was the notion that authoritarianism paved the way for antisemitism and pointed a finger of culpability at the German people and German culture.

By the late 1980s, a second line of thought emerged, focusing on the situational forces involved in genocide. Advocates from this social psychological perspective concluded that Nazism and fascistic mindsets were the result of good people caught up in bad situations. Place ordinary people in extraordinary circumstances and they will perpetrate. Consequently, men behaving badly are victims of prevailing social forces. The actions of the Nazis, the Hutus, and Islamic extremists are the actions of every man. Both arguments will be examined and their shortcomings addressed with a focus on development – the missing component in both arguments.

NAZIS AS NORMAL

One school of thought argues that those who participate and collude in another human being's destruction are not mentally ill but are temporarily murderers perhaps no different than those in prison who temporarily adapt and perform acts that upon discharge they would never do again. Psychiatrist Robert J Lifton:

> The disturbing psychological truth is that participation in mass murder need not require emotions as extreme or demonic as would seem appropriate for such a malignant project ... ordinary people can commit demonic acts.

"It is demonic that they were not demonic," exclaimed Holocaust survivor Elie Wiesel upon hearing psychiatrist Robert Lifton's report on the Nazis as normal.[3] His concern is valid. One wonders what good a definition of mental health is if one of the most pathological cultures and their functionaries are not considered insane.

The Nazis-as-normal hypothesis has received considerable support from a wide variety of sources, some of whom were there. The origin of this argument appears to have been advanced with *New Yorker* magazine correspondent Hannah Arendt's reporting of the Adolf Eichmann trial. Among other things Arendt was taken by Eichmann's mild-mannered style and her now-famous "banality of evil" observation offset the widely held notion of human monster.

> The trouble with Eichmann was precisely that so many were like him, and that the many were neither perverted, nor sadistic, that they were, and still are, terribly and terrifyingly normal. This normality was more terrifying than all the atrocities put together.[4]

"Utterly bourgeois and normal," remarked Nazi hunter Simon Wiesenthal upon Eichmann's capture.[5] Yet, this bourgeois and normal person orchestrated the murder of hundreds of thousands of other people. Several scholars have disagreed with Wiesenthal and Arendt, the latest being British historian David Cesarani. Cesarani begins by portraying an Eichmann who was very normal and ordinary.

Raised in a conventional middle-class northern Austrian household, notwithstanding the early loss of his mother, Eichmann had what appears by all accounts to have been a normal childhood. Adolescence was not remarkable either. "He was an idle teen but hardly exceptional," notes the biographer. Eichmann had Jewish friends, worked as a kerosene salesman for Jewish employers and had Jewish relatives by marriage. Eichmann's Nazism appears to have evolved out of convention and not vicious antisemitism per se. Eichmann soon learned to follow orders and to hate Jews. "All we knew was obedience to others," Eichmann repeated at the Nuremberg trials. Cesarani summarizes Eichmann with the following.

> Some called him servile to his superiors, bullying to subordinates and victims, arrogant and ambitious, an opportunist. Others saw him as solipsistic and thoughtless, even banal. One of Arendt's achievements was to make a case that normality was no protection against doing harm to others.[6]

Yet, when the Nuremberg trial notes of American psychiatrist Leon Goldensohn were recently discovered, the Nazis-as-normal argument was again supported. Despite his best efforts to identify Nazi psychopathology, Dr. Goldensohn did not find much there. Instead, the key Nazis appeared little more than ordinary *opportunists*, though he notes that many of them had minimal remorse. Leon Goldensohn concludes,

> With the exception of Rudolf Hess and in the later stages of the trials possibly Hans Frank, the defendants at Nuremberg were anything but mentally ill. Alas, most of them were all too normal and excluding Hess they were mentally competent throughout their careers. Most of them turned out to be "good family men"

and many had been highly educated or had received some kind of professional training.[7]

Normalizing the Nazis as victims "by circumstance and opportunity"[8] may point up the limits of mental health as a source of understanding. Or, we have to clinically read between the lines.

For instance, when Nazi elite were administered the Rorschach ink-blot test for authoritarianism, three dimensions were discovered: superstition and stereotypy, projectivity, and anti-intraception (anti-tenderminded) – traits that comprise a larger picture.[9]

Juxtapose those traits with findings from survivor-turned-sociologist John M. Steiner. Examining both SS and Wehrmacht Nazis, Steiner found the following traits: valuing of loyalty and honor over justice, tendency toward fascistic government, satisfaction with past military efforts, and a reading of *Mein Kampf* prior to Hitler's election.[10]

Those traits dovetail nicely with psychologist Doug Kelley's findings regarding the Fuhrer's elite. Kelley writes in his memoir,

> They simply had three quite unremarkable characteristics in common – and the opportunity to seize power. These three characteristics were: *overweening ambition, low ethical standards [and] a strongly developed nationalism* but no insanity per se.[11]

In yet further examination of the Einsatzgruppen killers, Dr. Hohne and his colleagues found a lack of major pathology per se.[12] The study's overseer Dr. Molly Harrower did not observe any overt psychopathology either. Specifically, her ten experts could not distinguish between high-ranking good bureaucratic Nazis and everyday citizens. She went on to conclude, "*well-integrated, productive and secure personalities are no protection against being sucked into a vortex of myth and deception.*"[13]

Herein lies the rub. There is no question that serious mental illness was not involved in either rank-and-file or the highest Nazis. But again, if we read between the lines, there are trends that tell the tale of proclivity toward fascistic thinking. If it is as Dr. Harrower concludes, that well-integrated personalities are no protection against myth and deception, then the questions we should be asking have more to do with identifying *those who believe* the "myths and deceptions." But before we can offer a developmental model, let us update this concept to include the mindset of terrorists.

TERRORISTS AS NORMAL

The genocidal mindset is the same as the Nazis' and Islamic terrorists'. It is the mindset that is of issue and not the cultural identity as exemplified by the Jewish doctor Baruch Goldstein's attack on unarmed Arabs praying, or the IRA blowing up a British pub, or the Japanese kamikaze fighters, or Hindu nationalists, or Tamil Tigers, and the never-ending litany of names and places destroyed by those who possess similar mindsets. Subsequently, the following analysis uses the current concerns of militant Islam but can be applied to any terrorism mindset.

"Suicide bombers who kill others by blowing themselves up may seem crazy to us," psychologist Scott Atran recently informed the *New York Times*,[14] "But these people show no signs of psychopathology." Colleague Robert A. Pape agrees, citing statistics that suicide bombers are not more religious, crazy, or poorer but just good strategists defending their sense of nationalism. Retired military psychologist Charles Ruby responded in an article entitled *Are terrorists mentally deranged?* with the notion that terrorists were as the adage goes, crazy – crazy like a fox, and concluded that suicidal bombers merely lacked the necessary resources to carry out a more advanced military attack; and had they better hardware, they would not bother to use their body as a weapon.[15]

Most who address the psychology of suicide bombers are not clinicians and have no training per se rendering their opinion as less than professional. So, it came as quite a blow when psychiatrist Marc Sageman found similar answers. Aside from age (average 26 years old) and ethnicity (Arab-Muslim) his examination of 174 Global Salafi Jihad members failed to uphold any of the usual clinical traits.

"There were no obvious mental health problems," Sageman began. Refuting the usual suspects of childhood trauma, personality disorders such as antisocial, authoritarian, or paranoid and psychoticism Sageman continued:

> I found that many jihadis were of middle class, educated backgrounds – three quarters of them were married and several with children. They all held strong beliefs but strong beliefs per se do not constitute a mental disorder even if they are of a religious, political, vocational or recreational nature. My only significant finding was that the terrorists felt isolated, lonely and emotionally alienated, joining the jihad through preexisting social bonds. I have detected no dedicated recruiter in my search. The pressure comes from the bottom up; prospective young men are eager to join the movement.[16]

The traditional explanations for "growing up Jihadi" have included poverty and dysfunctional families (e.g. Jerrold Post)[17] but Sageman found answers in social psychology. He offers a model that emphasizes an intensification of beliefs via social bonds.

> More likely it is the case that experts have underestimated the social bonds that produced the Japanese kamikaze fighter in World War II "the glue of in-group love." "What you have is a group phenomenon; maybe no different than gang membership."[18]

And while not everyone joins gangs, the *good men behaving badly* theorists focus on alternative explanations, e.g. careerism, peer pressure, group loyalty, not unlike the social psychological processes that affected the Nazis.

It seems that like the Nazis, serious mental illness is not the explanation for terrorism. (Hitler did not suffer from schizophrenia while Al Qaeda fired Zacarias Moussaoui for being too crazy.) A better understanding of what makes Jihadis and Nazis tick is to appreciate that these disaffected persons have an emotional vacuum created by social identity. Associated with that emotional vacuum is the hunger to fill up with what Radcliffe's Louise Richardson aptly calls "implicit surroundings" – that which the culture and politics esteems. From this perspective, if the culture esteems suicidal bombing, socially identified persons are all too ready to rush in and fill the identity void.

We have to dig a little deeper or we are reduced to accepting that the young Muslim men from Leeds who coordinated the attacks on London's transit system were simply "ordinary British lads."[19]

NAZIS AS NOT SO NORMAL

Years ago Hans Askenasy asked a question in his book of the same title: *Are we all Nazis?* A second camp of social scientists have a fairly clear answer to Dr. Askenasy – a resounding no! We are not all terrorists, or Nazis, or political murderers. The thinking along this line is that while Nazification occurred in ordinary people – those citizens never before in trouble with the law, that is not the whole mental health story.

Mental health professionals understand that terms such as "normal" and "mentally healthy" are relative and clinically worlds apart. Normal and average in the psychiatric sense has to do with meeting minimal levels of functioning such as lack of major mental health symptoms, e.g. hearing voices and seeing things that are not there. Average is part of the mental health definition in that the average person functions within an average range of psychiatric experience. By contrast, mentally healthy people are statistically in the upper percentage of those who live in a culture – that percentage may be only 10–20 percent. Perhaps it is like driving a car. The average drivers may include those who drive drunk, speed excessively, or cause accidents. Their actions are considerably different from good drivers who do not do those things.

Genocide scholar Israel Charny[20] has a similar notion. He likens mental illness to the plague and then poses the following question: If most of the people catch the plague, does that make it normal?

More to the point, the Nazis-as-normal research is not as pure as appearances would have us believe. For instance, Eichmann's psychiatric testimony was deemed "inconclusive" and contained several glaring omissions. While philosopher Hannah Arendt's banality-of-evil perspective is widely touted, the findings of clinicians who examined Eichmann were not as poetic.

As the trial prosecutor asked one expert (Professor Szondi) to blindly interpret Eichmann's test results, the professor responded that this was "a man obsessed with an urge for power *and insatiable tendency to kill.*"[21] Eichmann's Rorschach results from psychologists I.M. Kulscar and Gus Gilbert found "a fairly well discernible personality type – the *murderous robot* of the SS."[22] Gilbert specifically made a case for deviant Nazi personalities consisting of constricted *schizoid-like traits*, and an *authoritarian* style highlighting those too eager to take hold of Nazi ideology. When researchers Miale and Seltzer reexamined sixteen of Gilbert's original records in 1975 they also upheld an "ill-enough-to-kill" hypothesis, finding support for fifteen of sixteen protocols with signs of *depression, and psychopathy with proclivities towards violence.*[23] Danish rank-and-file Nazis fared no better. Sadism, sociopathy, and proclivity to violence were involved, though absent in the Nazi leaders.[24] Finally, Henry Dicks's research of Nazis observed high Fs (*authoritarian* tendencies) in personality *and multiple ego deficits.*[25]

From this perspective, Harrower's notion that the Nazis were "well-mannered" but prone to an "oversimplification in information processing, ineffective problem solving style, altered self-esteem and diminished regard for human experience" sounds like the very same brand of authoritarianism of which the Frankfurt school was trying to warn.

So, if both the Nazis-as-normal and the Nazis-as-not-so-normal camps have well-reasoned arguments, perhaps it's the wrong argument. Ill-enough-to-kill may not be to do with severe mental health problems as much as delineating those who are susceptible to social forces of culture including prejudice and hate beliefs.

TERRORISTS AS NOT SO NORMAL

Few social scientists criticize the politically correct position of cultural relativism, but they should as it colors opinions in mental health. Psychiatric disorders often get a pass when politics or culture are involved. A case in point is Dinesh Bhugra's description of Indian women who self-immolate. Universally, clinicians would agree that actions that destroy an individual are suicide. But when suicide occurs when making a social, cultural or political statement, it is given a pass. The author goes on to conclude that "there is little evidence to suggest that women who commit this act suffer from a formal mental illness."[26]

Are immolents mentally ill because they are susceptible to social norms? The short answer is that nobody seems to know. When it comes to diagnosing individuals, there are whole books, e.g. *Diagnostic and Statistical Manual of Mental Disorders (DSM)*, which have pages upon pages of criteria. Yet when it comes to social or political problems, there is no diagnosis book and no consensus if something is pathological – *even when people are emotionally traumatized, maimed, or killed.* For example, here is what we in the West would consider horrific.

> Eyewitnesses, including civil defense officers, reported that several
> members of the Committee for the Promotion of Virtue and the
> Prevention of Vice interfered with rescue efforts because the
> fleeing students were not wearing the obligatory public attire (long
> black cloaks and head coverings) for Saudi girls and women. The
> mutawwa'in, a law-enforcement agency that has sought to ensure
> the application of the kingdom's strict gender segregation and
> dress code for women, has drawn criticism for abusive practices
> including harassment, physical abuse, and arbitrary arrest.
> "Whenever the girls got out through the main gate, these people
> forced them to return via another. Instead of extending a helping
> hand for the rescue work, they were using their hands to beat us,"
> Civil Defense officers were quoted as saying. The officers also said

they saw three people beating girls who had evacuated the school without proper dress. "Women and girls may have died unnecessarily because of extreme interpretations of the Islamic dress code," said Hanny Megally, Executive Director of the Middle East and North Africa division of Human Rights Watch. "State authorities with direct and indirect responsibility for this tragedy must be held accountable." The March 11 fire at the girls' public intermediate school in Mecca claimed the lives of at least fourteen students.[27]

Psychiatry remains overly cautious when it comes to labeling political or cultural or social conditions as pathological. Fortunately, Western lawmakers have more temerity. It is no accident that most developed nations have banned the following cultural practices: *hate crimes, child abuse, childhood marriage, child prostitution, honor killings, acid throws, female genital mutilation, sati, suicide bombings.*

By the same token, criticism of any of those practices will guarantee a label ranging from cultural insensitivity to imperialist bias by implying that Western psychiatry knows best. UCLA psychiatrist Joe Pierre offers a simple way of understanding the origins of social pathology.

When beliefs are shared by others, the idiosyncratic can become normalized. Therefore recognition of social dynamics and the possibility of entire delusional subcultures is necessary in the assessment of group beliefs.[28]

With social pathologies it is a numbers game. So, if enough people believe the practice to be good, true, or ordained from God, then it must be okay.

Unless, of course, there is cultural maturation. For example there are reasons that Western nations no longer use children for income, sex, or beat them till they scar. Almost all these cultures commited some variation of what we now understand as abuse in earlier times and recognize them today as child abuse as science, medicine, and law have developed to reflect a more evolved consciousness. In a similar vein, we no longer endorse slavery though two centuries ago we did. Since that time, democratic nations have learned about the ugliness of racism and now have laws preventing the abuse. Less than two hundred years ago (1826), the Catholic church executed a schoolmaster for replacing Ave Maria with another prayer. The Church no longer hangs people for heresy or disobedience. We no longer challenge each other to duels and so on. We have progressed to the next level of consciousness and will not return. Nobody grows backwards.

Psychology is different from other sciences in that the mind has certain universal principles not subject to cross-cultural debate. Donald Brown's human universals are even more salient as they apply to mental heath.

All children need to be loved. All people require a safe and secure environment. We all need food. Pathology should not get a pass because there is a less evolved political or cultural perspective to consider. Besides, if all the social pathologies listed earlier were to be accepted, why do those who have experienced such abuse report clinical depression, trauma, and a host of other psychiatric problems?

Along similar lines, criminologist Anat Barko has studied dozens of jailed would-be suicide bombers and offers the following insight.

> There are lots of places in the world where there are ethnic
> conflicts, nationalist conflicts ... and people don't blow
> themselves up. But suicide bombers have become role models for
> Palestinian youth. In one study, 36 percent of 12-year-old boys and
> 17 percent of Palestinian girls want to die a shaheed/martyr. It is
> an epidemic phenomenon. There are songs about them ... They
> see their posters on the streets. They hear about them in the media
> and in the mosques.

Barko has also profiled the recruiters noting that the militant groups seek women in crisis who hope to redeem themselves.

The women are usually outcasts seeking to be idealized in a society where suicide bombers, or martyrs are folk heroes. Some were rebels who resented the rigid rules of their society and felt smothered by their families. A few had suicidal tendencies. Some were at an age where marriage prospects were slim. The female suicide bombers are like marionettes. Somebody can pull the wires and manipulate them.[29]

She recounts the case of a woman who became a suicide bomber to get back at her father. The father refused to allow her to marry because of a dowry dispute with her fiancé's family. Yet, becoming a shaheed/martyr/witness as delineated in the Koran (Sura 169) and to appreciate the martyr as not really dead *"Think not of those who are slain in Allah's way as dead. Nay, they live, finding their sustenance in the presence of their Lord"* covers up everything that was going on in the family.

There is one line from Dr. Barko's account that points to psychiatry's diagnostic dilemma – the "bombers are like marionettes." At this time, no clinician is examining the lack of emotional development in terrorists. Also, nobody is diagnosing social and political overidentification and asking why this is occurring. To this day, no clinician is pointing out the pathology of being so empty inside, so underdeveloped emotionally that to kill themselves and others for the good of the group, for the culture, for the religion, for the politics, makes total sense.

Genocide scholar Israel Charny is the exception.[30] He points to previous death cults, e.g. Nazis, Japan (kamikaze), and Stalin and then focuses on Arab-Muslim extremists. "Suicide bombers are not normal!" declares Charny. He then points a finger at the clinicians for caving in to exonerate mental pathology if politics are involved.

His basic tenet makes intuitive and well as clinical sense – *normal people want to live* – and this is the case irrespective of culture or politics.

The pity of it all is that suicide bombers did not start off that way. They were at one point children who wanted to be loved, nurtured, and live productive and meaningful lives. Along the way, they were not given the same opportunities to develop themselves as individuals. Instead, they were overfed a politics of hate. The ones who did not become shaheeds (martyrs) are nauseated, empty, and weary. One can only hope that their weariness will transform from the political to the personal and their emotional development begins.

THE LYNCHPIN OF CONFORMITY: WHO COMPLIES, WHO DEFIES?

> Everyone in the world would like to be different from others but instead, you Marcello want to be the same as everyone else
>
> Italo in Bertolucci's Il Conformi.

When is the last time you did not stand at a game when the national anthem was played? Would you even consider the same behavior at home watching television? What changed was the number of people around and complying with the collective.

Complying with the collective became known experimentally in 1936 when psychologist Muzafer Sherif asked several students to estimate the distance a dot of light in a dark room had moved. Although their estimates initially varied, they reached a group consensus – that the light had indeed moved a couple inches, even though it was completely stationary.

But the power of others to influence became clearer when University of Pennsylvania researcher Solomon Asch asked subjects to estimate line lengths (see Figure 2.1). The test was simple. Even though two lines in separate boxes were equal, a surrounding group stating that they were not informed the respondents. To Asch's surprise, thirty-seven of the fifty subjects conformed to the majority opinion at least once, even when they knew that the majority opinion was wrong. In a revised version of the experiment, subjects were permitted to write down their answers after hearing the answers

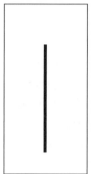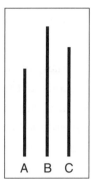

FIGURE 2.1 Asch's line length test

of others, and levels of conformity declined to about one third. Whether they agreed or not, they were going with the group – many of the defiers (nonconformers) said they felt conspicuous, and crazy. When asked why people conformed to social group opinion and gave up their own personal opinion, most said they did so because they wanted to be liked by the group or thought the group was better informed than they were. "The tendency to conformity in our society is so strong that reasonably intelligent and well-meaning young people are willing to call white black," observed Asch.[31]

While the findings are intriguing, equally as fascinating is what social psychologists did with them – they used the findings to underreport Asch's 25 percent who consistently demonstrated independence from social forces (they named them independents). A research team at New York State University at Stony Brook reviewed Asch's key studies and noted:

> Ironically, many accounts of Asch's work draw from it the very
> assertions he was intending to refute. He concluded that he had
> convincingly demonstrated powers of independence under certain
> highly demanding conditions. What we find, though, is that most
> writers have portrayed his findings as evidence that individuals are
> predominately weak in the face of the social pressures he studied.
> These portrayals have minimized or ignored what Asch
> particularly stressed and considered his major finding, namely the

capacity of few individuals to resist group pressure despite severe stress and doubt.[32]

Almost fifty years to the date, many of the same conformity qualities emerged in paranormal versions of the Asch experiment. When researchers created a fake séance, one third of the subjects swore they saw the table levitate. A similar percentage of persons also swore they saw bananas ripen under a pyramid if those around them reported that the bananas were ripening.[33] The authors concluded that people acquire a paranormal belief through observation, but their work also addressed conformity and the social influence of others.

When reality becomes ambiguous and we become uncertain of our own judgments, we look to others for direction. One laboratory experiment is particularly telling. Several subjects were injected with epinephrine (synthetic adrenalin) while others were given a placebo. All subjects were told of epinephrine's potential side effects, i.e. heart palpitations and hand tremors. Since some subjects experienced adrenalin's side effects, their explanations of high anxiety made sense. The rest looked for explanations outside themselves. When a member of the research team entered the room and became angry, so did they. On another occasion, he entered the room happy and they became happy. Those who were given the placebo or were forewarned remained unaffected. The study suggests that if people are anxious, they'll believe what the group/culture tells them.[34]

By the early 1960s, in what is now a classic and well-known experiment, Yale University researcher Stanley Milgram rigged a phony electrical shock apparatus and monitored how those involved responded to conformity.

A shock generator, appearing as a black instrument panel with a row of thirty toggle switches and identifying degrees of "slight to severe shock" (15–450 volts), was placed in front of a student. The unsuspecting subject was told to send an electric jolt when a wrong test answer was given. The experimenter reassured him,

"Although the shocks can be extremely painful, they cause no permanent tissue damage." No one was actually wired to any electricity. The research team's cries of pain were rigged to be heard from another room each time a lever was hit. At 75 volts, grunts and groans were heard. At 150 volts, pleading to be let out of the experiment was evoked. At 180 volts, there were more cries that the pain could no longer be tolerated. As the shocking levels approached the label Danger: Extreme Shock, pounding on the wall was added. Then, an eerie dead silence was heard. When the phony shock test was repeated in other cultures, the results were about the same – most people (65 percent) continued to shock obediently until the ersatz death of others was announced.

Parenthetically, there was plenty of variation in shock rates from 31–91 percent in the United States to 28 percent (Australia) and 88 percent (South Africa) – a finding perhaps not so surprising since Australia consistently ranks more individualistic than other nations. There was no real change in the degree of obedience from 1963 to when it was repeated in 1985, notes biographer Thomas Blass, who applauds that the findings are consistent over time and place.

> There was absolutely no relationship between when a study was conducted and the amount of obedience it yielded. In a second analysis, I compared the outcomes of obedience experiments conducted in the US with those conducted in other countries. Remarkably, the average obedience rates were very similar: In the US studies, some 61 percent of the subjects were fully obedient, while elsewhere the obedience rate was 66 percent … Milgram noted in a letter to Alan Elms: "We do not observe compliance to authority merely because it is a transient cultural or historical phenomenon, but because it flows from the logical necessities of social organization. If we are to have social life in any organized form – that is to say, if we are to have society – then we must have members of society amenable to organizational imperatives.[35]

The third classic conformity experiment, called The Stanford Prison Experiment (SPE), also yielded similar findings. In the SPE, some students temporarily dressed as prison guards and assumed guard roles while others became prisoners. But the guards became so brutal that the experiment had to be shut down a week prematurely. Lead experimenter Philip G. Zimbardo concluded this:

> The majority of "normal, average, intelligent" individuals can be led to engage in immoral, illegal, irrational, aggressive and self-destructive actions that are contrary to their values or personality – when manipulated situational conditions exert their power over individual dispositions.

But it turns out that the individual dispositions or traits never quite go away. The SPE was recently replicated on television and the results were at best inconclusive. As British psychologists attempted to remake the study for a BBC broadcast, the personalities of the guards and their rejection of their roles collapsed the entire study. [36]

Nevertheless Zimbardo sticks to his guns and in his most recent book, *The lucifer effect*, he insists that we blame the Iraqi Abu Ghraib prison abuse on the situation though he expands it to the system in total. His notion that "bad systems create bad situations, create bad apples, create bad behaviors, even in good people," p. 445, avoids all reference to personality traits and emotional development. It begs an immediate question. If trait and emotional development are not involved in creating "good people, then why in a genocide do some people rescue?"[37]

More to the point, consider that in all three classic conformity studies, a substantial number of subjects did not conform. In the Asch experiment, at times two thirds of those tested did not conform. In the Milgram experiment, one third of the shockers defied the experimenter's orders and as in the Asch experiment, the remaining persons would often argue and hesitate, and proceed in a stop-and-go fashion. Even in the Stanford Prison Experiment, a third of the guards emerged as "good guys." Zimbardo states,

There were three types of guards. About a third of the guards were hostile, arbitrary, and inventive in their forms of prisoner humiliation ... There were tough but fair guards ... There were "good guys" who did little favors for the prisoners and never punished them.[38]

Those findings fly directly in the face of the social psychology credo concerning the power of the situation. Milgram summarized his results in a statement that would anticipate Zimbardo and incorporate Asch's research as well. He had hoped that "the mutual support provided by men for each other is the strongest bulwark we have against the excesses of authority."[39]

Yet, wasn't it this same "mutual support" that under different circumstances blindsides people into bad judgments like groupthink or polarizes group members to take extreme positions, or creates an Abu Ghraib? Milgram was probably thinking about group support for the defiers. Like the intrepid scientist he was, Milgram continued to pursue all avenues. With the assistance of Yale graduate student Alan Elms, he reexamined 40 of the original 160 persons who had participated in the original four-part "Proximity Series" studies and matched for age, occupation and gender (all male) but now included defiance and obedience for the subjects. Those who had stood up to the experimenter were named defiants and those who did not were termed obedients. Now there were some new findings to consider: One out of three participants terminated their participation immediately. The shock rate also declined when other defiers/nonconformists were introduced and the respondents sat physically closer to those receiving the shock.[40]

Partway into the procedure, two of the conformists defied the experimenter and refused to continue – one at 150 volts the other at 210 volts. When this occurred, a full 90 percent of the subjects followed their example and dropped out at some point before the end. What was the ingredient that separated defying wheat from the chaff? You can hear it in the response of the respondents themselves. Here is how an upset 32-year-old Dutch defiant named Jan Rensaleer responded to social pressure.

RENSALEER: I can't continue this way; it's a voluntary program if the man doesn't want to go on with it.

EXPERIMENTER: Please continue.

RENSALEER: No I can't continue I'm sorry.

EXP: The experiment requires that you go on.

RENSALEER: The man, he seems to be getting hurt.

EXP: There is no permanent tissue damage.

RENSALEER: Yes but I know what shocks do to you. I'm an electrical engineer and I have had shocks ... and you get real shook up by them – especially if you know the next one is coming. I'm sorry.

EXP: It is absolutely essential that you continue!

RENSALEER: Well I won't. – not with the man screaming to get out.

EXP: You have no other choice.

RENSALEER: I do have a choice [incredulous and indignant:] Why don't I have a choice? I came up here on my own free will. I thought I could help in a research project. But if I have hurt somebody to do that, or if I was in his place, too, I wouldn't stay there. I can't continue. I'm very sorry. I think I've gone too far already probably ... I should have stopped the first time he complained. I did want to stop at that time. I turned around and looked at you. I guess it's a matter of ... authority, if you want to call it that: my being impressed by the thing and going on although I didn't want to."[41]

Compared to obedients, here is how defiants answered several of the test items.

> How close were you to your father when you were a child? (defiants said close)
> How were you usually punished? (defiants said less severe punishment)
> How do you get along with him [father] now? (defiants were consistently close)

Choose five words to describe your father's or the
experimenter's personality. (defiants chose positive words)
Did you ever shoot at a man in combat? (defiants shot less)

When tested, defiants possessed the following traits as well:
they were more socially responsible; they had lower authoritarian
scores (F-scale) and were less willing to shock others to the highest
levels, even when education was factored out (as low levels of education are often linked to authoritarianism).[42]

By and large, the most intriguing notion is something Jane
Loevinger would have predicted. When developmentalist Lawrence
Kohlberg examined the defiants with a battery of exams, *defiants
scored at the highest levels of moral development.*[43]

At times in psychology, parallel research occurs in an area and
yet remains separate from the main research. A closely related if not
identical concept is called nonconformity. The finding from the
nonconformity studies is fairly consistent with the defiance research
and suggests the following.

Nonconformity begins as a person grows out of his or her teens
(social conformity peaks at age 13 declining thereafter).

Nonconformity has been linked to the following traits: more
honesty and generosity, elevated levels of self-esteem, and elevated
levels of achievement and leadership.

Nonconformity is also correlated with decreased need for
others' approval, and declines in authoritarianism and conservatism.

A related concept may be dissent as portrayed in John Gwalt-
neys's *The Dissenters.*[44] Gwaltney compiled a collection of dissenters or, in his terms, "soldiers of conscience," that ranged from a
Puerto Rican mother protesting conditions at her daughter's school,
to nuns rebelling against their patriarchal hierarchy.

One may call the concept by a variety of names – dissent,
nonconformity, or defiance – but irrespective of name, a pattern has
emerged. This pattern suggests that those who follow orders (obedients)
function as socially identified and are at lower levels of autonomy

than more personally identified defiants. Many of the low and high traits parallel those who in a genocide become perpetrators (see Chapter 3). By contrast those who are independent-minded and stand up to the social forces (defiants) have the same traits as rescuers (See Chapter 5). Those with scores ranging between those extremes appear to become bystanders (See Chapter 4). In order to better understand the above differences, a developmental perspective should be introduced.

WHY A DEVELOPMENTAL PERSPECTIVE IS NEEDED

Every seven years British director, Michael Apted, films a new documentary of the fourteen children he began with in 1964 when they were age seven. The *Seven Up!* children are now in their fifties with the next installment, *56 Up!*, anticipated in late 2011. The series is a powerful reminder that with time some things change and some things stay the same.

Developmental research works along the same lines, reminding us that certain phenomena such as age, cohort differences, and key traits like self-concept remain relatively stable over time. Some researchers have made it their life's work to examine how neuroticism, extraversion, and openness to experience stay the same in people over time.[45] A separate thirty-year study found in both sexes self-esteem traits of "reliant, having rapid tempo, assertive rather than submissive, undiscouraged by adversity, without fluctuating moods, decisive, having a sense of personal meaning, initiating of and response to humor and unpreoccupied with ruminate fantasy."[46]

Adult developmentalists utilize the gambit of theorists who have addressed changes over time. The developmentalists focus on maturity and the notion of passing through key points that reflect childhood, adolescence, and adulthood in thinking.

Developmental levels may be best understood through Abraham Maslow's (1908–1970) notion of a hierarchy of needs (see Figure 2.2). From a Maslowian perspective, people must satisfy basic physiological needs (eating, sleeping, shelter) and when those needs

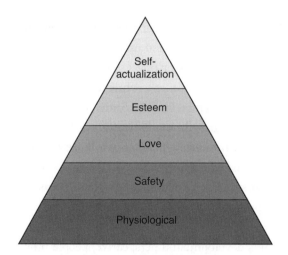

FIGURE 2.2 Maslow's hierarchy of needs

are satisfied, a person's concerns shift toward personal security, then to socially connecting, loving and bonding with others, and then to achieving for themselves. "Self-actualization" needs culminate in the realization of one's potential, a state of psychological health attained by people who are motivated by meaning instead of insecurity and social fit.

Self-actualized persons are thought to possess the following traits more than the average person: tolerance and appreciation of others, the capacity to be alone and enjoy solitude, greater spontaneity, playfulness and creativity, enhanced independence, and the ability to develop a philosophical stance and experience the mystical. On tests that measure self-actualization, respondents endorse statements such as "It is better to be yourself, than popular," and "if given the choice between having lots of money or personal meaning, I would pick personal meaning."

Related theorists such as Erikson and Fromm suggest that most multistage theories can be seen in terms of childhood, adolescence, and adulthood, designated as Tiers I, II, and III.

The theorist who anticipated much of postmodern discord is Erich Fromm (1900–1980). From a Frommian perspective, conformity is a key to understanding why people do what they do. His seminal work *Escape from Freedom*[47] can be summed up as follows.

In modern Western culture, one's character develops through completing a series of social tasks, all the while consuming its products. People then either regress and become materialistic automatons or become open and grow humanistically. Authoritarian societies seem to produce authoritarian persons while permissive consumer societies produce people who consume. To escape from both cultural trappings – consumerism and fundamentalism/fascism – requires avoiding the trappings of materialism, fundamentalism, and other authoritarian experiences.

According to Fromm's developmental perspective, people move from authoritarian states towards socially conforming ones and progress onto humanistic and productive states. This is the key to understanding emotional levels. Fromm's divisions were believed to be encouraged in a culture that esteemed emotional development, though he used the term common at the time – humanism. From a Frommian perspective, people could find true freedom if they embarked on a path of personal identity and emotional growth and avoided the seductions of social identity – religion, politics, and materialism. For Fromm, there was no other choice but to grow emotionally (see Table 2.1).

SOCIAL OVERIDENTIFICATION

Fromm would have said that most people are too fearful and culturally landlocked to develop themselves. Instead, they remain developmentally arrested, identifying and overidentifying with their culture, role, social group, and religion. Some do not fit and, unable to tolerate the anxiety of having no identifiable group, shift towards a more structured identity.

Cults and religious experts have known about this for years. In the television series the Wild Wild West, some would "go Indian" and adopt a new social identity. Others, e.g. born-again Christians and Islamicists, are well known for their political and religious conversions. You may recall the names of John Walker Lindh or

Table 2.1 *Stages of identity development*

Mode/Tier	I	II	III
Lifespan	childhood	adolescence	adulthood
Maslow	physical needs	social needs	esteem /actualize
Fromm	authoritarian	conformist	humanistic/ productive
Erikson	personal identity	social → personal	fulfillment
Freudian	false self	some authenticity	authenticity
Ego	preconformist	conformist	postconformist
Moral	preconventional	conventional	postconventional
Cognitive	preoperational	concrete	formal
Political	fascism	socialism	democracy
Religion	fundamentalist	conventional	universalism
Identity	diffused	foreclosed/ moratorium	achieved

Adam Gadahn as they shifted from being Californian to becoming Afghan Jihadi and Al Qaeda operatives. The following newspaper account depicts a young woman from Monceau-Sur-Sambre, Belgium.

> She was the typical girl-next-door – pretty daughter of a hospital secretary who grew up on a quiet street in this rust-belt town and finished high school before becoming a baker's assistant. Years later she was in Baghdad, carrying out a suicide bombing in the name of jihad – a disturbing sign of the reach of Islamic militancy. Neighbors say Muriel Degauque, who blew herself up last month at age 38 trying to attack US troops, had lived a conventional life but became heavily involved in Islam after marrying an Algerian. "She was absolutely normal as a kid," said Jeannine Samain, who lives a few doors down from the Degauque family home in the shadows of a towering coal pile. "When it snowed, they would go to the hill together with the sled." She recalled the last time she saw Degauque, eight months ago: "She was veiled. By that time she would just say 'bonjour' and that was it." Authorities say Degauque

carried out an attack Nov. 9 near an American military patrol in Iraq after entering the country from Syria a month ago, and was the only person killed. "It is the first time that we see a Western woman, a Belgian, marrying a radical Muslim and is converted up to the point of becoming a jihad fighter," federal police director Glenn Audenaert said. Authorities say Degauque had been a member of a terror group that embraced al-Qaeda's ideology. The group included her second husband, a Belgian of Moroccan origin who entered Iraq with Degauque and was killed in murky circumstances while trying to set up a separate suicide bombing. Experts said converts to Islam like Degauque are often easy prey for extremists because their search for a new identity can make them impressionable.[48]

When it becomes extreme is when it makes the news. In Holland, a 26-year-old of Moroccan origin named Mohammed Bouyeri took offense for his entire social group of fellow Islamicists. Hearing that 44-year-old filmmaker Theo van Gogh and Somali Dutch parliamentarian Ayaan Hirsi Ali had produced a movie depicting Islam in a negative light, he decided to do something about it. The documentary *Submission* consisted of interviews with several Muslim women and detailed conflicts with Islam and adjusting to Dutch culture. On the morning of November 2, 2004, as van Gogh was cycling to work, Bouyeri shot him and pulled out a machete and cut his throat. He then used another knife to pin on van Gogh's chest a long rambling note to Hirsi Ali calling for a holy war (jihad) against nonbelievers. The note read:

> I know for sure that you, Oh America, will go down. I know for sure that you Oh Europe will go down. I know for sure that you, Oh Netherlands, will go down. I know for sure that you Oh Hirsi Ali, will go down. I know for sure that you, Oh unbelieving fundamentalist, will go down.[49]

According to Dutch psychiatrists, Moroccan males are ten times more likely to be schizophrenic than a native Dutchman. But most schizophrenics could not care less about politics, let alone murder a film director on a busy street in Amsterdam. The smoking gun is an underdeveloped emotional life and all the signs of social overidentification were there.

Bouyeri began sprouting a Taliban-style beard, donning the djellaba, posting Islamist tracts on the Web, listening to the invective of a Syrian cleric, and watching videos of holy warriors cutting the throats of infidels. The enticements of Dutch culture, such as smoking dope, drinking alcohol, and being attracted to Western women proved to be too much. Add to that the two prior physical assaults of slitting of Dutch policeman's throat and assaulting his sister's boyfriend when he realized they had had sex. Bouyeri had to protect the group.

"Two kinds of personal identities may be most susceptible to terrorism," notes University of Miami's Seth Schwartz:

The aimless, diffuse identity and the oppositional authoritarian foreclosed identity. In both the diffuse and foreclosed cases, group ideals are adopted whole and without question. The aimless person is vulnerable to the allures of terrorism because terrorist ideologies which are filled with certainty, purpose, and commitment may provide a sense of direction to a previously unguided life ... Feeling unable to make identity decisions, these individuals seek out a group that will give them an identity. This makes such individuals particularly vulnerable to manipulation. They become willing to go to their deaths for ideas that they have appropriated from others rather than for ideas that they have chosen through independent thought and reflection.[50]

In the field, mental health tests are used to identify proclivities toward violence but none address social overidentification. Treatment plans are formed and patients are provided with a round of medications that slow down their violent tendencies and force delay of impulses and allow more time to reflect options other than violence. No one says to the patient – get a life and develop yourself emotionally. Most people, even those in the field of mental health, have never heard of such a thing.

WHAT IS EMOTIONAL DEVELOPMENT ?

The whole of the individual is nothing but the process of giving birth to himself; indeed we should be fully born when we die, although it is the tragic fate of most individuals to die before they are born.

Erich Fromm, *The sane society*[51]

Emotional development focuses similarly on human needs by way of stage progression, but expands the theory to encompass cognitive (style, complexity, impulse control preoccupation), moral (pre/conventional/post) and ego functions (differentiation/integration). These constructs and the reasons for progression, stagnation, or regression from one stage to another have to do with insight and the potential for advancing to a more evolved sense of self. There is integration of perceptions and cognitions, as well as a sense of control or mastery over relationships and anticipated future events. It is believed that few of us achieve the highest levels in all aspects of functioning.

This school of thought began at Washington University with the work of Jane Loevinger, in the early 1970s. For Loevinger, all human beings progress through a series of stages or developmental milestones. Each stage consists of increasing levels of awareness and the progression moves from impulsivity, self-protectiveness, and conformity, toward greater self-awareness, and increased conscientiousness, culminating in enhanced individuality and autonomous functioning. For reasons of brevity, several of these categories will be collapsed into tiers highlighting maturity, cultural compliance, and post-cultural functioning. Emotional development is a stage progression theory of social and emotional decision-making and in conjunction with what is known from social identity research, I will break these down into the following levels of identity as well. I will use the term personal identity as a synonym for emotional development.

The development of personal identity may be conceptualized along three Tiers paralleling childhood, adolescence, and adulthood.

A foreground-to-background shift offers a simple understanding (in Table 2.2, the background is represented by parenthesis). At the earliest stages of maturation (Tier 1), most of one's identity is social (the tribe/group/collective) and one's personal identity is yet to be developed. At the adolescent stage of identity development (Tier II), one's personal and social identities compete for prominence as social identity begins to decline and personal identity accelerates. At the adult stages of identity development (Tier III) one's personal identity has shifted to the foreground while one's social identity has reverted to the background. The shift at this highest level is not permanent and is fairly malleable. For instance, when one's social group is temporarily threatened, one's social identity proceeds to the foreground while one's personal identity reverts to the background. When the threat has ceased, previous levels of identity continue. Full development unfolds as cultural conformity lessens and progresses through three levels – preconformist, conformist, and postconformist.

Each level of development is fluid. An individual at a lower level may possess several traits of the next higher tier. Individuals of the higher tiers may not possess all those traits consistently. Under stress and pressure, a Tier II individual may not be concerned with cultural success, but may revert temporarily to a survival mode of functioning. As the stress passes, Tier II again becomes the dominant operating mode. Similarly, a Tier III individual may operate at the highest levels most of the time but revert to lower levels under stress.

As Table 2.3 shows, maturation cuts across several domains of functioning. In cognitive science, thinking evolves from simple to more complex thoughts with the integration of the logical and emotional parts of our minds (see Figure 2.3). In religious maturation, concretized forms of belief such as fundamentalism (Tier I) progress through an integration of personal and conventional beliefs (Tier II) culminating in universal ideas relevant to all religions (Tier III). Moral and ego development follow the same patterns. Beginning with

Table 2.2 *Personal identity tiers*

Tier I (personal identity) social identity	Tier I PRECONFORMIST (Childhood) This lowest level of functioning is characterized by basic social relating. Individuals are defined by narcissistic indulgences and characterized by self-absorption, impulsivity, naiveté, and opportunistic social exchanges. The lack of internal emotional development is offset by greater dependency on social norms and conventional morality. Their blatant or overt racism is marked by authoritarianism and by poor internal integration. Basic emotions (anger) and primitive defenses, e.g. numbness; splitting (good/bad) tolerance of ambiguity/others; are employed in the most defensive manner. They look to define themselves and their actions based on outside influences and are more vulnerable to superstitions, extremist religious/political beliefs, and hate beliefs. Relationships are one sided, manipulative, and status enhancing. Behavioral attributions and perceptions are based on group stereotypes, e.g. "He did that because he's an Italian." Identity is reflective of social norms that range from conservative to extreme. Tier I tend to be more manipulative and status seeking than the average person. Ego development researchers identify perpetrators at the earliest (preconforming) levels as having more psychopathology than other subjects. As the capacity for emotional development has been suppressed, higher level emotions such as empathy are rarely nurtured. As a consequence of the lack of empathy, relationships are marginal and often

Table 2.2 (cont.)

	exploitive. Such emotionally immature individuals are often abusive when compared with laboratory controls. The personal identity is diffuse, ready to merge with the prevailing culture.
Tier II personal identity social identity	Tier II CONFORMIST (Adolescence) This middle level of functioning is characterized by conflicts between personal and social aspects of the self and the need to fit into the social group. It is defined by cultural conformity and attempts at integrating others' needs and empathy. There is more emotional development and less reliance on social norms and conventional morality. There is enhanced ego strength and more sophisticated defenses, e.g. tolerance of ambiguity/others, rationalization, are utilized in a moderate defensive manner. Identity is reflective of conventional social norms. Tier II covert or "subtle racism" is characterized by restricted cognitive style. Relationships tend to be manipulative and status enhancing. Behavioral attributions and perceptions are based on group stereotypes and some recognition of personal identity, e.g. "He did that because he's got some Italian in him or maybe it's his arrogance." The personal identity is in moratorium or foreclosed, suggesting some exploration and development but short of full and achieved sense of self.
Tier III personal identity (social identity)	Tier III POSTCONFORMIST (Adulthood) This highest level of functioning is characterized by authenticity. Defined by the integration of social and emotional realms there is a need to fit in with one's authentic self. There is little social pretense

Table 2.2 (cont.)

and no social manipulation. Characteristics include insight, empathy, interdependence, greater tolerance of ambiguity/others, openness to experience, maturity, integration of opposites, applied universal justice, personal meaning and spirituality. Integration of one's emotions with one's cognitions occurs with the most sophisticated defense mechanism and the least defensive manner. Relationships are non-exploitive and respecting of the rights of others. Identity is reflective of emotional norms. Behavior attributions and perceptions are based on personal identity, e.g. "He did that because he's Jimmy." Religious beliefs tend to be unconventional and personal. The achieved identity is least susceptible to social forces.

selfish and self-protecting modes of functioning (Tier I), maturation proceeds toward convention (Tier II) through a series of stages marked by eroding cultural conformity, and culminates in an evolved sense of self. Persons with an evolved sense of self are authentic, conscientious, autonomous, and well integrated, having developed a capacity for caring, toleration of others, and upholding universal principles of justice (Tier III).

Differences in development are not so apparent in daily life but become clearer in extremis. For most, the only true test would be threat of death. The threat of death provides a window to levels of emotional development. Against death, people shed their social makeup. In a holocaust, some people are perpetrating, while some are rescuing. Most alternate their behavior somewhere between those two extremes, at times helping, at times killing, or just standing by.

Table 2.3 *Maturation tiers*

	Perpetrators Tier I	Bystanders Tier II	Rescuers Tier III
Stage	preconformist	conformist	postconformist
Mode	conflicted	conforming	conscientious
Norms	wholly accepts	partially accepts	resists/transcends
Control	external	moderate	internal
Openness	rigid	culturally conforming	open
Empathy	low	moderate	high
Defenses	angry/acting out	more sophisticated	well integrated
Self	self-centered	self- & other-centered	universal
Identity	preformed	social & personal	personal
Level	survival	social status	authenticity
Goal	protective	cultural success	meaning
Frame	distorted	culturally consistent	emotionally congruent
Vocation	limited	culturally confirmed	emotionally confirmed
Success	role-based	status/money/power	highest emotional/spiritual
Concerns	survival	social status	authenticity
Experience	limited	culturally confirmed	emotionally confirmed
Insight	poor	moderate	high

Table 2.3 (cont.)

	Perpetrators Tier I	Bystanders Tier II	Rescuers Tier III
Tolerance	low	moderate	high
Mental health	low	moderate	high
Relations	marginal	superficial/role	emotionally deep
Relating	exploitive	needs exchange	authentic concern
Play	exploitive	normative	creative
Fear	ambiguity	unconventionality	inauthenticity
Motivation	survival	power	growth
Politics	fascistic	conservative	liberal/democratic
Religion	fundamentalism	conventional	atheism – universalism

Adapted from S. K. Baum (2004) A bell curve of hate? *Journal of Genocide Research*, 6, 567–577.

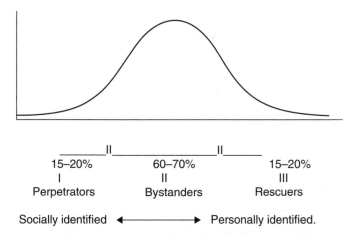

FIGURE 2.3 A bell curve of perpetrators, bystanders, and rescuers

Figure 2.3 depicts a bell curve distribution of emotional maturation. At one extreme is a less emotionally developed group representing 15 to 20 percent of the population. The opposite end of the curve is comprised of the healthy and mature segment of the population, also constituting 15 to 20 percent. The middle 60 to 70 percent consist of average, ordinary people. The curve of normal distribution with a mean of zero and a standard deviation of one is often called the bell curve because the graph of its probability density resembles a bell. We have no way of knowing if hate is evenly distributed within the population but if that assumption is justified, then about 68 percent of the values are at within 1 standard deviation away from the mean, about 95 percent of the values are within two standard deviations and about 99.7 percent lie within 3 standard deviations.

EMOTIONAL DEVELOPMENT AND THE GENOCIDAL MIND

Nationalism ... is certainly a dangerous mental illness wherever it appears.

Sebastian Haffner from *Defying Hitler*

The model of perpetrators, bystanders, and rescuers shown in Figure 2.4 is fairly simple. The two separate identities, social and personal, progress through culture and determine who will become a perpetrator, a bystander, or a rescuer. For example, those who were the lowest functioning people (Tier I), when placed in a culture of hate became the most likely perpetrators. Those same persons when

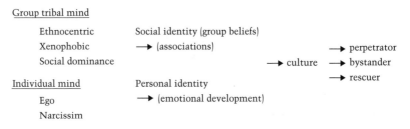

FIGURE 2.4 A model of perpetrators, bystanders, and rescuers

placed in a bystander culture became more bystander-like and when placed in a tolerant culture of rescue, became more rescuer-like.

The same pattern of moderate functioning would occur with bystanders. Raise bystanders in bystander conditions and they continue to stay passive but place them in a rescuer culture and more prosocial behavior occurs. Conversely, place bystanders in a culture of hate and they are inclined to perpetrate.

The same pattern of highest functioning would occur with rescuers. Raise a rescuer in a culture of hate and they will minimize their helping behaviors. Raise a rescuer in a culture of bystanding and they will seek a middle ground and be less inclined to assist than potentially is available. Raise a rescuer in a culture of helping and they will maximize their levels of rescue and aid to others.

Tier I (perpetrators)

Vulnerability to the prevailing cultural norms, namely normative hate/stereotyping, hallmarks those in the first (I) and to a lesser degree, the second (II) tiers. Tier I individuals have an underdevelopment of personal identity and an overdevelopment of social identity. Their personal voice and social voice are undifferentiated: all feelings, needs, and thoughts are the identified social group's feelings, needs, and thoughts. Their "personal and religious identities may have completely fused – often in the social camaraderie of adolescence, when unsettled identities become stabilized and institutionally detonated," adds Nicol Institute's Scott Atran.[51]

An example of Tier 1 development would be Mohammed Reza Taheri-azar. Taheri-azar was the 22-year-old Iranian immigrant and former University of North Carolina student who in March of 2006 rammed his Jeep SUV into a crowd of students, sending nine to the hospital. Taheri stated that he was "aveng[ing] the deaths of Muslims around the world." In court he smiled and said he was "thankful for the opportunity to spread the will of Allah."[52]

Tier II (bystanders)

Conventionality, cultural compliance, and social status are the hallmarks of Tier II individuals. A classic example of those in the more moderate tier can be seen in the Kitty Genovese example.

Catherine Genovese was a 29-year-old woman who was tragically stabbed to death in New York in March of 1964. What makes her death more tragic is that the thirty-eight people who witnessed it did nothing to stop it. Several witnesses were unaware that an assault or homicide was in progress; some thought it a lovers' quarrel or a drunken brawl or a group of friends leaving a nearby bar. Social psychologists are beginning to understand that an attack at 3:15 a.m. in a large apartment complex may create a bystander effect.

More trait-based examples of Tier II include average, law-abiding, church-going citizens. The movie *About Schmidt* captures a Tier II type well. The film depicts Warren Schmidt's life of routine and restrained Midwest conventionality. Several life-altering events (his retirement, his wife's unexpected demise, and his estranged daughter's marriage) act as wake-up calls for Schmidt to move up the ladder of emotional development.

Ordinary people are able to function on a daily basis and conform to the prevailing culture's standards, but are not emotionally evolved. When standard mental health tests are administered to the average person, most are found to possess "remarkably little insight and awareness, with only fair levels of emotional stability and poor resilience against stress."[53]

In contrast, emotionally evolved individuals have the highest levels of mental health: they possess insight, emotional stability and resilience against stress. This line of research consistently finds emotionally evolved people to be the least racist. A news item from South Africa of July 19, 2005 exemplifies the bystander experience. "At first I was angry, but now I realize it's just a sign of the times that people are just too scared to help each other." This was the reaction of Chris Botha after a bizarre incident in which his daughter Minette, 21, spent nearly four hours in the swimming pool of an Alberton home in the early hours of Sunday morning, after the car she was traveling in crashed through a wall surrounding the property, killing the driver, Vernon Laurie, 19. Laurie and Botha were cousins. Laurie apparently lost control of the car at about 3:00 a.m. A post-mortem revealed that he probably drowned. Botha had apparently screamed for help for hours before the woman staying at the house in Hartebees Street, Mayberry Park, alerted the authorities by pushing a panic button.[54]

Tier III (rescuers)

Tier III persons perceive others individually and personally rather than socially; they see another's psychological makeup, not cultural/ social group. They have more individuated impressions of others by integrating more complexities.[55] Tier III people make judgments often in terms of emotional needs, traits, and feeling states. Empirical studies suggest Tier III have better self-worth[56] and that those who function at higher ego development levels are more competent in the workplace.[57] Tier III individuals function autonomously and subscribe to universal ideals and principles, concepts which parallel Maslowian notions of self-actualization. Developmentalist Alan Waterman understands the notion as human potential.

> For each person there are potentials, already present though unrecognized, that need to become manifest and acted upon if the person is to live a fulfilled life. For many people, the task of

recognizing and acting upon these potentials is not an easy one as evidenced by the stresses associated with an identity crisis. Feelings of eudaimonia or person expressiveness can serve as a basis for assessing whether identity elements are well chosen. The presence of such feelings can be used as a sign that identity choices are consistent with an individual's potential and thus can provide a basis for self-fulfillment.[58]

Tier III individuals are also less racist and part of that is they are unlikely to adhere to social norms. In studies where more evolved people were compared to less evolved people, the evolved persons (low suppressors) did not follow what their social group said or did.[59] They tend to be politically liberal, and a longitudinal study found a host of positive traits associated with early and healthier childhoods, e.g self-reliant, energetic, having developed closer relationships, and somewhat dominating.[60]

There is related work regarding stages in prejudice development as well. In a major study on antisemitic prejudice, researchers found that prejudice is nurtured in those lacking the skills and sophistication to combat it and the converse of that was equally certain:

Judged on purely statistical grounds, level of cognitive sophistication accounts for more of the variance in the incidence of adolescent prejudice than any other factor examined ... There are two fundamental reasons we propose why the cognitively sophisticated are better able to resist prejudice than their unsophisticated counterparts. First, by virtue of their cognitive capabilities, they are better able to deal with the "truth content" of any stereotype. Second, they are better fortified to resist an intolerant response to "real" group difference.[61]

An example of Tier III in action is Sister Reine. I met this 48-year-old French Canadian nurse and nun who runs a 22-bed leprosy clinic by herself in the middle of the Peruvian Amazon. The atmosphere of heat, humidity, and squalor is oppressive. Yet, amid the chaos, she continues aiding the ill. I asked her why she continues and she replied:

> I guess you just get used to it. These people need my help. We give the medicines and the leprosy is halted. I remember the first day here on the job. It was pretty grim and there are no resources. Another nurse from the States was here and now I'm by myself. We're supposed to get some more personnel here, but you know cutbacks and all. This is a fifteen-bed unit and it gets tough running it alone at times. But it's worth it. It must be. I've been here for four years now.

Is Sister Reine hate-proof? Hardly. But the integration of logic with emotion and the synthesizing of opposites characterize her. Tier III individuals are able to integrate more comprehensively – to see the larger picture of experience. Marked by less impulsivity and greater tolerance of ambiguity, persons in this tier understand context and the relativity of their beliefs and actions. The highest levels of empathy hallmark them. Tier III people function with integrity. They are devoid of social pretense and convention. They are often not of high social status within a culture, as they do not define themselves materially.

Journalist Gitta Sereny understood the emotional development of genocide thirty years ago. Sereny interviewed the Treblinka concentration camp commandant Franz Stangl. After multiple experiences she concluded her book with the belief that Stangl had stopped growing emotionally. She concluded that a "moral monster" was not born but was produced by "interference with this growth."[62]

NOTES ON CHAPTER 2

1. E. O. Wilson (1998) *Consilience*. New York: Knopf. Alvin Poussaint, cited in an op-ed piece for the *New York Times* www.abcnews.go.com/sections/living/InYourHead/allinyourhead_58 hmtl. Orthopsychologists have criticized the notion of making racism a disease, offering instead the notion that "we must rearrange our priorities and dismantle

institutions that perpetuate and maintain racial privilege." Unfortunately, Poussaint minimizes the misconceptions, and has no explanation for very racist and nonprejudiced persons. He probably should have listened to James Golden and Richard Rieke (The rhetoric of Black Americans) when they said "communicating with white men about their beliefs and attitudes regarding black men may be more a psychiatric than a persuasive problem." See D. Wellman (2000) From evil to illness: Medicalizing racism. *American Journal of Orthopsychiatry*, 70, 28–32.

2. A. G. Miller (1982) *In the eye of the beholder*. Westcourt, CT: Praeger.
3. R. J. Lifton (1986) *The Nazi doctors*. New York: HarperCollins, p. 5. Wiesel's remarks are from the 1997 debate marking the 50th anniversary of Nuremberg as "you know it's demonic that they are human" (www. nijm.org).
4. H. Arendt (1963) *Eichmann in Jerusalem*. New York: Viking, p. 25.
5. Wiesenthal, cited in T. Blass (1993) Psychological perspectives on the perpetrators of the Holocaust: The role of situational pressures, personal dispositions, and their interactions. *Holocaust and Genocide Studies*, 7, 30–50.
6. D. Cesarani (2006) *Becoming Eichmann*. Cambridge, MA: Da Capo.
7. L. Goldensohn (2005) *The Nuremberg Interviews*. New York: Vintage.
8. Dick de Mildt (1996) *In the name of the people*. Den Hague: Marinus Nijhoff, p. 311.
9. M. N. Resnick & V. J. Nunno (1991) The Nuremberg mind redeemed: A comprehensive analysis of the Rorschachs of Nazi war criminals. *Journal of Personality Assessment*, 57, 19–29.
10. J. M Steiner (1980) The SS yesterday and today: A sociological view. In J. E. Dimsdale (ed.) *Survivors, victims and perpetrators*. Washington, DC: Hemisphere.
11. My emphasis: D. M. Kelley (1947/1961) *22 cells in Nuremberg*. New York: McFadden, p. 171.
12. H. Z. Hohne (1970) *The order of the death's head*. New York: Coward-McCann.
13. M. Harrower (1976) Rorschach records of the Nazi war criminals: An experimental study after 30 years. *Journal of Personality Assessment*, 40, 341–351, my emphasis.
14. "Indoctrination, careful training, and a relatively stable and positively reinforcing social milieu," comprises the education component of the

neophyte bomber (S. Atran (2002) *In gods we trust*. New York: Oxford University Press, p. 271).

15. R. A. Pape (2005) *Dying to win*. New York: Random House; C. Ruby (2002) Are terrorists mentally deranged? *Social Issues and Public Policy*, 2, 15–26.

16. M. Sageman (2004) *Understanding terrorist networks*. University of Pennsylvania, p. 135.

17. Political psychologist Jerrold Post and others have opted for the family maladjustment theory of terrorists; see J. Post (1984) Notes on a psychodynamic theory of terrorist behavior. *Terrorism*, 7, 241–256.

18. M. Sageman (2004) *Understanding Terrorist Networks*, University of Pennsylvania.) p. 135; personal communication, June 3, 2004.

19. L. Richardson (2006) *What terrorists want*. New York: Random House, p. 49; *San Francisco Chronicle*, 7/14/05, p. A1.

20. H. Askenasy (1978) *Are we all Nazis?* New York: Lyle Stuart. I. W. Charny (2006) *Fascism and democracy in the human mind*. Lincoln: University of Nebraska Press.

21. Léopold Szondi, cited in D. Cesarani (2006) *Becoming Eichmann*. Cambridge, MA: Da Capo.

22. US psychologists Kulscar and Gilbert: "without the support of normal and respectable leaders in that society, without a considerable following among the masses of people ... it would hardly have been possible for the Nazi leaders to precipitate as great a social catastrophe as they did," cited in G. M. Gilbert (1950) *The psychology of dictatorship*. New York: Ronald, p. 287.

23. F. Miale & M. Selzer (1976) *The Nuremberg mind*. New York: Quadrangle.

24. E. A. Zillmer, M. Harrower, B. A. Ritzler & R. P. Archer (1995) *The quest for the Nazi personality*. Hillsdale, NJ: Lawrence Erlbaum.

25. H. V. Dicks (1950) Personality traits and national socialist ideology: A war-time study of German prisoners of war. *Human Relations*, 3, 111–154.

26. D. Bhugra (2005) Sati: A type of nonpsychiatric suicide. *Crisis*, 26, 73–77, quote on p. 73.

27. Saudi girls school: http://news.bbc.co.uk/2/hi/middle_east/1874471.stm retrieved Sept 10, 2007.

28. Citing p. 163 from J. M. Pierre (2001) Faith or delusion: At the crossroads of religion and psychosis. *Journal of Psychiatric Practice*, 7, 163–172.

29. D. Brown (1991) *Human universals*. New York: McGraw-Hill. Barko www.americanintifada.com/2004/3/3-21-5.htm

30. I. W. Charny (2007) *Fighting suicide bombing*. Westport, CT: Praeger International Security. Also see F. M. Moghaddam (2005). The staircase to terrorism. *American Psychologist*, 60, 161–169.

31. S. E. Asch (1956) Studies of independence and conformity. A minority of one against a unanimous majority. *Psychological Monographs*, 70.

32. R. Friend, Y. Rafferty & D. Bramel (1990) A puzzling misinterpretation of the Asch conformity study. *European Journal of Social Psychology*, 20, 29–44.

33. B. Markovsky & S. Thye (2002) Social influence in paranormal beliefs. *Sociological Perspectives*, 44, 21–44. Also see R. Wiseman, E. Greening & M. Smith (2003) Belief in the paranormal and suggestion in the séance room. *British Journal of Psychology*, 94, 285–297.

34. S. Schacter & J. Singer (1962) Cognitive, social, and physiological determinants of emotional state. *Psychological Review*, 69, 370–399.

35. T. Blass (2004) *The man who shocked the world*. New York: Basic, p. 108. Also see his article in *Psychology Today*, Mar/Apr 2002 and the original S. Milgram (1974) *Obedience to authority*. New York: HarperPerennial. Also see A. G. Miller (1986) *The obedience experiment*. New York: Praeger.

36. S. Richer & S. A. Haslam (2006) Rethinking the psychology of tyranny: The BBC prison study. *British Journal of Social Psychology*, 45, 1–40.

37. His later description of heroes suggests good people are created by "human nature." See P. Zimbardo (2007) *The lucifer effect*. New York: Random House, p. 461.

38. Zimbardo quickly adds: "Even the 'good' guards felt helpless to intervene, and none of the guards quit while the study was in progress. Indeed, it should be noted that no guard ever came late for his shift, called in sick, left early, or demanded extra pay for overtime work." www.prisonexp.org/slide-37.htm. Yet one wonders, had the experiment continued, how the good guards would have acted.

39. S. Milgram (1974) *Obedience to authority*. New York: HarperPerennial.

40. *Ibid.*

41. Rensaleer, cited in S. Milgram (1974) *Obedience to authority*. New York: HarperPerennial, p. 51.

42. A. C. Elms & S. Milgram (1966) Personality characteristics associated with obedience and defiance toward authoritative command. *Journal of*

Experimental Research in Personality, 1, 282–289. Also see S. Milgram (1964) Group pressure and action against a person. *Journal of Abnormal and Social Psychology*, 69, 137–143.

43. L. Kohlberg & L. Candee (1984) The relationship of moral judgment to moral action. In W. Kurtines & J. L. Gurwitz (eds.) *Morality, moral behavior and moral development* (52–73). New York: Wiley. Also see L. Kohlberg (1969) Stage and sequence: The cognitive-developmental approach to socialization. In D. A. Goslin (ed.) *Handbook of socialization theory and research* (347–480). Chicago: Rand-McNally.

44. Nonconformity is linked to the following traits: for honesty and generosity, see J. Arndt, J. Schimel, J.Greenberg & T. Pyszczynski (2002) The intrinsic self and defensiveness: Evidence that activating the intrinsic self reduces self-handicapping and conformity. *Personality and Social Psychology Bulletin*, 28, 671–683. For declines in authoritarianism and conservatism and decreased need for others' approval, see L. E. Petersen & J. Dietz (2000) Social discrimination in a personnel selection context: The effects of an authority's instruction to discriminate and followers' authoritarianism. *Journal of Applied Social Psychology*, 30, 206–220. For elevated self-esteem, see R. T. Santee & C. Malasch (1982) To agree or not to agree: Personal dissent amid social pressure to conform. *Journal of Personality and Social Psychology*, 42, 690–700. For elevated levels of achievement and leadership, see B. R. Strickland & D. P. Crowne (1962) Conformity under conditions of simulated group pressure as a function of the need for social approval. *Journal of Social Psychology*, 58, 171–181. Similar conclusions with other references are available in Kevin Wren's chapter on Independent Behaviour, see K. Wren (1999) *Social influences*. London: Routledge. See also J. Gwaltney (1986) *The dissenters*. New York: Random House.

45. R. R. McCrae & P. T. Costa Jr. (1997). Personality trait structure as a human universal. *American Psychologist*, 52, 509–516.

46. J. Block & J. Block (2006) Venturing a 30-year longitudinal study. *American Psychologist*, 61, 315–327, citing p. 321.

47. Fromm's theory is more social based, evolving from escaping the Nazis in Berlin. After moving to New York in 1934 he completed his doctorate in sociology and psychoanalytic training. At Columbia University, he went on to develop a social psychoanalytic school then took a position at the National University in Mexico City where he established a similar

training institute, somewhat radical for the times. He then took teaching positions at Michigan State and New York Universities before retiring to Muralto, Switzerland.

48. Identity: www.usatoday.com/news/world/2005-12-01-belgians-bomber_x.htm

49. The van Gogh murder follows on the heels of a murder by a 33-year-old Dutchman named Volkert van der Graaf, who believed the outspoken professor Pim Fortuyn posed a threat to "vulnerable members of society." Van der Graaf had over-identified with the Muslim immigrants. For Bouyeri & Buruma see *New York Review of Books* October 5, 2006, p. 33. Also see I. Buruma (2006) *Murder in Amsterdam.* New York: Penguin.

50. Seth Schwartz, writing with colleagues Curt Dunkel and Alan Waterman, Terrorism: An identity theory perspective; paper submitted for publication. Also see V. Saroglou & P. Galand (2004) Identities, values, and religion: A study among Muslim, other immigrant, and native Belgian young adults after the 9/11 attacks. *Identity*, 4, 97–132; E. Fromm (1955) *The Sane Society.* New York: Rinehart.

51. S. Atran (2002) *In gods we trust.* New York: Oxford University Press, p. 271.

52. www.danielpipes.org/blog/576

53. *About Schmidt* (2002) NewLine. See also J. Shedler, M. Mayman M. Manis (1993) The illusion of mental health. *American Psychologist,* 48, 1117–1131.

54. Botha www.news24.com/News24/South_Africa/News/0,,2-7-1442_1740060,00.html

55. J. W. Sherman, St J. Stroessner, F. R. Conrey & O. A. Azam (2005) Prejudice and stereotype maintenance processes: Attention, attribution, and individuation. *Journal of Personality and Social Psychology*, 89, 607–622.

56. For more on ego development see S. Hauser, A. Jacobson, G. G. Noam & S. Powers (1983) Ego development and self-image complexity in early adolescence. *Archives of General Psychiatry*, 40, 325–332.; R. R. Irwin (2002) *Human development and the spiritual life.* New York: Kluwer/Plenum; G. Noam (1988) Solving the ego development mental health riddle. In P. M. Westerberg, A. Blasi & L. D. Cohn (eds.) *Personality development.* Mahwah, NJ: Lawrence Erlbaum; A. Norenzayan & S. J. Heine (2005) Psychological universals: What are they and how can we know? *Psychological Bulletin*, 131, 763–784; J. Pals & O. P. John

(1998) How are dimensions of adult personality related to ego development?: An application of the typological approach. In P. M. Westerberg, A. Blasi & L. D. Cohn (eds.) *Personality development.* Mahwah, NJ: Lawrence Erlbaum; S. T. Hauser (1993) Loevinger's model and measure of ego development: A critical review. *Psychological Inquiry,* 4, 1–25; J. N. Knutson (1973) Personality in the study of psychology. In J. N. Knutson (ed.) *Handbook of political psychology.* San Francisco: Jossey-Bass. Most studies on personality show a consistency over time with a mellowing over the years. There appears to be an increase in conscientiousness and agreeableness with decline in extraversion. R. Helson, C. J. Soto & R. A. Cate (2006) From young adulthood through the middle ages. In D. K. Mroczek & T. D. Little (eds.) *Handbook of personality development* (pp. 337–352). Mahwah, NJ: Lawrence Erlbaum.

57. D. W. Evans, L. Brody & G. G. Noam (2001) Ego development, self-perception and self-complexity in adolescence: A study of female psychiatric inpatients. *American Journal of Orthopsychiatry,* 71, 79–86.

58. A. S. Waterman (1992) Identity as an aspect of optimal psychological functioning. In G. R. Adams, T. Gullotta & R. Montemayor (eds.) *Advances in adolescent development.* 4, *Identity formation during adolescence* (pp. 50–72). Newbury Park, CA: Sage, p. 59.

59. C. Crandall, A. Eshleman & L. O'Brien (2002) Social norms and the expression and suppression of prejudice: The struggle for internalization. *Journal of Personality and Social Psychology,* 82, 359–378.

60. J. Block & J. Block (2006) Venturing a 30-year longitudinal study. *American Psychologist,* 61, 315–327.

61. C. Y. Glock, R. Wuthnow, J. A. Piliavin & M. Spencer (1975) *Adolescent prejudice.* New York: Harper & Row, p. 165.

62. G. Sereny (1983) *Into that darkness.* New York: Vintage, pp. 232–233.

3 Perpetrators

A Rembrandt masterpiece of science and art put together.

Bo Gritz, on the Oklahoma City bombing.

On the cover of Ron Rosenbaum's book *Explaining Hitler* is a compelling portrait of human contradiction. After your eyes leave the title, they are drawn to the background, where a photograph of an infant Adolph Hitler becomes more obvious. As one stares into the infant's eyes to search for clues, there are none to be found. This is a baby with all a baby's innocence, awe, and excitement of human life. The picture stands in stark contrast to the name that became synonymous with hatred and misery for millions. The simple juxtaposition of name and photo commands the observer to ask: between then and now, what happened?

DEFINING PERPETRATORS

The search for answers began with those who had fled an adult Hitler. Pioneering work by Theodor Adorno and his Frankfurt School colleagues resulted in an investigation called *The authoritarian personality*. Among other findings, their psychoanalytically based work emphasized childhood experiences feeding fascism. Yet their work fell short of linking punitive childhood experience directly to the adult genocidal mind. The lacuna was in part due to a lack of delineation between the groupings of perpetrators, bystanders, and rescuers. In spite of the shortcomings, Adorno and his colleagues made several important discoveries.

The first discovery of the Frankfurt school was that there were indeed *personality* components to antisemitic persons – specifically types who in thinking were rigid, fearful, and closed to new experience. This finding was soon echoed by Gordon Allport's esteemed *The nature of prejudice*.[1] Both books emphasized that those who disliked Jews tended to dislike other ethnic minority, racial, and religious groups as well (Mormons, Hispanics, African-Americans, gays). This notion of a prejudiced personality remains today one of two research avenues (the other being social group membership) that researchers of prejudice pursue.

Many of Adorno's findings were yielded from a test called the Fascism or F-scale. The test contained thirty items such as:

Obedience and respect for authority are the most important virtues children should learn.

A person who has bad manners, habits, and breeding can hardly expect to get along with decent people.

What this country needs most, more than laws and political programs, is a few courageous, tireless, devoted leaders in whom the people can put their faith.

Adorno's second discovery holds true to this day. It is the notion that those who are inclined to obey authority and act aggressively towards others possess the following traits:

CONVENTIONALISM: Rigid adherences to conventional values

SUBMISSION: Uncritical attitude towards their own group's idealized moral authority

AGGRESSION: Punishment for those who violate convention

ANTI-INTRACEPTION: Intolerance of tender-mindedness

SUPERSTITION AND STEREOTYPY: Rigid categorization and belief in the supernatural

POWER AND TOUGHNESS: Preoccupation with power and dominance, strength/weakness

DESTRUCTION AND CYNICISM: General hostility

PROJECTIVITY: Placing their sexual and aggressive impulses onto others

SEX: Preoccupation with sexuality and morals of others

Respondents would endorse each statement to varying degrees on a scale ranging from strongly disagreeing to strongly agreeing. Those who scored high in authoritarianism tended towards the political Right, opposing social programs, favoring tough law and order for crime, and concerned for morality.

Psychologist Bob Altemeyer psychometrically picked up where Adorno left off. Noting little support for the nine traits that Adorno proposed, Altemeyer created a new measure called the Right-Wing Authoritarianism (RWA) scale. With improved measurement qualities he found only three factors involved in authoritarianism – conventionalism, authoritarian submission, and authoritarian aggression. Authoritarianism as the basis for the genocidal mindset was becoming clearer, especially in perpetrators.

Who are perpetrators? According to historian Ben Valentino, in an average population, the number of perpetrators ranges between 2 and 15 percent. Supporting estimates are based on hardened Nazis. For instance, historian Michael Mann noted that a third of the Nazis had records of prewar extremist activity. Elsewhere the estimates are more theoretical, based on the percentage of authoritarians within a population. They are estimated to range between 15 and 20 percent. Estimates of perpetrators within the Muslim community also suggest 15 percent.[2]

There are anecdotal estimates as well. Jane Elliott, the grade school teacher who performed the now-classic experiment on in-group prejudices, summarized her work with the following. Approximately 80 percent of the people in the community are compassionate, caring people concerned about their school, their kids. "But," she adds, "the 20 percent, the vocal, vicious minority, intimidated the rest of them."[3]

No two perpetrators are alike and distinctions may be based on the degree of psychopathy. Some perpetrators function as antisocial personalities compared to the relatively more evolved narcissists and more rigid persons. From lawless antisocial tendencies to obedient authoritarians, all perpetrators have one trait in common – they can kill without much remorse. Instead of being concerned with the traditional concerns of "what would the neighbors think?" the concern of the perpetrator is "would those in authority (church, employers, police) approve?"

BACKGROUND

No single line of theory or research points to how a perpetrator mindset evolves. Terri Moffitt suggests perpetrator traits may be passed down genetically. Others point to biobehavioral considerations. For instance, a 20 to 30 percent decrease in cortical and subcortical development has been observed in neglected children with declines in the anger-balancing neurotransmitter serotonin. A low active gene has also been implicated. Some differences are striking. Non-abused children are known to respond immediately to others with concern, sadness, and empathy. However, abused toddlers remain unresponsive to cries of other children. In addition, it is not uncommon for abused children to become easily distressed, lashing out without provocation. Similar findings occur in primates research. Abused and neglected monkeys were unable to read feeling states such as anxiety, anger, and despair – non-abused primates can.[4]

Perpetrators seem to evolve from perpetrator homes. Researchers have long documented criminogenics or the relationship between criminal home life and family and later criminal activity.[5] Some child-rearing practices may be involved. Specifically, punitive, authoritarian, and rigid child-rearing practices in German and Rwandan culture have been addressed.

Psychoanalyst Alice Miller points to the influence of a popular physician in prewar Germany who, like Dr. Spock in America, set the standards of child-rearing. She describes the content of Dr. Schreber's lauded writings.

> In these works it is stressed again and again that children should start being trained as soon as possible, even as early as their fifth month of life, "if the soil is to be kept free of harmful weeds." I have encountered similar views in parents' letters and diaries, which provide the outsider with a clear indication of the underlying causes of the serious illnesses that developed in their children, who were later to become my patients. But initially, these patients of mine were unable to derive much benefit from

these diaries and had to undergo long and deep analysis before they could begin to see the truth in them. First they had to become detached from their parents and develop their own individuality.[6]

Punitive child-rearing practices may create authoritarianism though there are many facets of perpetrator mentality. Historian George Browder emphasized low socioeconomic status, and religiously dogmatic families. Yet the findings are at times mixed. For instance, several years ago political psychologist Gerda Lederer examined both American and German teens with respect to authoritarian thinking. Surprising, at least to most Americans, was the finding that Americans had higher rates of authoritarianism.[7]

Many times, teachers are able to identify perpetrators. "Their play is filled with warnings," notes educator Maria Piers. "They invent chaos in order to show that everything is under control. They portray fear to prove that it can be conquered. No theme is too large or too small for their intense scrutiny." Her analysis comes none too soon. Every 7 minutes a child is bullied and that affects 1 out of 4 kids, with slightly fewer (1 out of 5 kids) admitting to being a bully. Teachers are also assaulted, robbed and bullied. There are 84 crimes per 1,000 teachers per year.[8]

Workplace and school shooters have the same genocide mentality. The FBI report after the Columbine High School massacres reveals the same underlying process. Here are the report's highlights:

The shooters were members of an antisemitic, anarchistic, nihilistic cult called the Trench Coat Mafia, who played off each other's doomsday fantasies complete with the Web page statement, "I live in Denver and I would love to kill almost all its residents."

The two teenagers had an astonishing arsenal of weaponry – three dozen homemade bombs, a 9-mm assault rifle, a semiautomatic pistol and two sawed-off shotguns.

They had a prior history of breaking into cars, making a video in which they talked about blowing up the school, and having a preoccupation with the explosive *Doom* computer game. Being armed and dangerous, it was just a question of obtaining weapons and selecting a due date. The day of choice was April 20, Hitler's birthday.

Workplace shooters adopt a similar mindset, but no longer care if they have the support of the people. Don, a middle-aged, single, White male from the Midwest explains to me how he "got into such a head-space" at an auto assembly manufacturing plant. Humiliation, both personal and professional, so often a component of perpetration, had developed into an obsession. Here is how he thought:

> I was all set to take down the people at Chrysler. I know I wasn't thinking right but I didn't care anymore. I had been working there for 25 years with no recognition of my job. Then one day I got the idea of making myself known. I'd walk into the plant and just start shooting. I was so filled with hate I didn't care if I got shot [smiles]. At least my message would get out and they'd finally know my name, and they would finally say "Gee, he had a point – we should have listened!"

PERPETRATOR DEVELOPMENT

In terms of research, directly applying Jane Loevinger's theory, the findings are fairly clear. Ego development is correlated with traits in that less mature people are more sociopathic.[9] Genocide scholar Israel Charny correctly identifies the mindset as fascistic and goes on to describe it as a mindset:

> based on earlier or more childish forms of thinking where right and wrong and truth and falsehood are neatly divided from each other. It is based on the mind's need for logic and consistency. It is also based on people's weakness in needing so much to be part of a confirmed social consensus or "to be in the right" even when one has to decide in favor of a position that runs contrary to one's own senses and logic.[10]

Psychopathy is a personality disorder affecting about 3 percent of men and 1 percent of women, characterized by impulsivity, self-centeredness, and lack of remorse for one's actions. Distinctions between perpetrators' levels of psychopathy are subtle. French foreign correspondent Jean Hatzfeld observed the differences in the psyches of nine Rwandans known as the Kibundo gang. These genocidaires were mostly farmers from the same small region in Rwanda and killed an estimated 50,000 out of their 59,000 Tutsi neighbors.

"I got into it, no problem," says one gang member. "Killing is easier than farming," reported another. Each describes what it was like the first time he killed someone, what he felt like when he killed a mother and child, how he reacted when he killed a cordial acquaintance, how cutting a person with a machete differed from cutting a calf or a sugarcane. One of the perpetrators recounts his experience:

> Some offenders claim that we changed into wild animals, that we were blinded by ferocity ... that is a trick to sidetrack the truth. I can say that outside the marshes our lives seemed quite ordinary. We stand on the paths ... we had our choice amid abundance. We chatted about our good fortune, we soaped off our bloodstains in the basin, and our noses enjoyed the aromas of full cooking pots. We rejoiced in the new life about to begin, feasting on leg of veal. We were hot at night atop our wives and we scolded our rowdy children ... We put on our field clothes. We swapped gossip at the cabaret, we made bets on our victim, spoke mockingly of cut girls, squabbled foolishly over looted grain. We sharpened our tools on whetting stones. We traded stories about desperate Tutsi tricks, we made fun of every "Mercy!" cried by someone who'd been hunted down, we counted up and stashed away our goods.

For Hatzfeld, ordinary war criminals differed from the Kibundo gang on the basis of remorse. Specifically, lower level perpetrators were incapable of remorse. While equally guilty of savagery, bystanders seem to reflect on the effort and demand forgiveness from both their victims and themselves. "But," he notes,

> The [perpetrator] killers of the Kibundo gang, while they speak frequently of forgiveness and hope to receive it, do not use the questioning language of self-examination. The way they see it, pardon – whether collective or individual, useful or useless, painful or not – comes on its own and is available upon request.[11]

Hatzfeld is correct. This lack of remorse and other key emotions are the hallmarks of perpetrator experience. Other key traits include impulsivity, numbed feelings, splitting (all-or-none thinking), intolerance of ambiguity, and projection of such lacunas and multiple deficits in ego function and character.

TRAITS

Table 3.1 shows the range of traits shown amongst perpetrators. If one could imagine a continuum of perpetrators, the more pathological end may be characterized by psychopathy, e.g. manipulative, self-centered, impulsive behavior, while more developed perpetrators would show traits of rigidity, closed mindedness, and intolerance.

Conventionalism/conformity

Social conformity is an important dimension in authoritarianism. Social conformity is key, in part because the authoritarian has no internal guide to distinguish right from wrong and is dependent on an external standard. Those experiences that are too open and without structure cause undue anxiety. Identity and feelings and needs must be laid out and described in black-and-white terms. Anything other than traditional, conventional, and cognitively simple thinking creates even more anxiety in a person with the most limited coping skills.

Simplistic thinking has been statistically linked to having more prejudices and the reasons seem obvious. "Although fascist thinking creates a certainty and hence a sense of safety, security and pleasure in having all loose ends tied down, slowly but surely its

Table 3.1 *Tier I perpetrator development levels*

	Antisocial	Preauthority	Authoritarian
Emotional	anti-to-high conformity	conformity	conformity
	least coping	some coping	some coping
	cognitive simple	moderate	more complexity
	superstitions/ myths	stereotypes	stereotyped
	impulsive	impulsive	less impulsive
Relations	self-centered	self-centered	less self-centered
Experience	survival	survival	survival/social status
Play	bullying	competitive	sense of fairness
Interaction	exploitive	manipulative	manipulative
Identity	none	presocial	social
Remorse	none	some	capable
Retaliation	high	high	moderate
Motivations	fear/power	fear/power	fear/power
Politics	fascist	fascist	conservative
Religion	primitive	fundamentalist	fundamental→ conservative

relentless quest for power and certainty destroys everything that stands in its way and eventually its own life as well," notes a genocide expert.[12]

Irrespective of culture, there appear to be open- and closed-minded people – and the closed-minded authoritarians cannot tolerate change. In examining the psychological makeup of White supremacists like the Ku Klux Klan, many were found to be fearful not of Blacks and Jews per se, but of diversity and new experience.[13]

Emotional insight into one's beliefs, feelings, and behavior hallmarks higher cognitive and emotional functioning. By contrast, a perpetrator's level of insight is low and often subject to distortion. It is as if they are hurt and someone has to pay for their pain. Their hurt produces a suspiciousness of outsiders, often projected onto outsiders as xenophobic. They are keepers of the fort and stay continually on guard for a pending threat.

Not surprisingly, when shocks were delivered in a verbal learning task, those who shocked more had higher authoritarianism scores.[14]

Submission to authority

Spanish filmmaker Luis Bunuel once quipped, "God and Country are an unbeatable team – they break all records for oppression and bloodshed." He must have been thinking about perpetrators and their need to submit to a higher authority.

Not all fundamentalists become perpetrators, though the opposite is fairly certain in that perpetrators have marked tendencies to extreme religious and political beliefs. The extreme sense of submission to a father-like figure may have evolved from living in an autocratic family where punishment was extreme and abusive.

Authority within the family generally translates to a paternalistic family culture. And such authority translates from cultural group to the culture at large.

When religion stops people from thinking about the larger questions, when it invokes infallibility and loyalty and avoids criticism, when it criticizes the followers for not believing enough, when it asks for full submission – then the cult is placed into religious culture and abuse occurs.

Putting the cult into culture, is exactly the process in fundamentalist anything. One does not have to be a Richard Dawkins, Christopher Hitchens, or Sam Harris aficionado to appreciate submission to authority as a limitation fostered by fundamentalist thought.

"The books promote an interest in witchcraft," writes a Christian reviewer of the popular children's book series *Harry Potter*.

No parishioners would dare to question why Harry's version of sorcery is taboo and Gandalf's activities in *The lord of the rings* are "approved." But one is supposed to believe and trust in the Lord. Trying to create a closed culture in an open and free society is difficult but not impossible. Educational materials regarding human sexuality, homosexuality, and Darwinian-based science are immediately rejected in favor of abstinence, Rev. Phelps-style homophobia and Intelligent Design. Trust in the Lord is extended toward one's unenlightened neighbor with prayers for the soul. Materialism is esteemed, especially regarding purchases from Christian-approved businesses. These businesses run the gamut from workouts at The Lord's Gym to purchasing a rapture-ready toilet.

It is an uphill battle for most born-again Christians but they are quick to remind themselves that their battles with secular humanists and other devil-based groups pale in comparison to the burden of the larger Christian group. It is all in the name of spreading the message by all available means. For instance, Cedar Hill, Texas, Trinity Church erects an annual haunted house for teens. But this particular exhibit is different than most, employing fire and brimstone at every turn. Says their spokesperson, "A part of salvation is being afraid of going to Hell. Hell house scenes depict botched abortions, adulterous wives, suicidal drug abusing teens, and Gay men dying of HIV. After witnessing the multitude of sins, the tour group is led into a room and asked if they accept the Lord Jesus Christ as their personal savior. Not surprisingly, most do without question."

Concerned about born-again Christianity as a political movement trying to fuse church and state, writer Michelle Goldberg says

> It makes no sense to fight religious authoritarianism abroad while letting it take over at home. The grinding, brutal war between modern and medieval values has spread chaos, fear and misery across our poor planet. Far worse than the conflicts we're experiencing today however would be a world torn between competing fundamentalisms. Our side, America's side, must be

the side of freedom and Enlightenment, of liberation from stale constricting dogmas. It must be the side that elevates reason above the commands of holy books and human solidarity above religious supremacism. Otherwise God help us all.

Writer Chris Hedges is equally concerned. The son of a Presbyterian minister, Hedges points to the hundreds of senators and members of congress who have achieved approval scores from the Christian Right advocacy groups with calls to dismantle church–state separation. He points to the increased politicalization supported by the Christian-approved television and radio shows reinforced by the Christian curriculum and home schooling. He makes no bones about these *American fascists*, paralleling the yearning for apocalyptic violence with the fascist movements of 1930s Germany and Italy.[15]

Devoid of complex choices, fundamentalist thinking is thinned and put into two files, right or wrong. Such polarized thinking helps simplify, e.g. saved/unsaved, and combines with selective information to keep the thinking closed. As with all groups, ethnocentrism, xenophobia and a proclivity toward social dominance translate to fear and loathing of outsiders. To help secure the group, an ever-changing enemies list is maintained that indicts all unsaved Christians, non-Christians, secular humanists, gays, Jews and to a lesser extent Catholics, feminists, pro-choice abortion advocates, anti-school-prayer proponents, church–state separatists, and those who would limit the movement's evangelization of the community. Restricted or approved media – for example in the US, movies, television (250 stations) and radio (1,600 stations), arts, theater, counseling, and literature – censor out potentially conflicting information.

When psychological tests are administered, religious fundamentalists score lower academic achievements. But it is not about achievement as much as mindset. As individuals, religious fundamentalists are more easily hypnotized and test as vulnerable to guilt and manipulation. Moreover, fundamentalists alternate between self-serving passivity in the face of authority and a greater sense of omnipotence. In the main, researchers have evidence to suggest that fundamentalists are more paranoid, racist, and homicidal than mainstream believers.[16] With a whole culture behind you, who needs the rest of the world?

Certainly not fundamentalist Islam. By contrast, the politically savvy born-agains' Christianity appears fairly tame. Islamicism, be it the Shia-based Iranian version, the Saudi-based Sunni Wahhabism, or the Salafist (world-wide jihad), is much more frightening, as the current state of the world attests.

Islam means *submission to Allah*. Submission to God and subjugation of nonbelievers are important components of that religion. One must submit and not question the religious law and practices which vary from Muslim nation to Muslim nation.

Aggression, specifically law-and-order concerns

Under the Taliban version of Islam, an aggressive law-and-order culture evolved. There were severe penalties for violation of any of the following laws. Kite sellers were to be imprisoned. Photos could not be posted in public places. Unclean things were forbidden, e.g. lobster, pork, alcohol, human hair, films, computers, music, and Westernized appearances. Homosexuality and abandoning Islam through conversion to another religion, or marrying out of faith, were punished by stoning to death.

In the United States, the analogue may be the militia movement, though here the emphasis is less on religion and more on state control and patriotism. Historian Michael Parenti describes some traits of the militia's love of control and order.

> Some superpatriots claim that they love America because of the freedom it gives us. Yet most of them seem to love freedom only in the abstract, for they cannot stand the dissidence and protests that are the actual practice of a free people. They have trouble tolerating criticisms directed against certain US policies and institutions. If anything, superpatriots show themselves ever ready

to support greater political conformity and more repressive measures against heterodoxy.[17]

From the militia's perspective, they are trying to return America to a simpler, bygone era – a simpler time. From their embattled perspective, they have a multitude of reasons. They rage against corrupt elites who have betrayed the common man and have to be corrected. They rage about a racial and ethnic takeover. They rage against the government who they see as Jewish infiltrated (Zionist Organized Government). There are any number of conspiracies, from communist to democratic, which are part of their law-and-order platform.

Although the American patriot movement may have begun as early as 1850, it was not until the 1990s, with the government-based actions at Ruby Ridge (1992), Waco (1993), and Montana (1996), that the state-based militia groups took hold. By 1995, there were 224 active militias in 39 states, though there have been declines related to the unpopularity of the militia-based Oklahoma City bombing. At least 32 of those groups had ties to other White supremacist movements.

There are other law-and-order groups focused primarily on American heritage and the restoration of the South to its former glory in the Confederacy, e.g. the League of the South Council of Conservative Citizens, United Daughters of the Confederacy. The neo-Confederate movement appears more political, rather than violent like their militia cousins, but there is no mistaking the camouflaged hate. Recently, the group's members erected a statue of Nathan Bedford Forrest in Nashville (Forrest was a Confederate general and the first Ku Klux Klan Imperial Wizard). Shortly afterwards, the world's largest Confederate flag was unfurled on the steps of the South Carolina State house and neo-Confederates demanded that officials refuse to bend to an NAACP boycott aimed at bringing the flag down on the state capitol.[18]

If, as Samuel Johnson observed, "patriotism is the last refuge of the scoundrel," there appears to be no shortage of either.

PERPETRATOR CULTURES

In enmity there is unity.

David Barash

Shame, lost honor, and not showing respect is the domain of gangs, the Mafia, as well as whole cultures. These are honor societies and dissing (disrespecting) a fellow gangbanger or Islamicist can have life-and-death consequences.

In honor cultures, shame is everywhere to be corrected by the honor-based gesture. In honor cultures, violence is glorified and passed on via shared public norms. In such cultures, restoring one's honor is culturally linked – there is no sense of an individual self.[19] I. W Charny has rightfully called such cultures fascistic, noting that

> they punish you for not obeying; they instill in you a sense of superiority toward all those you consider inferior because they don't know or observe the one and only correct way to do things. They open the door to violence and then to denials of the very violence they have you wreak on anyone who doesn't obey, including yourself. Fascist mind compels the person, couple or family to conform and obey the totalistic dictates of its ideology. Any deviation is treated as deserving of retaliatory punishment by unforgiving symptoms in the functioning of the self or of the interpersonal system.[20]

Writer Umberto Eco[21] sees perpetrator culture (Ur – eternal fascism) as a hotbed of populism, fostering intolerance of the weak (usually defined as homosexual) and containing the following: non-traditional, uncritical thinking and valuing of loyalty, esteeming of tradition, creation of a myth of heroic dying for the group, maintaining a strong leader, using propaganda, slogans and language like Orwellian Newspeak.

Genocide expert James Waller calls these "cultures of cruelty"[22] and I suggest that they are, simply, cultures of hate.

Hitler's architect Albert Speer recalls some of the conditions of perpetrator culture.

In normal circumstances people who turn their backs on reality are soon set straight by the mockery and criticism of those around them. In the Third Reich, there were not such correctives. On the contrary, every self-deception was multiplied as in a hall of distorting mirrors becoming a repeatedly confirmed picture of a fantastical dream world which no longer bore any relationship to the grim outside world. In those mirrors, I could see nothing but my own face reproduced many times over.[23]

NeoNazi recruiter Ingo Hasselbach describes how little has changed since Speer.

Instead of considering an issue objectively you always thought about things from the perspective of an embattled German man. Within the group, tests of Aryan purity now included eye color (the more blue, the more Aryan). The movement is intentionally designed to be as decentralized and anonymous as possible so that its members can distance themselves from acts of violence committed in its name. This deniability helps keep its members both morally and legally in the clear. Though I trained young people to hate, I could still profess shock that any of them would go out and actually commit murder. Our racist propaganda always put hatred in a positive light – it expressed racism as racial pride – and removed from the reader any responsibility for its bloody consequences. All responsibility rested with the victim who was biologically inferior and brought trouble on himself by mixing with the master race, or so the thinking went.

Currently, many Muslim cultures are honor and shame based, where rigid adherence to religious standards and political interpretation makes daily life intolerable for some.

Ayaan Ali Hirsi can tell us about the problems of living in an honor culture from direct experience. The Heritage Foundation Fellow and author[24] candidly addresses the abuses in her native Somalia beginning with female genital mutilation and ending in Holland and the United States with ongoing death threats.

Though Muslims may criticize other religions, those who are critical of Islam are to be punished. The dishonor one brings to Islam by any criticism must be dishonored or shamed or punished back. In the United States, key critics of Islam, i.e. Stephen Emerson, Daniel Pipes, and Robert Spencer, must take protective measures due to death threats. Ali Hirsi herself and other critics of Islam, e.g. Salman Rushdie, Irshad Manji, Taslima Nasreen, Muhammed Abu, are under 24-hour guard by non-Muslims. Her colleague Theo van Gogh is dead.

Citing several examples of what Melanie Phillips[25] has named predatory Islamicist ideology, Ali Hirsi shows how many Western values insult Muslims. She points to the events of the 2002 Miss World beauty pageant in Nigeria. The first and probably last time an Islamic nation hosted a Miss World Competition offended Islamicist sensibilities and left 200 Nigerians dead and 500 injured. A shaming of Islam occurred in May 2005 when *Newsweek* reported that a soldier at Guantánamo Bay flushed the *Koran* down a toilet. Retributed justice resulted in 16 deaths. Then, in 2006, defamed images of the Prophet resulted in 139 dead and the world froze waiting for Muslim anger to subside.

But in an honor society, the anger never subsides because, like bullies waiting for a pretext to rage, everything that threatens, everything that they cannot control, everything that is not their way or the way of their version of God is to be punished.

Women in such cultures are particularly vulnerable. Recently a 15-year-old Jordanian girl was stoned to death by her brother who spotted her "walking toward a house where young boys lived alone." Arab Islam society perceives a raped woman not as a victim, but as someone who debased the family honor, and relatives will opt to undo the shame by taking her life. Failure to do so further dishonors the family. Murder however is not the only option. A compromise is marrying the woman off to the person who violated her honor. Middle East expert Y. Feldner explains:

> In cases where the rapist is a brother, and marriage is impossible, the family may find someone else who will marry the victim. This procedure of getting the woman married is felt to rectify the

offense supposedly committed by the rape victim against her family and as such has won the legal approval of the state. If a rapist-victim marriage takes place in Jordan or some other Middle Eastern states, the criminal investigation is stopped, though the rapist may still face criminal charges if he divorces his wife within five years "without a legitimate reason." This custom enjoys support in some unlikely places; a lawyer at a Cairo human-rights advocacy group says that "putting a rapist in jail does not help anyone ... but if he marries the victim, then it helps both of them, giving them a chance to start fresh and to protect the girl from social stigma.[26]

In such societies, it is almost impossible to develop a sense of individual self. The lack of personal identity development means that every assault in the collective or social or religious or political realm is a personal attack. In this "Islam is Me" world, to Parisian Arab teens, not being hired is an assault not on all unhired teens but on all Muslims of all ages, so retribution by rioting must occur as it did twice in Paris and neighboring cities in 2006. The twin towers coming down on 9/11 not only restored lost honor to offended Arabs in America, e.g. in Dearborn (Michigan), but also led to a rejoicing in the streets by Muslims in Gaza (Palestine), Ede (Holland), and Birmingham (England).

Fatwa recipient Salman Rushdie spoke of the problem of Islamicist thinking and honor culture:

> The fundamentalist seeks to bring down a great deal more than buildings. Such people are against, to offer just a brief list, freedom of speech, a multi-party political system, universal adult suffrage, accountable government, Jews, homosexuals, women's rights, pluralism, secularism, short skirts, dancing, beardlessness, evolution theory, sex. These are tyrants, not Muslims. (Islam is tough on suicides, who are doomed to repeat their deaths through all eternity.) However, there needs to be a thorough examination, by Muslims everywhere, of why it is that the faith they love breeds

so many violent mutant strains. If the West needs to understand its Unabombers and McVeighs, Islam needs to face up to its bin Ladens.[27]

But it won't – because when it comes to religion, most abuse gets a pass. The Catholic church never excommunicated Hitler. A fatwa (religious edict and death threat) has been issued on writer Salman Rushdie but not on Osama bin Laden. At the present time, the world is being terrrorized by social identity and religion gone wild.

PERPETRATORS AS LEADERS

Why, of course the people don't want war. Why should some poor slob on a farm want to risk his life in a war when the best he can get out of it is to come back to his farm in one piece? Naturally the common people don't want war; neither in Russia nor in England nor in America, nor for that matter in Germany . . . it is the leaders.

Goering

Interesting, the leaders do not subscribe to the same mindset as do those who follow. "I'm proud of everything I did," offered a defiant Slobodan Milosevic of his Bosnian war crimes. "I am a terrorist and I am proud of it," sounded WTC bomber Ramzi Yousef upon hearing his 240-year prison sentence. "I don't think so," responded an unrepentant Albert Speer at his Nuremberg trial when asked if he would have behaved differently. While the names change over time, the psychology of perpetrators remains the same.

At one time, Charles Munyaneza was a popular local mayor. Yet in April 1994, Munyaneza was involved in planning, inciting, and implementing multiple Rwandan murders. In speeches, Munyaneza exhorted Hutus to massacre Tutsis. He was said to have coordinated a series of massacres at an agricultural research center in Rusatira, at the Catholic parish in Cyanika/Karama, and in Ruhashya and Rusatira. Munyaneza organized the distribution of weapons and helped to train civilians in the use of firearms. In addition, he was involved in a large number of civilian deaths. In 2002 Munyaneza was granted "Indefinite Leave to Remain" status and resides in Britain.

"Dictators come in many forms," notes writer Ian Buruma.

While some are religious maniacs, and some total cynics, some are mama's boys with a lust to dominate, and some are compelled by a higher cause or mission; some just wish to be worshipped as gods, some just want to be feared, and most are probably a mixture of all these things. But they all have one quality in common: striving for absolute power consigns them to a world of lies.[28]

Whether orchestrating a cult or perpetrating genocide, the leaders are generally brighter and more manipulative than the groups they are running. George Washington University political psychiatrist Jerrold Post likens such leaders to malignant group therapists:

Shared fantasies of power and glory, family and friendship are associated with identification with each other and the leader. Shared fantasies are embodied in social and national myths. Great orators including demagogues know how to appeal to infantile hunger for love and narcissistic supplies ... and to sanctions for aggressive behavior and violence ... directed to outsiders, preserving group bonding and cohesion.[29]

Group leaders tend to be more charismatic than most people, with better social skills. A former skinhead recruiter describes his experience:

I did get a certain enjoyment from searching out people's psychological and intellectual weaknesses and exploiting them for the sake of political training. It's hard for me to remember any of these young men now because I never became interested in them as people. Somehow it all remained a very abstract exercise to me, while to them it was as personal as could be – all about their fears and sense of self-worth.[30]

Perpetrator leaders and followers exist in civilian life as well as genocide. Table 3.2 lists some brief biographies of perpetrator leaders and their legacies.

Table 3.2 *Perpetrator leaders*

Ion Antonescu	AKA "Red Dog" Romania	300,000 Jews and 500,000 soldiers	Born in 1882 in Pitesti into a middle-class family. Vehemently antisemitic, he became engaged to two separate Jewish women and married a third. His father also divorced his mother to marry a Jewish woman. Antonescu received his education in French military schools and pursued a career in the army. On June 19, 1941, Antonescu ordered the expulsion of 40,000 Jews from villages and towns in "Old Romania" to detention camps and urban ghettos.
Prince Yasuhiko Asaka	Japan	200,000–350,000 Chinese	Born in 1887 in Kyoto, Japan. He was a member of the Japanese imperial family and uncle-in-law to Emperor Hirohito. He graduated from the Japanese military academy and was commissioned into the army as a sub-lieutenant.
François Duvalier	AKA "Papa Doc" Haiti	20,000–60,000	Born in 1907 in Port-au-Prince, Haiti. Completed a degree in medicine at the University of Haiti, serving there as a hospital staff physician until 1943; became a member of Le Groupe des Griots, a group of writers committed to Black nationalism and voodoo mysticism.

Table 3.2 (cont.)

Francisco Franco Bahamonde	AKA "El Caudillo"/ The Leader Spain	200,000	Born in Galicia Spain in December of 1892 to a Navy paymaster father and navy-based mother. During his youth he suffered at the hands of his aggressive, alcoholic father.
Nicolae Ceausescu	AKA Genius Romania	5,000 +	Born in a village in 1919, he moved to Bucharest at the age of 11 to become a shoemaker's apprentice and joined the illegal communist party. Arrested for agitating during a strike at age 13 and eventually imprisoned for two years by age 17.
Enver Hoxha	Albania	thousands	Born in 1908 at Gjirokastër. Hoxha's father was a wealthy Muslim landowner and cloth merchant with experience of traveling to and working in the United States. Hoxha attended Albania's best college-preparatory school, the National Lycée in Korçë, 80 km northwest of Gjirokastër and later he attended the American Technical School in Tiranë.
Saddam Hussein	AKA "Great Uncle"/Lion. Iraq	up to 2 million	Born in 1937 near Tikrit Iraq into a landless but influential Sunni family. He was a member of the al-Khatab clan and later had his genealogy fabricated to

support his claim to be a direct descendant of the prophet Mohammed. Hussein's father died while his mother was pregnant with him. When an older brother also died during the pregnancy, Hussein's mother tried to abort the fetus and commit suicide but was stopped by a neighboring Jewish family. After Hussein was born his depressed mother placed him in the care of his maternal uncle, army officer Khairalla Msallat, a nationalist and Nazi. When Hussein was three, his uncle was imprisoned for participating in a failed coup. Hussein was returned to his now-remarried mother but was mistreated by her and his stepfather. When his uncle was released from jail, Hussein ran away from home to live with him in Tikrit. Unable to read or write, Hussein now began his formal schooling. After his graduation from primary school Hussein followed his uncle to Baghdad and enrolled at the Karkh high school. While in Baghdad he became involved in the Arab nationalist movement, though was denied admission to the Baghdad Military Academy.

Table 3.2 (cont.)

Radovan Karadzic	Bosnia-Herzegovina	up to 200,000	Born in 1945 in Petnjica Montenegro, he studied medicine at the University of Sarajevo, graduating as a physician and psychiatrist. He also published poetry and books for children. In 1985 he was sentenced to three years imprisonment for embezzlement and fraud but never served his time.
Felicien Kabuga	Rwanda		Hutu businessman accused of financing the 1994 Rwandan genocide. He first attempted to enter Switzerland, but was ordered to leave, then went to Kinshasa and possibly resides in Kenya but his whereabouts are unknown. The International Criminal Tribunal for Rwanda issued an international arrest warrant for Kabuga in August 1999, charging him with eleven counts, including genocide, conspiracy to commit genocide, and complicity in genocide.
Kim Il Sung	AKA "Great"/ Eternal /Supreme Leader N. Korea	3 million killed in the Korean War	Born on April 15, 1912 in Mangyongdae into a middle-class family. His birth name was Kim Song Ju and he was the eldest of three sons. Kim's younger brother died

Name	Country	Death toll	Biography
			early. His youngest brother served with him until the mid-1970s. Kim's father was a Christian and Kim attended church throughout his teens. Father died early and mother also died before Kim was age 19.
King Leopold II	Democratic Republic of Congo Belgium	between 5 and 15 million Congolese	Born on April 9, 1835 in Brussels, as the eldest son of Leopold I, first king of the Belgians. He entered the Belgian Army at an early age, serving in the grenadiers, where he was appointed as a second in command and a Belgian Senator.
Mao Zedong	AKA Chairman Mao China	60 million	Born on December 26, 1893 in Shaoshan in Hunan Province to a prosperous family of peasant farmers. He lived with his mother's family in a neighboring village until he was eight then returned to Shaoshan to begin his education, but ran away from school by age 10. He was expelled from three other schools and entered an arranged marriage at age 14 with an older (age 18) cousin who died three years later.
Ferdinand Marcos	Philippines	thousands	Born in 1917 in Sarrat. Both his parents were teachers. After completing his schooling, Marcos enrolled at the University of the Philippines to study law.

Table 3.2 (cont.)

Slobodan Milosevic	AKA "Butcher of the Balkans" Serbia	240,000	Born in 1941 in Pozarevac, the second son of a former Orthodox priest and a Serbian communist schoolmistress. Both parents committed suicide (father in 1962/ mother in 1973). Met his future wife AKA "Red Witch" and the "Lady Macbeth of the Balkans," and married in 1965. Had two children, Marija and Marko.
Jose Rios Montt	AKA "The General" Guatemala	70,000	Born June 16, 1926, his army career included the School of the Americas and the Western Hemisphere Institute for Security Cooperation. He was a "born-again" evangelical Protestant.
Benito Mussolini	AKA "Il Duce" Italy	400,000 Italians and 30,000 Ethiopians	Born on July 29, 1883 near Predappio into a working-class family. His father was a blacksmith, his mother a schoolteacher. Had a difficult childhood during which he was twice expelled from school for attacking fellow students, but easily passed his exams. Mussolini obtained a teaching diploma and worked for a year as a schoolteacher at Gaultieri, northeast of Parma, until he was dismissed.

Name	AKA / Country	Death toll	Biography
Ante Pavelic	AKA "Butcher of the Balkans" Croatia	300,000 to one million	Born on July 14, 1889 in Bradina, about 35 km southwest of Sarajevo, he studied law at the University of Zagreb. Following his graduation he established a small law practice in Zagreb, the capital of Croatia. In his youth Pavelic joined the Croat Party of Rights (Hrvatska Stranka Prava, HSP), an extreme, right-wing nationalist political group advocating Croat separatism.
Augusto Pinochet	Chile	over 3,000	Born in 1915 at Valparaiso to a middle-class family headed by a customs official, started a military career.
Pol Pot /Saloth Sar	AKA "Brother Number One" Cambodia	1–3 million	Born 1925 in Kampong Thom province, his father was a prosperous farmer and his family had connections to the Cambodian royal family. At the age of six he moved to Phnom Penh to live with his brother, an official at the royal palace. He learned the rudiments of Buddhism during a brief stay at a pagoda near the royal palace before receiving his formal education at a number of French language schools and at a Catholic college, although he never obtained a high school diploma. While serving with the anti-French resistance under Vietnam's Ho Chi Minh, he joined the outlawed

Table 3.2 (cont.)

		50,000	Indochinese Communist Party and won a government scholarship to study radio electronics in Paris. He failed to obtain a degree but became enthralled with revolutionary socialism.
Anastasio Somoza Debayle	Nicaragua	50,000	Born on December 5, 1925 in Leon, Nicaragua. He attended school in Florida and then La Salle Military Academy on Long Island, New York, after which he pursued a career in the military, graduating from West Point on June 6, 1946.
Josef Stalin	AKA "Koba"/ Uncle Joe USSR	60 million	Born Iosif Vissarionovich Dzhugashvili 1879 in Gori, Georgia, the only surviving child of a poor and struggling family. His cobbler father died when Stalin was 11.
Mohamed Suharto	Indonesia	up to 2 million	Born 1921 in the village of Kemusu Argamulja in Central Java, Indonesia. Though his family were simple peasants, Suharto received a relatively good education.

Young Turks (1914–1918)	Turkey	100,000 Assyrians, 300,000 Greeks and 600,000 Armenians	Amet Cemal son of a military pharmacist; Ismail Enver from a military family; Mehmet Talat, whose father was a minor Ottoman official and trained as a telegraphist.
Jorge Rafael Videla	AKA "The Bone"/ "Pink Panther" Argentina	up to 30,000	Born in 1925 in Mercedes, a graduate of the National Military College, and the son of an army colonel.
Ne Win	AKA "Big Father"/ Old Man Burma	3,000–10,000	Born in 1911 at Paungdale to middle-class parents. His father was a minor public servant. He studied at University College, Rangoon (now Yangon), from 1929 to 1931, and left after failing a biology exam.

(For further information see www.moreorless.au.com/killers)

WHERE ARE THEY IN PEACETIME?

The following is taken from daily newspaper accounts of how perpetrators conduct themselves in daily life:

Denver:	Two heavily armed young men dressed in fatigues and black trench coats, opened fire in a suburban Denver high school Tuesday in what police said was a "suicide mission" that left as many as 25 people including the gunmen dead.	*New York Times* 4/20/99 p. 1; Associated Press, 3/6/01
Baton Rouge, LA:	Gov. Mike Foster was fined $20,000 Thursday by the state Board of Ethics for failing to report more than $150,000 in payments to ex-Ku Klux Klan leader David Duke for a computerized voter list. Foster had no comment.	www.stateline.org/ Louisiana 6/22/01
Fayetteville NC:	The murder of a young African-American couple in downtown Dec. 7, and the arrest of three members of the 82nd Airborne division for committing the heinous crime touched off calls for a probe of Ku Klux Klan infiltration of the US military.	Capusa.org 1995
Jakarta, Indonesia:	The November 22 killings were a first for Jakarta but in the past few months there have been 250 lynchings across the archipelago. The killings seem to be a product of fear, economic frustration and a breakdown of law and order as security forces are withdrawn from	*Time* 12/7/98 p. 35

the provinces to cover demonstrations in the cities. "The more people see that they can murder without facing any consequences, the more it becomes part of the culture," said Univ. of Indonesia's Sarlito Wirawan Sarwono Ph.D.

San Francisco:	A 62-year-old woman was attacked and her hip was broken. The man who assailed her thought she was Chinese though she was Korean and had lived in the US for 58 years.	A.P.A.org/hate. Cited from May, 1997
Anchorage:	But while Afoula, who was 17 at the time, was hitting victim Katsura Matsui, he repeated several times that he "hated Japanese." The defendant was Samoan.	*Anchorage Daily News* 3/23/03 alaska.com
McKees Rocks PA:	A man opened fire in several suburban Pittsburgh communities Friday killing five people and critically wounding one in what police called a racially motivated shooting spree. The suspect, Richard Baumhammers, 34, a lawyer from Mt. Lebanon, was charged Friday night with criminal homicide and reckless endangerment.	*Detroit Free Press* 4/29/00 p2A
Chicago:	Self-proclaimed white supremacist Matthew Hale was arrested by federal agents in the lobby of the Dirksen Federal Building for allegedly	ABC7 Chicago. com Federal agent's arrest 1/10/03

trying to hire someone to
kill a federal judge. Hale, 31,
reportedly targeted Judge Joan
Humphrey Lefkow who was
presiding over a trademark
case involving Hale's church.

London:	A bomb shattered a Gay pub in the heart of London's teeming restaurant district yesterday killing two people, injuring more than 70, and fueling fears that right-wing extremists are waging a murderous campaign against the capital's minorities.	*Marin Independent,* 5/1/99 p. A7
Turen, Indonesia:	Thirty motorcyclists recently drove slowly through town in a victory celebration, one of them waving an impaled head shouting Allah Akbar (God is great!). Communities are so terrified of black magic that vigilante groups are forming daily to seize, torture and execute anyone suspected of being a sorcerer. At least 150 people have died.	*International Herald Tribune,* 10/21/99 p. 8
Oldham, England:	Bricks and burned-out cars litter the streets of a British town following one of the country's worst outbreaks of racial violence in years. Chief Superintendent Eric Hewitt said he was shocked by the ''ferocity and sheer carnage'' of the rioting, which raged for seven hours on Saturday night. Ashid Ali, leader of the Oldham	*USA Today* 5/23/01 p. 1

Bangladeshi Youth Association,
said the incident was the result
of increased tensions because of
provocative actions by the
ultra-right-wing National Front.

Ivory Coast:	The BBC's Joan Baxter describes the scene at a mass grave in the Ivory Coast, where government troops are being blamed for the deaths of more than 100, mainly immigrant, workers.	BBC.com 12/09/02

NOTES ON CHAPTER 3

1. R. Rosenbaum (1998) *Explaining Hitler.* New York: Random House;
   T. W. Adorno, E. Frenkel-Brunswik, D. J. Levinson & R. N. Sanford
   (1950/1964) *The authoritarian personality.* New York: Wiley, p. 40.
   Perpetrator estimates 15–20 percent, Christopher Browning (personal
   comm. 4/8/02). M. Mann (2000) Were the perpetrators of genocide ﹐
   "ordinary men" or "real Nazis"? Results from fifteen hundred biographies.
   Journal of Genocide and Holocaust Studies, 14, 331–366: One in three
   Nazis were prewar extremists. Jane Elliot estimated 20 percent of her
   school children as authoritarian, as has Daniel Pipes in his estimates of
   15–20 percent of Muslims as militant Islamists. See D. Pipes (2002)
   Militant Islam reaches America. New York: W. W. Norton. See also
   G. Allport (1954) *The nature of prejudice.* Reading, MA: Addison-Wesley.
2. Chris Browning, personal communication, 2004.
3. www.janeelliott.com/
4. S. Scarr (1981) The transmission of authoritarian attitudes in families:
   Genetic resemblance in social-political attitudes? In S. Scarr (ed.) *Race
   and social class and individual differences in IQ.* Hillsdale,
   NJ: Erlbaum. For Terri Moffitt's work on genes, see www.self-esteem-
   international.org/Research/Low%20SE%20&%20Aggression.pdf
5. S. Glueck & E. Glueck (1950) *Unraveling juvenile delinquency.*
   Cambridge, MA: Harvard University Press.
6. Alice Miller (1990) *For your own good.* New York: Farrar, Straus and
   Giroux, p. ix; Rwandan version in D. N. Smith (1998) The psychocultural

roots of genocide: Legitimacy and crisis in Rwanda. *American Psychologist*, 53, 743–753. Also see that when parents withdraw love to be punitive, the children are more rule oriented and conventional: in F. Hoffman (1970) Conscience, personality and socialization techniques. *Human Development*, 13, 90–126. Primate research cited in *Newsweek*, 5/3/99, p. 34; Main and George research cited in *Newsweek*, 5/3/99, p. 34. See M. Kemmelmeier, E. Burnstein, K. Krumov, P. Genkova, C. Kanagawa, M. S. Hirshberg, H. Erb, G. Wieczorkowska & K. A. Noels (2003) Individualism, collectivism and authoritarianism in seven societies. *Journal of Cross-Cultural Psychology*, 34, 304–322.

7. G. Lederer (1993) Authoritarianism in German adolescents: Trends and cross-cultural comparisons. In W. F. Stone, G. Lederer & R. Christie (eds.) *Strength and weakness*. New York: Springer-Verlag.

8. Maria Piers (1987) Book review. *American Journal of Education*, 95, 498–500. For statistics, see the US Department of Justice, Bureau of Justice Statistics – Recent School Crime & Safety Statistics.

9. FBI (2000) *The school shooter*. Federal Bureau of Investigation. B. S. Connelly, S. O. Lilienfeld & K. M. Schmeelk (2006) Integrity tests and morality: Associations with ego development, moral reasoning and psychopathic personality. *International Journal of Selection and Assessment*, 14, 82–86.

10. I. W. Charny (2006) *Fascism and democracy in the human mind*. Lincoln, NE: University of Nebraska Press, p. 6. Also see Jessica Stern (2003) *Terror in the Name of God*. New York: Ecco, who found Arab perpetrators often misperceived persecution and trust, seeing everything as an attack.

11. J. Hatzfeld (2005) *Machete Season*. New York: Farrar, Straus, and Giroux, p. 198.

12. The study reports a link between less cognition and racism, see J. Waller (1993) Correlation of need for cognition and modern racism. *Psychological Reports*, 73, 542. The quote is from I. W. Charny (2006) *Fascism and democracy in the human mind*. Lincoln, NE: University of Nebraska Press, p. 4.

13. Irrespective of culture there are open- and closed-minded people, see M. Kossowska & A. Van Hiel (1999) Personality and current political beliefs: A comparative sample of Polish and Belgian samples.

Polish Psychological Bulletin, 30, 115–128. Also see D. Green, R. Abelson & M. Garnett (1999) The distinctive political views of hate-crime perpetrators and White supremacists. In D. A. Prentice & D. T. Miller (eds.) *Cultural divides*. New York: Russell Sage.

14. B. Altemeyer (1996) *The authoritarian specter*. Cambridge, MA: Harvard University Press, p. 200. Also see K. Stenner (2005) *The authoritarian dynamic*. New York: Cambridge University Press.

15. www.lordsgym.org; for rapture-ready toilets, see www.landoverbaptist. org. M. Goldberg (2006) *Kingdom coming*. New York: Norton, p. 210; C. Hedges (2006) *American fascists*. New York: Free Press.

16. B. Spilka, R. W. Hood, B. Hunsberger & R. Gorsuch (2003) *The psychology of religion*, 3rd edn. New York: Guilford.

17. M. Parenti (2004) *Superpatriotism*. San Francisco: City Lights, p. 6. Also see Michael Mann (2004) *The Dark Side of Democracy*. Cambridge: Cambridge University Press, who, addressing the worshipping of state power, also points out the "pursuit of a transcendent and cleansing nation-statism through paramilitarism."

18. www.splcenter.org

19. J. A. Vandello & D. Cohen (2004) When believing is seeing: Sustaining norms of violence in cultures of honor. In M. Schaller and C. S. Crandall (eds.) *The psychological foundations of culture* (pp. 281–304). Mahwah, NJ: Lawrence Erlbaum. Also see R. E. Nisbett & D. Cohen (1996) *Culture of honor*. Boulder: Westview Press.

20. I. W. Charny (2006) *Fascism and democracy in the human mind*. Lincoln: University of Nebraska Press, p. 3.

21. Eco's *Eternal fascism: Fourteen ways of looking at a blackshirt*, originally in *New York Review of Books*, 6/22/95, www.themodernword. com/eco/eco_blackshirt.html

22. J. Waller (2002) *Becoming evil*. New York: Oxford University Press.

23. A. Speer (1970) *Inside the Third Reich*. New York: MacMillan.

24. I. Hasselbach (1996) *Fuhrer-Ex*. New York: Random House; A. Ali Hirsi (2006) *The Caged Virgin*. New York: Free Press; Ayaan Ali Hirsi (2007) *Infidel*. New York: Free Press.

25. M. Phillips (2006) *Londonistan*. San Francisco: Encounter.

26. Y. Feldner (2000) Honor murders – why the perps get off easy. *Middle East Quarterly*, 7 www.meforum.org/article/50

27. S. Rushdie *New York Times*, 10/6/01.

28. See Ian Buruma's article Master of Fear *New York Review of Books* 5/13/2004, p. 4.
29. J. M. Post (1999) The psychopolitics of hatred: Commentary on Ervin Staub's article. *Peace and Conflict*, 5, 337–344.
30. Hasselbach, I. (1996) *Fuhrer-Ex*. New York: Random House.

4   Bystanders

The diligent executors of inhuman orders were not born torturers, they were not, with few exceptions, monsters – they were ordinary men.

Primo Levi

Can we explain bystander mindsets and actions? How much of bystander behavior is trait and how much is situationally based? Or, are there personality dispositions involved in being bystanders? Why do the vast majority of persons do nothing at times? The key question regarding bystanders is this: who becomes what kind of bystander and why and how do they differ from their perpetrator and rescuer counterparts?

DEFINING BYSTANDERS

A bystander is generally one who is present but refrains from involvement. Yet there is an active component to bystanders – they can temporarily perpetrate or at times rescue. With fewer dependency traits than perpetrators or rescuers, bystanders are vulnerable to social norms, and make choices of action as the situation dictates.

Conformity to cultural norms co-opts much of who they are. Social roles and social status are very important to the bystander, whose primary identity is social. Traditionally religious, though not extreme, politically conservative, and at times even liberal, the Tier II group is defined by its moderate stance between perpetrators and rescuers. Bystanders employ more sophisticated defenses and thinking compared to perpetrators.

The percentage of bystanders within a population may be between 50 and 65. Within Tier II there is a range of differences as well. No two bystanders are alike. Some are lower functioning, such as the antisocial personality, and others are higher functioning and more emotionally evolved. But all are similarly motivated. The bystander is primarily concerned with safety and regulation of identity and a place in the world.

Bystanders may be called the salt-of-the-earth types. Bystanders abide by the laws of their nation, attend houses of worship, and protect their families. In Germany, the average home focused on children, church, and kitchen (*Kinder, Kirche, Küche*). The focus is the same everywhere for the bystander.

BACKGROUND

Fear not your enemies, for they can only kill you. Fear not your friends, for they can only betray you.

Fear only the indifferent, who permit the killers and betrayers to walk safely on the earth.

Edward Yashinsky, poet

GENETICS

At present there are no studies addressing a genetic component to bystanding. Much of the bystander's makeup appears to serve an adaptive function regarding feelings of safety. Longitudinal research reveals that certain bystander-like dispositions may be lifelong, e.g. instability, dogmatism, intolerance of ambiguity, lack of openness to experience, uncertainty, tolerance, the need for order, the need for structure, the need for closure, integrative complexity, fear of threat and loss, and poor self-esteem.[1]

FAMILY AND DEVELOPMENTAL TRENDS

Perpetrators tend to come from perpetrator families. Rescuers generally hail from homes where helping behavior is esteemed and altruistic values are imbued. There is no comparable research on bystanders. It would make sense that the home life of bystanders would be average. What does average mean? Is average statistical, e.g. 2.2 children? Can average be expressed in more psychological terms, e.g. freedom from trauma? Or, can we begin to unravel who bystanders are, based on comparisons?

Table 4.1 *Bystander and rescuer differences*

	Bystanders	vs.	Rescuers
Rescue opportunity	lower		higher
Concerns	material losses		people
Mental health	lower		higher
Cultural dependent	lower		higher
Internal control	lower		higher
Self esteem	lower		higher
Empathy	lower		higher
Postwar volunteering	41 percent		75 percent
Organ donation	12.4 percent		44 percent
Past helping	lower		higher
Life satisfaction	lower		higher
Goal achievement	lower		higher

Rescuers experience more opportunities to help (Perry London cited by Tec. Bystanders relate less well with more insecurity and money-motivated behavior (see Oliner *et al.*). Bystanders are more self-centered and emotionally constricted than others (see Block & Drucker; Fogelman; Oliner & Oliner; Oliner, p. 57). Also see Midlarsk *et al.* and related work in Jones & Corley.[2]

PASSIVE AND ACTIVE BYSTANDING

The available data examines either perpetrators alone or rescuers alone and not bystanders per se. Table 4.1 compares several studies of bystanders to rescuers and the patterns reveal the following. Compared to perpetrators, bystanders are more developed on multiple measures. Compared to rescuers, bystanders are less developed emotionally. The same pattern occurs from the earliest studies to the latest studies. The passive bystander may show a trait in that under all conditions, he or she remains passive or becomes more active. Passivity changes bystanders, notes genocide expert Ervin Staub.

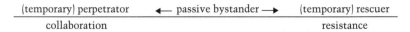

FIGURE 4.1 Different types of bystanders (a continuum)

It is difficult to see others suffer and do nothing. To justify their passivity, reduce their guilt, and reduce empathy with the victims that would make them suffer, passive bystanders tend to distance themselves from victims, in part by increasingly devaluing them. This makes it even more likely that they will remain passive. It also leads some bystanders to join perpetrators.[3]

It remains uncertain as to the qualities that create the provisional or temporary perpetrator and the provisional or temporary rescuer. Bystanders may include subcategories as well (see Figure 4.1). For instance, those who collaborate may be considered (temporary) perpetrators and those who join the various resistance movements would be subsumed under the rubric of (temporary) rescuers.[4]

How do bystanders function in genocide? Some theorists like Robert Lifton have focused on psychological processes such as a "functional second self" or the psychic numbing that is specific to bystanders. Other experts continue the same line of thought:

> Numbness, that is, manifests an important challenge to the liberal ideal that we can empathically project ourselves into others with whom we share a common humanity, whether strangers or neighbors. For numbness is not only a psychological form of self-protective dissociation; it is arguably a new, highly self-conscious narrative about the collective construction of moral availability, if not empathy, and may thus constrain humanist aspirations in ways we do not yet recognize. Because numbness may also be a necessary dimension of our ability to absorb a mass atrocity, it paradoxically confirms ideas about our common humanity – we can only respond numbly to what we feel in excess – while also rendering humanitarian practice increasingly vexed. It may be that

numbness merely exposes in new and dramatic terms the limits of the ideally expansive liberal "we."[5]

Ethologists suggest that human animals function no different from their mammalian counterparts. Animal behavior expert Hans Kruuk has observed the high frequency of gawking and bystanding instead of helping their fellows amongst gazelles. On the surface it appears as a simple fascination and fear.

"We were all born with a powerful herd instinct," notes Rwandan hotelier Paul Rusesabagina. As he watched the 1994 Rwandan genocide unfold he observed the numbing as well as the herding component.

Still others focus on the situational or risk factors that create bystanding. Psychologist Daniel Bar-On has questioned the premise that it is natural to help if an increased risk of violence occurs. He believes that there are rational (cost/benefit), cultural, personality (authoritarian), and social reasons to stand by in which we can often rationalize and blame the victim.

> There are many forms of by-standing behaviors. There are many different positions (eyewitnesses, distant listeners, those far away who should be concerned), as well as different levels of exposure to the victimization process. We may all have the capacities to perform most of these behaviors in many different situations. Very few of us find ways to overcome these constraining forces, thereby becoming rescuers or performing acts of resistance. Still, all bystanding behaviors relate to certain violent actions that the victimizers inflicted upon their victims against their will, most involving direct injury to the physical and psychic health, even the lives of the latter.[6]

Bystanders have great potential power to do good," notes Ervin Staub. "When two people hear sounds of distress from another room, what one person says can greatly influence whether the other witness helps or not."[7] Scott Straus's investigation of the motives of

Rwandan ordinary-people-turned-genocidaires led him to conclude similarly: "My findings indicate that all other things being equal, most Hutu men would have just as easily complied with orders for peace as with orders for violence."[8]

In a genocide, bystanders can be overwhelmed easily and switch sides on a whim, divesting themselves emotionally where they can.

Chanty Chhang age 45 was a bystander in the 1975 Cambodian genocide. After the Vietnamese invaded and liberated the Cambodian people from the Khmer Rouge, 600,000 Cambodians fled to Thai border camps. He was one of those who lived on the border, eventually making his way to Canada. When he was 15 the Pol Pot regime came to his area (Batdambang, a region about 300 km from Phnom Penh) and because he was a city dweller he was taken away to work in a gulag for 18 hours a day.

> You see movie *Killing Field*? It was worse. We knew the Khmer Rouge were to come but we did not know where to go. Then we hear my policeman father, they bamboo him [quick death blow to back of head with bamboo stick] and then my uncle and cousins by axe. They cut power to town so no electricity. We were so scared and hungry – one time I eat cowskin because I weigh 65 lbs (His normal adult weight is 160 lbs). We go to work [camps] and it is bad. Many people die [malaria] and my friend they take him away, I always thought I was next. I still have nightmares – when I returned a few years ago with my wife to Torslang [one of the killing fields] I started having many nightmares. I cry – something you were not allowed to do. If you cried, they would kill you and your family. The Khmer were stupid [uneducated] people who want power – crazy for power. Collaborate? Everyone do what Khmer Rouge say – no one want to be killed.

Threat, anxiety, and stress cause an increased need for structure. From this perspective, compliance to the Nazi regime by ordinary Germans is more understandable than antisemitism per se.

In the obsessive compulsive culture of prewar Germany, with its great emphasis on orderliness, cleanliness, and routine, suspension of those conditions were too overwhelming for the average ordinary citizen. Great efforts were made by the Nazi leadership to create a semblance of normal daily activities. Author Victoria Bennett reminds us that most Germans kept their jobs in the private and public sectors. As bystanders continued to lead normal lives, the institutions (e.g. churches) and people made similar accommodations in order to maintain the pretense of normality. Such compliance was necessary to ensure what sociologist Zygmunt Bauman called the illusion of rationality.[9]

Many Germans simply busied themselves with bureaucracy. As historian Raul Hilberg notes, even Jewish institutions became an extension of the German bureaucratic machine.

Rewards for complicity and turning the other way were offered in the form of money, property, and status. In the Armenian genocide, the Turkish government directly gave money to those willing to help with the deportation of, and murder of, Armenians.[10]

The average citizen strives for "predictability, influence ability and exploitability." Theorists cite specific German cultural patterns which were involved (e.g. loss of control, orderliness, anti-modernism, strong leadership and circumstances, social unrest, political crimes, loss of tradition); the ordinary German was provided with sufficient good explanations, predictability, and the illusion of control.[11]

The striving for normality has been asserted by authors Detlev Peukert, Marion Kaplan, Victor Klemperer, and by Oliver Pretzel's father in Sebastian Heffner's *Defying Hitler*. The packaging of the normal and the convivial is a general theme that runs through Andrew Stuart Bergerson's *Ordinary Germans in extraordinary times*.[12] Bergerson interviewed the townsfolk of Hildesheim Germany and uses terms to describe them which are all too reminiscent of bystanders, e.g. "uniformity," "naturalized customs of everyday life," and "concern to fit in the *volksgemeinschaft* [community]."

One of Bergerson's interests was the ordinary seduction of habits such as neighborhood pride and cleanliness. Linking morality with purification, Bergerson notes, was successful such that ordinary Hildesheimers "tried to preserve their normalcy by framing this expanding state into the pre-existing cultural framework of neighborliness."

Discrimination against Jews proceeded based not on the usual tenets of "paved with indifference" or antisemitism as much as the need to "preserve a coherent sense of self."

Rudi Florian, age 73, recalls ordinary life growing up in Schneidemühl, Germany.

> By the time I entered first grade [1940] I was surrounded by Nazi curriculum, Nazi books, and Nazi teachers. The Jews were very integrated and thought of themselves as Germans first, Jews second, but by the time I was six, there were no Jewish children in my class. The only Jewish person I ever met was the family doctor who we later learned had fled to England. By age ten I had to join the Jungvolk [Hitler Youth], sort of like Cub Scouts for Nazis but there were rallies as well. I attended five meetings and thanks to my parents, very little of the Nazi poison affected me. My mother had the perfect excuse – I had to baby-sit my younger sister. The Youth leader came to our house a few times but my mother used the same excuse every time and he eventually gave up. For some reason, they left us alone.
>
> Even though I was no longer part of the Nazi Youth, it [Nazism] was all around me. They had created a totally paranoid atmosphere – in the media, in the classroom, monitoring and controlling. For instance; the Nazis knew children don't lie so they would have the children report on the parents' activities. Parents knew that as well. The result was that nobody ever said anything to their kids – nobody said anything to anyone. So often you'd see the propaganda like a picture book that showed Jews preying on Christian girls [Poison Mushroom] and you'd hear the stories.

I remember one in particular. In the park near where we lived, there was a gazebo that we had heard that the Jews had practiced their evil rituals there. I didn't know if it was true or not. But after that, every time I passed it, I was unnerved.

I don't remember but I was living in Albuquerque and it was back in 1988 or 1992 and my mother had given us kids a book on our hometown. I went through the book and came to the picture of a plaza where I played as a child. But the photo was different because it included a synagogue and I never saw one when I was a child. Then my mother told me that the synagogue had "vanished" on November 9, 1938 [Kristallnacht]. Yet there it was in black and white.

In any culture, the majority of people will go along with the group. They will think, "if everyone else does it, it must be okay." Nobody likes to go against the grain and be an outsider or alone – let alone the threat of what they would do to you or your family. I recall seeing a film in 1947 about what happened and thought "my people couldn't do that" – but they did. It does no good to deny or minimize any of this – or like most Germans of my generation – they just don't want to talk about it. I think people have to become aware of their frailties and move beyond. To this day I keep a photo in my room from the war, of a mother and her two children and know that nobody speaks for them – so I must.

In Table 4.2, we see the suggestion that bystanders who came from more conflicted homes would be prone to anger and acting out while those bystanders who evolved from less conflicted homes but were more passive stay passive. Bystanders from higher functioning backgrounds may be more apt to temporarily help and rescue when tilted by the social forces. These distinctions between who becomes what appear to incorporate other traits as well, e.g. identity (see Table 4.2). At the time of writing, however, such trait-based ideas must remain theoretical until situational determinants or the interaction of both can yield fuller understanding.

Table 4.2 *Tier II levels of bystanding*

	Temporary perpetrator	Bystander	Temporary rescuer
Early Life	conflicted	conventional	conscientious
Emotional	rigid	conforming	nonconforming
	least coping	average coping	high coping skills
	cognitive simple	more complex	integrated
	superstitions/myths	stereotypes	individualist
	social identified	social + emotional	emotional identity
	role	role + personal	integrated
Identity	social	social/personal	personal
Self	false	semi-authentic	authentic
Motivation	fear/anger	safety/social status	openness
Politics	fascist	conservative	liberal democrat
Religion	fundamental	conventional	universalistic

Nowhere is the need to appear normal more apparent than in the bystander mindset. For the bystander/ordinary person, the term normal is not a concern for mental health so much as for social fit and social status. In the bystander's mind, average equates to social acceptance (not deviating very much from what is expected) and being able to predict and anticipate their world.

While the identity of the perpetrator is all social with no personal development, the bystander is more a mixture of the two. There is some personal identity formation, but it is limited in scope, co-opted by the tugs of the social world.

ORDINARY PEOPLE

The opinion of the ignorant and numbed masses in matters of
reasoning and philosophy is to be mistrusted, its voice being that

of nastiness, of stupidity, of inhumanity, of insanity, and of
prejudice

Diderot, French philosopher 1713–1784

Average and normal may have distinct meanings in most people's minds but for mental health practitioners, the term normal means only average levels of mental health. The idea of normalcy evolves from a statistical average within the general population and is based on minimal standards for psychiatric hospitalization. It turns out that the average person is not mentally healthy. UCLA psychologist David Shapiro reminds us of the bystander's limits:

> These are the ones whose lives are usually governed by various
> rules and authoritative principles, [who] often have great difficulty
> in making decisions that rest inescapably on personal
> preference ... They can make choices – where there is or appears
> to be a right answer. But they may be thrown into anxiety by even
> inconsequential decisions when there is no rule or authority to
> refer to. To the dutiful person of this sort who lives with
> a constant awareness of what he should do ... the process has
> distorted self-awareness and has produced a state of neurotic self-
> estrangement.[13]

In a separate study conducted earlier at the University of Michigan, clinical psychologists surveyed ordinary people with mental health tests. The authors of that study noted that while most people were able to function on a daily basis and conform to the prevailing culture's standards, such persons were average but not mentally healthy. Upon closer examination of those who they had rated "well adjusted," they found "remarkably little insight and awareness, with only fair levels of emotional stability and poor resilience against stress."[14]

Epidemiology researchers have even more to say on the matter. In what may be the most extensive study of its kind, a National Comorbidity Study examined 10,000 people in the US with regard to mental health. Their findings were less than impressive. They found that about half the population had or had had a diagnosable form of mental illness with half of those requiring immediate psychiatric attention.

> The first of these two results was significant because it addressed the issue of stigma that has for so long interfered with rational thinking about mental illness. The mentally ill are not some distinct set of "them" out there who are distinct from "us" sane people. Instead, the vast majority of us has been touched by some form of mental illness at some time in our lives, either through personal experience or through the illness of a close loved one. In many cases these illnesses are either mild or transient or both, but they certainly should not be considered in any way foreign.[15]

TRAITS

Conforming

More than any other trait, the desire to fit in and conform to external forces is what motivates the bystander. From an evolutionary psychology perspective, this makes sense. Otherwise how would we learn to adapt to the environment?

Where conformity ends and rigidity begins is not certain for either ordinary people or the experts. Psychological tests of conformity invariably include items regarding rigidity and vice versa to the point that some have asked if the two constructs are one. I. W. Charny addresses the conformity inherent in socially distorted minds:

> Like every other aspect of fascist society, fascist mind is geared to producing conformity to the über alles dictates of rules that must be followed unquestioningly regardless of their appropriateness, and to achieving set goals no matter the cost.[16]

Recall Milgram's shock study? In that study, most people (65 percent) complied with the experimenter's demands to shock someone to dangerous levels. And while there was a core group who defied (35 percent), one has to wonder if under different circumstances

Milgram could have influenced the majority to rescue instead of obediently to shock. In a later version, Milgram attempted to repeat the study to separate out conformity from obedience to authority and found that there were some differences. In other words, some were responding to the authority of Milgram and others were highly conforming persons.

Highly conforming bystanders cannot tolerate too much change. Their patterns of behavior are those expected within a particular society in a given situation. The shared belief of what is normal and acceptable shapes and enforces the actions of people in a society.

Lack of emotional development
The findings of a Danish study are noteworthy. Danish rank-and-file Nazis, many of whom could be considered bystanders, were found to be *ambitent* – socially full but emotionally empty; with no consistent mind of their own; relying instead on others and adapting to whoever was in power.[17] In the same study, researchers observed the following criteria: the "ordinary Nazis" were not deep thinkers, with deep feelings or deep emotional attachments; they had poor coping skills and were highly vulnerable to stress, had lower self esteem, were cognitively simple, racist, and rigid, and, like perpetrators, often saw themselves as victims. In her study of *Nurses in Nazi Germany*, Bronwyn McFarland-Icke similarly suggested that what motivated the Nazi nurses was an "abstinence from thinking."[18]

Thinking beyond the box of convention is a higher order process – one process that the average person does not have. The reader is reminded of the moral developmentalist Lawrence Kohlberg's research regarding higher levels of moral development in those who administered the fewest Milgram shocks. Those findings are noteworthy and bear repeating – highly conforming people are more likely to follow orders, and are less emotionally developed. People who were more compliant to the prevailing culture scored lower on several psychological indicators including a pattern of greater tendency towards authoritarianism.

Bystanders can be swayed to follow one direction or the other. Bystanders can be pulled into temporary states of rescue or perpetration, but immediately revert back to the bystander and uninvolved stance. "One should not ask too much of the average man," observed Walter Lippmann in *Public opinion*. "He would arrive at a problem in the middle of the third act and leave before the last curtain."[19]

TEMPORARY PERPETRATORS

Wartime collaborators may have accounted for only 5 percent of the population but they were a dangerous percentage. By definition, such persons would have been bystanders. One World War II veteran, Pieter Broersma, age 81, spoke of his experience with the collaborators.

> My friend was with me in the underground and got caught and they beat him so badly he lost an eye – the bastards. I know there were some NSB [Dutch Nazis] – they were poor and not too bright and duped by the Nazis promises – the collaborators were manipulators and wanted to play both sides but nobody talked to them after the war. I know in theory there were some good Germans, but my father used to say the only good German is a dead German. I guess I'm like my sister. To this day, the hair on the back of my neck stands up if I hear someone speaking German. I know of two NSB that live here in our little city. Of the Dutch immigrant community that moved here, nobody till this day has anything to do with them.

Koos Hummelen, age 69, of Zoutkamp, Netherlands recounts his war experience with collaborators.

> Yes, I knew them. Some colluded for the money; one of my friends' father was one. He was the mayor. Some did it because they thought Germany would be the stronger country and they wanted to go with the winner. Some did it because they were scared for their own lives. Some even helped Jews if they were paid enough; others took the cash and turned them in.

PROFESSIONAL COLLABORATORS

Having a high IQ and being formally educated appears unrelated to morality. One has only to recall that the architects of 9/11 held advanced engineering degrees and seven of the fifteen Wannsee Conference attendees had doctorates. (Of the fifty-six leading Nazis, 27 percent were MDs and 27 percent were lawyers, while the rest were engineers, or professors whose IQs fell into the superior range.) An intelligence test administered by Dr. Gilbert showed that all the Nuremberg defendants but one (Streicher) were above average in intelligence (average intelligence ranges between 90 and 110). Of the twenty-one tested, seven had IQs as high as the 130s and two more reached the 140s.[20] The lack of emotional development is made clear by the deeds of Nazi German physicians during World War II. While some physicians refused to join the Nazi party (Tier III), the vast majority did join. They went on to collude and collaborate and devise the various medical experiment programs. Some even became high-ranking members of the Reich.

Psychoanalyst Robert J. Lifton and historian Henry Friedlander remind us how the Nazi physicians developed and implemented Tiergartenstrasse (T-4), a euthanasia program dedicated to killing 70,000–100,000 "useless eaters" and those "unworthy of life." Many of the victims included the mentally retarded, the institutionalized mentally ill, and the physically impaired whose existence was inconsistent with Aryan superiority. Physicians also conducted the infamous pseudoscientific medical experiments utilizing thousands of concentration camp prisoners without their consent. Most of the victims, primarily Jews, Poles, Russians, and Gypsies, became disabled or died as a result.

In general, psychiatrists, psychologists, and nurses had no higher moral development than physicians. When Hermann Goering's nephew took over the prestigious Berlin Psychoanalytic Institute, he immediately dismissed the Jewish psychoanalysts. Instead of protesting, fellow Christian analysts rewrote Freudian theory to fit Nazi ideology, with some participating in exterminations. German psychologists fared no better, with right-wingers quickly ceding to Nazi destruction of the psychological sciences.[21] Nurses collaborated as well and while some rescued, the majority assisted in the medical murders of tens of thousands of outlawed minorities.[22] In Rwanda, clergy collusion is well known and is still being documented, as the following news report notes:

> A local Rwandan traditional court has sentenced a Catholic nun to 30 years in prison for helping militiamen kill hundreds of Tutsi hiding in a hospital during the country's 1994 genocide, an official told Reuters on Friday. Theophister Mukakibibi was sentenced by the traditional gacaca courts on Thursday for working closely with Hutu militiamen to kill Tutsi hiding in Butare hospital where she worked. She was also accused of dumping a baby in a latrine. "She would select Tutsi [and] throw them out of the hospital for the militia to kill," said Jean Baptiste Ndahumba, president of the local gacaca court in Butare town. "She did not even spare pregnant mothers." Focusing on confession and apology, the traditional gacaca courts have been used in Rwanda to ease the backlog of genocide cases. They are also intended to ease the way to national reconciliation. Under gacaca, those who confess and plead guilty before a set date will have their sentences reduced. Those sentenced to prison will serve their time in a Rwandan jail. Mukakibibi is the first nun to be sentenced by a Rwandan court for her role in the genocide. A Belgian court convicted two Roman Catholic nuns in 2001 for aiding the mass murder.[23]

TEMPORARY RESCUERS

Some bystanders helped and rescued and some became full-time rescuers – why? Consistent with trait theory, the impact of other rescuers created a rescue-and-helping atmosphere. Whether Denmark, or Bulgaria, or Le Chambon-sur-Lignon, when a culture of rescue prevails over a culture of perpetration and hate, then bystanders save lives (see section on bystander culture below). The temporary rescuer exceptions to bystanding tended to be those from the helping professions, e.g. social workers, some psychologists, some nurses, and some clergy (see Chapter 5). In this category are those who rescued Jews because others did, so unfortunately the fickleness and dependency on external forces makes the chance of informing and even perpetration high as well.

HOW TO MAKE BYSTANDERS KILL

The people can always be brought to the bidding of the leaders. That is easy. All you have to do is tell them they are being attacked and denounce the pacificists for lack of patriotism and [for] exposing the country to danger. It works the same way in any country.

Goering

A most important contribution to genocide studies has been the application of social psychological principles. Prior to 1990, there were key conformity studies, and a myriad of speculations and top-down theories that seemed to offer no comprehensive explanations. It was the pioneering work of Herbert Kelman on the My Lai massacre in Vietnam, and Ervin Staub regarding genocidal mindsets, that offered new social psychological conceptualizations.

"Yes, just about anyone could have," replies Princeton University social psychologist Susan Fiske, when asked how American 18-year-olds could have tortured prisoners at Iraq's Abu Ghraib. After reviewing over 25,000 studies she concluded that the "social context – specifically authority figures and peer pressure – are at work."[24]

It may be a little too easy to create what occurs in a genocide notes Whitworth College social psychologist James Waller. Waller outlined the conditions for extraordinary evil in *Becoming evil*. Deemphasizing traits and highlighting situational determinants, Waller's model incorporates all the related research in the growing field of genocide studies.

His work primarily builds on historian Christopher Browning's examination of 500 German Reservists (Police Battalion 101) and the mass killing of 38,000 Jews during World War II. Most of the killing was done on a one-on-one basis with a rifle placed to the back of the victim's head in an open field, over a brief period of time. Violence adaptation, careerism, and self-interest emerged from Browning's study. Browning highlighted the fact that these were not fanatical Nazis, but ordinary people – civilian police sent to Poland to do a job.

To increase American soldiers' shooting power, Lt. Dave Grossman observed the firing power of the average soldier in three conflicts and understood the manipulation involved in increasing shooting. Grossman notes that the firing rates increased between World War II (15–20 percent) and Korea (55 percent); and again between Korea and Vietnam (95 percent).[25]

Herbert Kelman's and V. Lee Hamilton's analysis of compliance to several events, including the Vietnam My Lai massacre, offers more insights into the perpetrator and rescuer mindsets. When the soldiers were asked why they would personally shoot or refuse to shoot, two clear mindsets emerged – consistent shooters and consistent refusers. The answers were not unexpected and follow along perpetrator and rescuer lines (see Table 4.3).

Prior to the 1990s, a number of theories advanced a pathology picture – antisemitism, violent pasts – much of which proved wrong. Browning's order police were very ordinary. A related study by Dick de Mildt[26] of 129 war criminals' trials similarly concluded "their background profile far more closely matches that of rather ordinary citizens with a well-developed calculating instinct for their private interests." It begs the question – What goes on in the situation that would guide previous policemen in Hamburg Germany to become blood robots for days on end?

I will propose that most evil is the product of rather ordinary people caught up in unusual circumstances. They are not equipped to cope in normal ways that have worked in the past to escape, avoid or challenge these situations. At the same time they are being recruited, seduced, and initiated into evil by persuasive authorities or compelling peer pressure.

Table 4.3 *Shooters and refusers*

Shooters	Refusers
Orders are orders (42 percent)	Victims are innocent (44 percent)
Self-protection (22 percent)	Immoral, inhumane, murder (37 percent)
Punishment for noncompliance (21 percent)	Couldn't get myself to do it (14 percent)

Source: H. C. Kelman & V. Hamilton (1989) *Crimes of obedience.* New Haven: Yale University Press.

Social psychologist Phil Zimbardo's shopping list of genocide ingredients includes rationalize by ideology; a nurturing-to-authoritarian leader; the use of small steps (dehumanize) to culminate in larger acts (discriminate); minimize dissent; provide models of compliance where killing is esteemed; maintain anxiety by changing rules often or deliberately keeping them vague.

Colleague James Waller's list contains some of the same items: an external/fatalistic orientation; authoritarianism; an ideology of commitment, moral disengagement; the use of euphemisms; moral equivalent arguments; careerism. Both Zimbardo and Waller are convinced that the setting is seductive and creates the conditions for extraordinary evil.

"Social pressure certainly made a difference for the average person," recalls Rwandan genocide witness Paul Rusesabagina:

> Ordinary citizens just like you and me were bullied and cajoled into doing things they would never have dreamed possible without the reinforcing eyes of the group upon them. And in this way, murder becomes not just possible but routine. It even gets boring after a while.[27]

Rusesabagina himself was not seduced and instead became a rescuer. Yet some may become temporarily enchanted or seduced.

Greek military police did not exhibit sadistic behavior before or after their tour of duty, but one recruit was able to acknowledge:

> Torturing became a job ... If the officers ordered you to beat, you beat. If they ordered you to stop, you stopped. You never thought you could do otherwise. It became a function – standard operating procedure.[28]

You ritualize, desensitize, and routinize, notes Waller, who points out that the Nazis often numbed themselves with alcohol and often got non-Germans, i.e. Lithuanians or Ukrainians, to do many of the killings.

What else do the experts know? It turns out that the average person does not like to kill, but certain conditions such as anonymity make abuse and killing easier. Harvard University anthropologist John Watson[29] created a classic experiment and found that 80 percent of people were more hostile and destructive when they wore masks or war paint. In variations of Milgram's study, people shocked more if they knew they had anonymity.

There are well-known variations on anonymity that create bystanding. Evolving from the Kitty Genovese tragedy, psychologists found that more people creates less help. For instance, in a group of three people, 80 percent help while in a six-person group, only 62 percent help, and so on. People help the most when there is one-on-one contact and others are not around.

Dehumanization of the enemy is one of the key ways in which combat infantry soldiers prepare themselves to overcome a normal, innate human repugnance at killing other humans, e.g. thinking of Tutsis as cockroaches. You can also essentialize the other ("they can't change, it is in their blood"). Dehumanized group members are excluded from the moral community; one feels no obligation to apply moral standards that are reserved for the fully human to them. The increased dehumanization appears similar to the socialization patterns in criminals.[30]

Social bonding helps us kill as well. Social connection was the glue that held Sageman's jihadis together. And US military psychologist Lt. Dave Grossman, thinks that it is the same glue that creates effective soldiers. "A soldier feels that he is 'letting his friends down' if he doesn't kill," observed Grossman.[31] Christopher Browning came up with the same explanation in his study of ordinary Nazis. He observed that those who did not shoot risked isolation, rejection, and ostracism. This ostracism created "a very uncomfortable prospect within the framework of a tight-knit unit stationed abroad among a hostile population so that the individual had nowhere else to turn for support and social contact."[32]

Careerism was also part of the equation. In any war, there are those who care little for anyone but themselves and use whatever means they can to advance up the ladder of wartime success. So for some, if the quota of daily murders were to be exceeded, it meant exceeding one's own quota. "I had lunch and after about half an hour's rest, then another round and more work at the office," World War II commandant Franz Stangl said of his concentration camp activities.[33]

There are some experts who still look to prewar German culture for answers for the stormtrooper storm but they will find none. German culture had marinated in antisemitism for a millennium but so had the rest of Europe. One investigator reviewing the European news media at the time found levels of antisemitism to be higher in Hungary and Eastern Europe. In addition, other groups such as Gypsies and homosexuals were targeted as well. Were bystanders slaves to the bureaucratic machinery as Baumann, Katz, Bartov, and others contend? Were bystanders careerists and looking for money – were they real winners by jumping on the Nazi bandwagon?[34] Or, were bystanders mere conformists devoid of emotional backbone and psychological development and seduced by any social norms? Nobody seems to know.

"The majority [of temporary perpetrators] were not distinguished by their background, personality, or previous political affiliation or behavior as having been men or women unusually likely or fit to be genocidal executioners," concludes James Waller.[35] Fellow genocide expert Ben Valentino agrees, "We should take heed of the fact that the capacity for violence or indifference to violence directed at others exists in nearly all human beings and societies."[36]

But the larger question is why didn't everyone jump in and kill? Why are some able to rise above the fray? How do you explain the intestinal fortitude of the people that saved an egg for the Jewish underground? How do you explain those who grew up hearing the same antisemitic tales, being ordered to join the ranks and kill, yet do not? How do you explain the rescuers?

BYSTANDER CULTURE

During World War II, whole cultures became perpetrators while others became rescuer nations. Why? Nations such as Denmark and Bulgaria made rescue legendary. By contrast, some bystander nations became rescuer nations where outlawed groups were scurried away to safety zones. Sweden may have come a bit late to the table but to those who were the recipients, it was perfect. The facts regarding Sweden's involvement and the shifting from bystander to rescuer nation are just now coming to light.

The largest rescue effort inside Germany during World War II was conducted by the Swedish Red Cross when over 17,000 concentration camp prisoners were transported via Denmark to Sweden in the Spring of 1945. Led by Count Folke Bernadotte of Wisborg, a series of small white buses arrived in Berlin on February 16, 1945. While Bernadotte's original instructions had been to intervene for Scandinavian Christian prisoners in Germany, the Swedish government extended his mandate to include non-Scandinavians in March. By April 21, Himmler consented to have the Swedish Red Cross transport women of all nationalities out of Ravensbrück camp. Some 3,000 women were brought out from Ravensbrück by the white buses, and, with an entire German train made available, some 4,000 more female prisoners were transported from Ravensbrück to Denmark.

SHIFTING OF CULTURES FROM BYSTANDER
TO RESCUER

Identity researchers suggest that the middle levels of development are comprised of some identity exploration, though with no real commitment (moratorium) or vocational commitment, but the individual has taken on the parent's identity (foreclosed). There are the rudiments of personal identity but it remains underdeveloped, subject to the overpowering of the social identity. According to theorists, some perturbation is required to shift to the next highest level. Ego developmentalists have empirical evidence to suggest "insight" as the key component in making developmental shifts. Insight is an understanding of the origin, nature, and mechanisms of beliefs, feelings, and attitudes and opinions of oneself and others. How a culture stimulates development of higher levels is not certain but education, specifically in empathy, may be a start.

In his Depression-era novel *It can't happen here*, Sinclair Lewis[37] writes that most Americans would be drawn to the political Right and his protagonist Doremus Jessup is sent to a concentration camp. Jessup later becomes part of the resistance that includes all decent citizens. "Blessed are those who don't think they have to go out and do something about it!" says Jessup. If it is, as Edmund Burke is popularly supposed to have said, sufficient for evil to triumph, that good men do nothing, then good and ordinary men and women must learn to be rescuers.

WHERE ARE THEY IN PEACETIME?
George Wallace (Alabama governor)
The evidence that this four-term Alabama governor was "the dominant and most important issue maker of his time," shifting national campaign rhetoric to the right, is convincing. The origins and development of Wallace's powers of hucksterism and his need for an audience, lay out his "extraordinary racial schizophrenia": because of his political ambition, Wallace allowed his populist support for bills that often benefited Blacks to be overshadowed by his racist political

positioning. From Bull Connor's brutality in Birmingham to the admitting of Black students to the state university, Wallace nonetheless tapped the "Southernization" of suburban and ethnic White America, thereby fueling his two presidential bids. Wallace's populism, unlike that of Reaganite Republicans, took on the rich, and Wallace, crippled in a 1972 assassination attempt, developed a humanity that led him to make public apologies for his former racism.

Paul Althaus (pastor)

Martin Luther's reformation ideas spurred on the lifework of Paul Althaus (1888–1966), perhaps the best example of *trahison des clercs*. During World War I, he preached in Poland, returning to the University of Rostock in 1920, and then moving to Erlangen University in 1925, where he was a professor of Systematic Theology. From there he provided the Nazi party with Christian rationale and justification for their acts of destruction. Known more as a sincere Christian, he sought a middle ground between the Church and the Nazis, believing the nationalist extremism would be tempered by Christian ethics in a fusing of church and state. Describing Hitler as a "gift and miracle of God" he criticized the peace movement and interpreted the Nazi party as a religious event where God was acting in history. More an ideologue than an ardent Nazi, he rejected notions that Hitler was the new Jesus/Messiah of a Germanic faith, and he never wrote about this again after 1937, though he never renounced allegiance to Hitler. When informed of the Jewish extermination in 1943, he did not speak openly and was cleared of Nazism in 1947, returning to the university until his death in 1966. In later writings he wrote that the aura of Luther's ideas may have contributed to the Holocaust.

George Burdi (former racist)

George Burdi's background is not even typical of temporary perpetrators. Born to a middle-class suburban Toronto family, the former altar boy was popular and had a successful upbringing, including his football team membership, student council activity, and straight-A report cards. His parents were not racist, but at age 18, his girlfriend's father brought him into a racist movement. Trying to win the father's approval landed him knee-deep in hate literature. He soon gained notoriety as the creator of Resistance Records, the largest distributor of oi (hate) music in North America. In 1997, he was arrested for beating an anti-racist woman protester and was briefly sentenced to prison. Today he is out of the fold, married to an Indian woman, and plays in an ethnically diverse rock band.

Louis Darquier (collaborator)

Louis Darquier was a collaborator in Vichy France. Darquier was made commissioner of Jewish affairs and was vehemently anti-semitic. Some credit his antisemitism to the influence of an older brother, but by 1936 he was beating up Jews in cafés and was out-spokenly antisemitic. It is unclear how many Jews he turned over to the Nazis. In 1947 the French High Court of Justice sentenced him to death in absentia (he had fled to fascist Spain). Spain refused extra-dition. Unrepentant, he once declared to a French journalist that gas was not used to kill Jews and that such allegations were falsities perpetrated by "the Jews."

NOTES ON CHAPTER 4

1. J. Block & J. Block (2006) Venturing a 30 year longitudinal study. *American Psychologist*, 61, 315–327.
2. See: N. Tec (1986) *When light pierced the darkness*. New York: Oxford University Press; P. M. Oliner, J. Wiegus & M. B. Gruber (1998) Religious culture and outgroup altruism. Presentation at the 106th Annual Convention of the American Psychological Association, San Francisco; G. Block & M. Drucker (1992) *Rescuers*. New York: Holmes & Meier; E. Fogelman (1994) *Conscience and courage*. New York: Anchor/ Doubleday; S. P. Oliner & P. M. Oliner (1988) *The altruistic personality*. New York: Free Press; P. M. Oliner (2004) *Saving the forsaken*. New Haven: Yale University Press, p. 57. Also see E. Midlarsky, S. F. Jones & R. K. Nemeroff (2006) Heroic rescue during the Holocaust: Empirical and methodological perspectives. In R. Bootzin & P. McKnight (eds.)

Strengthening research methodology: Psychological measurement and evaluation. Washington, DC: American Psychological Association; S. F. Jones & R. P. Corley (2005) Personality correlates of heroic rescue during the Holocaust. *Journal of Personality*, 73, 907–934.

3. E. Staub (2001) Individual and group identities in genocide and mass killing. In R. D. Ashmore, L. Jussim & D. Wilder (eds.) *Social identity, intergroup conflict, and conflict reduction*. New York: Oxford University Press, p. 173.

4. Nazis have never been considered freedom fighters – why? Because freedom fighting for fascism is an oxymoron. The same is true for fundamentalism. Those who defend fascistic and religiously fundamentalistic ideologies are not freedom fighting – they are fighting to uphold fascism via religion. I would argue as vehemently against fundamentalist Jews, Christians, Hindus etc. And Palestinian Muslims who are extremist are not exempt. To wit, popularly electing a religiously extremist government Hamas.

5. C. J. Dean (2004) *The fragility of empathy*. Ithaca: Cornell University, p. 5.

6. D. Bar-On (2001) The bystander in relation to the victim and the perpetrator: Today and during the Holocaust. *Social Justice Research*, 14, 125–148.

7. E. Staub (1995) How people learn to care. In P. Schervish, V. A. Hodgkinson, M. Gates & Associates (eds.) *Care and community in modern society*. San Francisco: Independent Sector/Jossey-Bass, p. 4.

8. S. Straus (2006) *The order of genocide*. Ithaca, NY: Cornell University Press, p. 13.

9. V. Bennett (2000) *Bystanders*. Westport, CT: Praeger; Z. Bauman (1989) *Modernity and the Holocaust*. Ithaca, NY: Cornell University.

10. C. Simpson (1993) *The splendid blond beast*. New York: Grove.

11. D. Frey & H. Rez (2002) Population and perpetrators. In L. S. Newman & R. Eber (eds.) *Understanding genocide* (188–221). New York: Oxford University Press.

12. D. Peukert (1989) *Inside Nazi Germany*. New Haven: Yale University Press; M. Kaplan (1999) *Between dignity and despair*. New York: Oxford University Press; V. Klemperer (1999) *I will bear witness*. New York: Modern Library; S. Heffner (2003) *Defying Hitler*. New York: Picador; A. S. Bergerson (2004) *Ordinary Germans in extraordinary times*. Bloomington, IN: Indiana University Press: "uniformity" p. 39, "naturalized customs of everyday life" p. 64, "tried to preserve their

normalcy" p. 213, "preserve a coherent sense of self" p. 247. I. Kershaw (University of Sheffield: b.eaton@sheffield.ac.uk); D. J. Goldhagen (1996) *Hitler's willing executioners.* New York: Knopf.

13. D. Shapiro (1984) *Autonomy and rigid character.* New York: Basic; D. Shapiro (2000) *Dynamics of character.* New York: Basic.

14. J. Shedler, M. Mayman & M. Manis (1993) The illusion of mental health. *American Psychologist,* 48, 1117–1131.

15. Ronald Kessler, see www.in-cites.com/papers/DrRonaldKessler.html

16. I. W. Charny (2006) *Fascism and democracy in the human mind.* Lincoln, NE: University of Nebraska Press.

17. E. A. Zillmer, M. Harrower, B. A. Ritzler & R. P. Archer (1995) *The quest for the Nazi personality.* Hillsdale, NJ: Lawrence Erlbaum.

18. B. F. McFarland-Icke (1999) *Nurses in Nazi Germany.* Princeton, NJ: Princeton University Press; also see M. Dudley & F. Gale (2002) Psychiatrists as a moral community?: Psychiatry under the Nazis and its contemporary relevance. *Australian & New Zealand Journal of Psychiatry,* 36, 585–594.

19. L. Kohlberg & L. Candee (1984) The relationship of moral judgment to moral action. In W. Kurtines & J. L. Gurwitz (eds.) *Morality, moral behavior and moral development.* New York: Wiley.

20. R. Gellately (2001) *Backing Hitler.* New York: Oxford University Press, p. xxvii.

21. R. J. Lifton (1986) *The Nazi doctors.* New York: Basic; H. Friedlander (1995) *The origins of Nazi genocide.* Chapel Hill, NC: University of North Carolina Press; G. Mander (2002) Psychologists and the National Socialist access to power. *History of Psychology,* 5, 190–200.

22. B. F. McFarland-Icke (1999) *Nurses in Nazi Germany.* Princeton, NJ: Princeton University Press.

23. Rwandan nun sentenced to 30 years for genocide. www.abc.net.au/news/newsitems/200611/s1786176.htm

24. E. Staub (1989) *Roots of evil.* Amherst, MA: University of Massachusetts; Fiske, see www.newscientist.com/channel/opinion/dn6727 dated 11/25/04.

25. C. R. Browning (1992) *Ordinary men.* New York: HarperCollins; D. Grossman (1995) *On killing.* Boston: Little Brown; R. Rhodes (2002) *Master of death.* New York: Knopf. J. Waller (2002) *Becoming evil.* New York: Oxford University Press.

26. Dick de Mildt (1996) *In the name of the people*. Den Hague: Marinus Nijhoff, p. 311.

27. Zimbardo's original lecture, 3/9/99, California State University, Sonoma, http://www.sonoma.edu/users/g/goodman/zimbardo.htm; P. Rusesabagina (2006) *An ordinary man*. New York: Viking, p. 193.

28. Torturers employ five techniques: hooding, noise bombardment, food deprivation, sleep deprivation, standing at wall. Originally inspired by the Soviet Union, China, and North Korea, this was adopted by the European Court of Human Rights as inhuman and degrading but not torture. It had been inflicted on people across the British empire, in Palestine, Malaysia, Kenya, Cyprus, British Cameroon, Brunei, British Guiana, Aden, and the Persian Gulf. J. Conroy (2000) *Unspeakable acts, ordinary people*. New York: Knopf. For My Lai details see H. Kelman & V. L. Hamilton (1989) *Crimes of obedience*. New Haven: Yale University. See Lifton's *Nazi Doctors*; also M. Haritos-Fatouros & J. Gibson (1988) The official torturer: A learning model for obedience to an authority of violence. *Journal of Applied Social Psychology*, 18, 1107–1129.

29. J. Watson (1973) Investigation into deindividuation using a cross-cultural survey technique. *Journal of Personality and Social Psychology*, 24, 342–345.

30. Daniel Bar-Tal (2000) *Shared beliefs in a society*. Thousand Oaks: Sage; H. Kelman & V. L. Hamilton (1989) *Crimes of obedience*. New Haven: Yale University; Ervin Staub (1989) *Roots of evil*. New York: Cambridge University Press; E. Staub (2003) *Good and evil*. New York: Cambridge University Press.

31. D. Grossman (1995) *On killing*. Boston: Little Brown.

32. C. R. Browning (1992) *Ordinary men*. New York: HarperCollins.

33. G. Sereny (1974/1983) *Into that darkness*. New York: Vintage.

34. F. Bajohr (2006) The folk community and the persecution of Jews: German society under national socialist dictatorship 1933–1945. *Holocaust and Genocide Studies*, 20, 183–206. Also see C. Browning (1992) *Ordinary men*. New York: HarperCollins.

35. J. Waller (2005) *Becoming evil*. New York: Oxford University Press, p. 8.

36. B. A. Valentino (2005) *Final solutions*. Ithaca: Cornell University Press, p. 60.

37. S. Lewis (1935) *It can't happen here*. Available on the internet at http://gutenberg.net.au/ebooks03/0301001h.html

5 Rescuers

Do not stand while your neighbor's blood is shed.

- *A chimpanzee named Nim Chimsky regularly sought to comfort people. If he saw a person crying, he would climb up to the individual and try to wipe the tears away.*
- *A scientist forgot his lunch and tried to knock some bananas down with a stick. An observant chimp climbed down the tree and handed a banana to the researcher.*
- *A mother chimp died, then her son adopted his year-old sister, taking her into his sleeping nest and carrying her around wherever he went.*

Recall the news story a few years ago of Binti Jua, a gorilla from the primate exhibit at Chicago's Brookfield Zoo. One summer's day a three-year-old boy fell eighteen feet down into the exhibit. Terrified patrons looked on as Binti picked up the child and cradled him, giving him a few pats on the back before handing him over to zoo staff. "I could not believe how gentle she was," observed the zoo director.[1]

Similar behavior has been seen in chimps who "comfort" each other after an attack or other trauma. It begs an immediate question as to why it is seems not as common in humans – or is it?

"This is not happenstance" child researcher Marian Radke-Yarrow told the *New York Times*. She and NIMH colleague Carolyn Zahn-Waxler's study of more than 300 children revealed that children as early as 12 months old touched, patted or offered some other sympathetic gesture to a person who appeared distressed.[2] Or perhaps adults are just picky and given the right circumstances, we give. For instance, in any given year, some 59 million Americans (27.6 percent) volunteer for work in various agencies. And in times of crisis, our capacity to care is even more pronounced.

"We tried to save as many as we could," said one survivor of the September 11 terrorist attack. People who would never acknowledge each other on the street helped each other out of harm's way. There was unprecedented pain and unprecedented help. Three quarters of the American public are said to have given money or clothes following the September 11 attack on America. But helping under any circumstances is a bit complex. To further understand helping behavior, let us examine what we now know about the motivations behind helping and rescue.

DEFINING RESCUERS

Helping and rescuing is somewhat difficult to define. Part of the difficulty lies in assessing the intention behind helping behavior. Even perpetrators help, though their motivations are different from most people's. In terms of our divisions, the motivations follow accordingly. While perpetrators are concerned with "what's in it for me?" or "what would those in authority say?" and bystanders are concerned with "what would the neighbors say?", by contrast, rescuers can be defined by an internal motivation expressed as "what do I say?"

The type of helping behavior we are addressing is not self-congratulatory or self-serving. It is the innate empathy-based morality of David Hume. And while some philosophers would argue that there is no purely unselfish helping – the actions of the helper are performed in order to make the helper feel less guilty or to think of themselves in a better light – others point to cultural definitions of character, honor and courage. Still others seek religious definitions of morality and taking the high road.

We can't really trust all the numbers. In the Holocaust, the exact number of altruistic rescuers is not really known. Yad Vashem, the Israeli organization that honors those who risked their lives for saving Jews, gives estimates which are quite low (20,000 acknowledged rescuers out of a general European population of 750 million) as the authentication process is quite stringent, due in part to the number of false rescuer claims.

Yad Vashem acknowledges that more rescuers may come to light in the future but those honors are now limited by the advanced age of the rescuers. Mordecai Paldiel, the Yad Vashem director and author of *Saving the Jews*, acknowledges that the number of those who helped Jews was much higher than those who were awarded Righteous status but is reluctant to say how much higher.

It would seem to be considerably higher. My fiancée's family in Holland put aside a small portion of food each week for the Jewish underground. No one acknowledges help on that level. Pieter Broersma's family did considerably more as his interview revealed that his parents' house in Groningen, The Netherlands, was used as a safe house to get the town's Jews into the countryside. Yad Vashem does not acknowledge that act. Middle East historian Robert Satloff has recently documented Arab-Muslims in Nazi-occupied Paris, Tunisia, Algeria, and Morocco who aided and abetted Jews during World War II. He cites Khaled Abdelwahhab who hid a Jewish family on his olive farm in Tunisia and Si Kaddour Benghabrit who may have saved a hundred Jews by issuing Muslim identity certificates and providing shelter at the Great Mosque in Paris. Consistent with the idea of perpetrators, bystanders, and rescuers in an Arab population, Satloff concludes,

> most were indifferent, some played a supporting role in the persecution; and a smaller group did what they could to protect Jews, defend them, or just ease their suffering.[3]

Judging by the examples above, the Yad Vashem estimates may be doubled or tripled if the definition is expanded to include helping behavior as well as bona fide rescue. Survivor and sociologist Sam Oliner similarly estimates the percentage of helpers to be higher than Yad Vashem's figures. Consider as well that historian Christopher Browning estimates that between 10 and 20 percent of Nazi soldiers evaded killing Jews. Philosemitism may not directly translate to Jewish rescue, nor may the non-prejudicial and anti-authoritarian acts surveyed by psychologists Gordon Allport and Erich Fromm.[4] But all the above estimates range between 10 and 20 percent of the

Table 5.1 *Stages of rescue development*

Level	Stage	Motivation
1	Egocentric	Helping to relieve your own discomfort.
2	Instrumental	Giving in order to get back.
3	Mutual	Helping to be thought of as a good person.
4	Conscientious	Helping as social responsibility/ good citizenship.
5	Autonomous	Helping to uphold internalized utilitarian values.
6	Integrated	Helping to uphold universal humanitarian, just, impartial values.[1]

[1] This table is based on the work of D. Krebs & F. van Hesteren (1992) The development of altruistic personality. In P. Oliner, S. Oliner, L. Baron, L. Blum, D. Krebs & M. Smolenska (eds.) *Embracing the other*. New York: New York University Press.

population, contingent perhaps on one's emotional development as Table 5.1 suggests.

RESCUER BACKGROUND

The findings of all the postconventional rescuing and helping studies can be summarized into one statement: Rescuers came from mentally healthier homes and are emotionally more evolved. When explaining to Bill Moyers the motivation behind the Le Chambon hiding of 5,000 Jews during the war, film director Pierre Sauvage said quite simply, "I think it was the mental health that shines through from these people. These people sort of exude that sense of mental health."[5]

Early research by Perry London and Sam Oliner observed that for the majority of rescuers and resisters, the family home was a determining factor in development of helping behaviors. Related research on the Carnegie heroes similarly addresses positive parental influence. These emotionally healthier mothers transmitted healthier goals of independence and social competence and were slightly older and better educated than mothers of non-rescuers.[6] Rescuers were closer to their parents.[7] The families of those who rescued were often described as loving. In rescuer families, punishment was less physical and non-authoritarian and conflicts were reasoned out.[8] For instance, rescuer parents directly taught universal values [39 percent compared with 13 percent of bystanders' parents] and may have conveyed much more indirectly. Rescuers had well-developed inner values and a good sense of personal responsibility.[9]

Some of those homes were religious, most were not. Political psychology researcher Kristen Monroe interviewed Holocaust rescuers and addressed a universal philosophy.

> The core of a universal morality was human welfare, not religious exhortations, systems of moral rules, or adherence to abstract ethical concepts such as fairness or justice. It was this belief in the sanctity of human life that was so integrated into the rescuers' sense of self. The integration of this particular moral value then left rescuers with no other option, even when presented with what appeared at least to others as agonistic choices. It meant rescuers would discard their learned rules of behavior when necessary to save a human life.[10]

Her colleague Pearl Oliner reanalyzed Holocaust rescuer data with findings that surprised religious scholars – most of those people who rescued were "irreligious," perhaps better thought of as post-religious. Oliner's irreligious possessed the same traits as in the other studies – they were more empathic than those who did not rescue, and held liberal democratic values. Concludes Oliner,

> The irreligious rescuers were more fortunate in their family relationships ... They had a much better start in life. They had

better family relationships generally and they were far less likely to perceive their parents as authoritarian. They emerged from these experiences with significantly higher self-esteem and a stronger sense of personal integrity. Rescuers were no more likely than non-rescuers to identify and affiliate with secular secondary institutions. Rescuers had significantly better relationships and attitudes toward out-groups. Their parents had made them conscious of Jews in positive ways, sometimes as a positive stereotype as intelligent, hardworking and taking care of their own and sometimes about individuals they knew: someone who was particularly generous, told good jokes, was a good teacher, or just a good friend.[11]

Pearl's husband Sam, himself rescued, continues to conduct research on rescuers. His most recent study is also germane. Included in the Oliner survey were philanthropists, volunteers, World War II rescuers and resisters, military, 9/11 and Carnegie Heroes. Sam Oliner's findings suggested that the following traits were involved in helping others: valuing social responsibility, valuing kindness and virtuous behavior, efficacy, immediacy, reciprocity, and a religious predisposition to help.[12]

Fritz Graebe is not a household name but perhaps should be. An engineer working for the German army in Ukraine, Graebe forged work papers and passports and food ration cards. At one point he stood pistol-to-pistol with an SS commander and walked away taking a hundred Jewish workers with him to safety. By the end of the war, he led Jews in his own train into Germany and across the Allied lines. His autobiographer summarizes his motives this way.

> [Fritz's] motives in the Nazi era can be traced back to the instruction of his mother Louise Graebe. She taught him to be an independent thinker and to care for the less fortunate and for those who were the victims of society. She showed him how to be hospitable and instilled in him a profound sense of justice that enabled him to resist ill-willed inhumane authorities.[13]

Dutch rescuer Hetty Voute also highlights the rationale of her home life.

> I think both my parents were rather independent. They were never impressed by what other people said. They always went their own way and thought their own thoughts and that's the way they raised us. My father took a strong stand on certain community issues. He didn't care what kind of flak he got. And when I went to school, I was the same way.[14]

Anne Frank's Austrian rescuer Miep Gies recounts the influence of her large adopted Dutch family:

> Kindness in my depleted condition was very important to me. It was medicine as much as the bread, the marmalade, the good Dutch milk and butter and cheese, the toasty temperature of the warm rooms.[15]

Kindness can become its own motive. "We are made kind by being kind," wrote longshoreman Eric Hoffer. Gies transferred the kindness she received into rescuing others. Her efforts are now considered exemplary.

TRAITS

Rescuers are more emotionally developed than bystanders. In one of the few studies to examine both groups, seventy-two postwar North Americans' scores for mental health suggested vast differences in rescuers compared to bystanders (83.3 percent vs. 36.8 percent). Rescuers have the highest moral standards of conduct. This inner conduct translates to strength allowing for what some have termed the altruistic urge. According to key researchers: "three important and striking behavior patterns flowed naturally from this altruistic perspective. These concern spontaneity, choice and the constancy and universality of the altruistic bond."[16]

From an early age, rescuers have amassed wisdom on how life is to be lived above the fray and beyond cultural boundaries. Rescuers have the ability to compassionately connect or be empathic and caring with others.

As addressed earlier, the psychologist Abraham Maslow[17] believed that when you are no longer dominated by your needs (physiological, social, and personal), then you are able to self-actualize, or achieve the highest levels of emotional development. He cited such examples as Abraham Lincoln and Eleanor Roosevelt but most rescuers' names will never be known. The traits of self-actualizers parallel rescuer traits and include the following:

- autonomy and independence
- resistance to enculturation
- democratic values
- tolerance/acceptance of others
- spontaneity vs. calculating
- honesty over social pretense
- appreciation of that which others take for granted
- intimate relations with a few friends
- social awareness, concern for social justice.

Rescuers possess what has been termed a democratic mindset. "They just indicated a belief in the universality of human nature, suffering and concerns," observes author Robyn Dawes.[18] But it is more than just subscribing to a particular philosophy. Rescuers possess a mindset of a higher level of functioning that is reflected by their more highly evolved philosophy. In his work with London School of Economics lecturer Matt Mulford, they found that a universal mindset was statistically linked to heroism and included accuracy in judging others.

Along those lines, Charny would suggest that rescuers possess a democratic mindset. One which

> invites responsibility for choosing one's direction in life with
> awareness that there are multiple ideations from which to choose.
> It supports question and testing of behaviors so to speak
> scientifically against their outcomes, accompanied by a readiness
> to change ideas as new information comes in. In the process, it

encourages experiences of anxiety and humility, abhors superiority and strives for a basic equality with other people even when one is in a leadership role. Democratic mind rejoices in one's existence and claims the inherent right to self-defense against dangers and extremes. But along with protecting one's own life, it is always committed to deep respect for the rights of others to live and to rejoice in the quality of their lives. Democratic thinking leaves one more uncertain and more aware of one's incompleteness and inability to solve all problems. It is anxiety provoking because it is known that one must often integrate contradictory ideas into a single policy and choose between imperfect possibilities. But because democratic thinking is sworn to protect the integrity of life and one's continuous opportunities to choose between competing ideas, it is ultimately safe for human life and generates a joy in being alive to choose and do … [It] carefully enjoins violence as anti-sacred, but if one does end up nonetheless doing some kind of harm to others, it calls for acknowledging and accepting responsibility for having done this harm and ceasing to do it.[19]

WISDOM AS INDEPENDENT SPIRIT AND AUTONOMY

Alright then, I'll go to Hell!

Mark Twain, *Huckleberry Finn*

In Twain's classic *Huckleberry Finn*, protagonist Huck is caught between the two realms of social and personal life. In order to do his civic duty Huck writes a letter to Miss Watson, telling her where to find her slave Jim:

> Miss Watson, your runaway nigger Jim is down here two mile below Pikesville, and Mr. Phelps has got him and he will give him up for the reward if you send. HUCK FINN.

The prevailing social order dictated that one should turn in runaway slaves. At the same time, Huck had realized that Jim was more than a slave, or another person; he was his friend.

I took it [the letter] up and held it in my hand. I was trembling, because I'd got to decide forever, betwixt two things and I knowed it. I studied a minute, sort of holding my breath, and then says to myself 'alright, then, I'll go to Hell' – and tore it up.

Our definition of autonomy can be defined as:

To act in accord with one's self – it means feeling free and volitional in one's actions. When autonomous, people are fully willing to do what they are doing and they embrace the activity with a sense of interest and commitment. "Their actions emanate from their true sense of self, so they are being authentic"[20]

In the Second World War, active resistance may have accounted for only 5 percent of the population, but it is an important 5 percent. Recall the response of 32-year-old Dutch engineer Jan Rensaleer, when implored by Milgram experiment to shock others and told he had no choice in the matter. "I do have a choice!" retorted Rensaleer.

Sheltered from the Nazis by multiple Christian rescuers from age 11 to 14, University of Connecticut sociologist Nechama Tec has since studied the choices Polish rescuers made.

Her findings reaffirm that rescuers rose above cultural convention: "Individualism was the outstanding trait"[21] (in 2001, she reported 98 percent self-rated as independent holding universalistic perceptions). Perry London's[22] earlier study concluded, as well, that rescuers were autonomous, with strong moral principles, and willing to take risks.

Tec reports that rescuers didn't quite fit in with the average person and neither did they seem to mind. All rescuers had individuality, a personal identity that enabled them to stand up for their beliefs. Her work was consistent with a separate analysis of a rescuer. Those who were rescuers tended to be the intellectuals, liberals, and politically resistant people. 82 percent originated from apolitical families. Helpers tended to be politically liberal and non-materialistic;

conversely, materialistic people tended to be unhelpful[23]: findings that are consistent with status-oriented, materialistic people.[24]

Out of several rescuer traits, Rev. Douglas Huneke believed the common denominator to be the ability to see each person individually, by which he meant in terms of personal (not social) identity. By contrast, lower functioning, socially identified people cannot separate out the personal from the cultural group. Rescuers saw others as individuals, not as part of a group or collective. Most rescues began spontaneously – on an unplanned basis, as a simple response to requests for help. Rescuing occurred out of public view and was performed repeatedly. "All were people of high moral principles, independent spirit and the courage to act on their convictions."[25]

COMPASSION AND EMPATHY

Compassion alone stands apart from the continuous traffic between good and evil.

C. S. Lewis

"There was goodness, there was kindness and there was love and compassion,"[26] recalls Anti-Defamation League's Abraham Foxman of his rescue during the Holocaust by a Christian nanny. Empathy, kinship, and friendship were the constants. A quarter of the rescuers knew those they had rescued. Some had family bonds, or Jewish relatives. Mixed marriages accounted for 29 percent of rescues in one study. The majority (84 percent) lived with somebody who would have been taken away if not rescued.[27]

Experts in this area record that rescuers were "ordinary people" for whom situational factors were key – the right conditions would produce a rescuer as easily as a bystander.

But rescuers are anything but ordinary. Research into personality traits finds in them extraordinarily high levels of altruism, courage, and independent mindedness. Altruistic personality variables (anti-authoritarianism, empathy, moral reasoning, and social responsibility) correctly identified most of the rescuers (83.4 percent) and bystanders (91.8 percent). In experiments, when given the choice, these less egoistic persons are consistently more inclined to respond to the distress of others.[28]

Oliner and Oliner[29] found more internal sense of control, self esteem, and empathy/social responsibility. Yet the best predictor of current helping was past helping.[30] Other predictors were intrinsic religious motivation, altruistic moral judgment, risk taking, and an anti-authoritarian attitude.

Some rescuing also occurred as a protest against fascism. At times rescuing occurred in spite of personal dislike for the people rescued. Most (76 percent) rescuers continued to focus on the needy condition of the person irrespective of cultural prohibition. Typical of this group was a long history of good deeds and empathic gestures such as visiting hospitalized people, caring for the poor, and assisting stray animals.

The findings of a recent Belgian study are of interest. Religiosity as measured on scientific scales had little or nothing to do empathy[31] and Pearl Oliner's rescuer study observed that those who classified themselves as "irreligious" did more to rescue Jews than did those who identified themselves as Catholic or Protestant. According to Tec,[32] all rescuers had a history of helping and a commitment to assist the needy. Most (95 percent) rescuers said that they felt prompted to rescue based on victim neediness while a smaller percentage reported that they rescued due to friendship. For those who could put Christian principles into practice, about a quarter (26 percent) stated that they rescued for religious reasons.

At times, empathy with Jewish victims transformed into an identification. Holocaust rescuer Nicholas Winton had a Jewish grandfather, which may have influenced his decision to help. Other rescuers wondered similarly if "Jewish blood" was somewhere in their family lines. Still others had Jewish spouses amongst their family members. Recall Rudi Florian, the Hitler Youth turned

Holocaust Museum docent (see Chapter 4) who reported on the following experience:

> It was 1975 and I was traveling to Israel with a tour group. I went up to the Wailing Wall and just stared at the parchment requests that people put in the cracks of the wall and for the next few minutes had what you call a déjà vu experience of some sort. I truly believe I had been there before and it was part of some larger picture. I had never had the experience before and I never have had one since. But maybe this is all part of why I do the work I do?

As previously mentioned, all rescuers downplayed their actions. "I had no choice but to rescue," was a common response. "We did what any human being would have done," says an 82-year-old Dutch rescuer, Johtje Vos.[33] "We did not think about it, you started off storing a suitcase for a friend and before you knew it you were in over your head."

After the war, Vos underscored that rescuers continued down the path of empathy, care, and personal responsibility. Rescuers continued to rescue in a variety of ways such as staying involved in community affairs and working for a number of charitable causes. For those who rescue, the responses were almost universal. "You'd have done the same for me if the situation was reversed." This simple statement explained the motivation for helping and pointed to why many of the rescuers were from the helping professions (e.g. social workers, teachers, counselors, and nurses). "They just simply had to do it because that's the kind of people they were," quipped survivor psychiatrist Emmanuel Tanay.[34]

Marcel Marceau was fifteen years old when he and his brother Alain left Limoges and joined the underground where Marceau altered French youths' identity cards to provide proof that they were too young to be sent to labor camps. Masquerading as a Boy Scout leading campers on a hike in the Alps, he later saved hundreds of children's lives by smuggling them into Switzerland. Alain and Marcel later fled to Paris; their mother moved to Perigueux and their father was sent to Auschwitz. Like most rescuers, Marcel was modest and almost dismissed the process of helping: "I really do not want to speak about my experiences because I didn't do anything compared to others – let alone those who helped and died."

Positive psychologists will tell you that they have found six major traits that define virtue: wisdom and knowledge, courage, humanity, justice, temperance, and transcendence. Rescuers knew what was right, good and just through their evolved emotional development and nature. "They had," as the Dalai Lama says, acted in accordance with "an opened heart."

COURAGE

It is curious that physical courage should be so common in the world and moral courage so rare.

Mark Twain

President Kennedy's 1957 Pulitzer prize-winning book, *Profiles in courage*, recounts the stories of eight US Senators who risked their careers by taking principled stands for unpopular positions. In 1989, the Kennedy family created an award for public officials who displayed such courage. Recipients include families of New York fire fighters and police, and more recently congressman John Murtha (D-PA) for, among other things, his initially unpopular stand against the Iraq war.

Courage can be defined as the bold need to help beyond reason. Many rescuers (up to 50 percent) at times were involved in the resistance or underground. As we have seen over and over, such acts of rescue were often unpremeditated and often were seen as matter of fact by rescuers, though as Tec noted, almost all (85 percent) of Jews thought of their rescuers as courageous.[35]

Some liked the idea of being above a law that was wrong. "There's a hell of a lot of fun – though that's not quite the word ... It's stimulating to be outside the law," wrote Holocaust rescuer Varian Fry. Perhaps Fry's temerity is captured by Anais Nin's notion when she wrote, "Life shrinks or expands in proportion to one's courage."

Life expanded for Marion Pritchard, though in ways she never thought possible. The quiet Amsterdam homemaker and social work student had never fired a pistol. But when a policeman arrived at her door at 2:00 a.m. searching for the three Jewish children and the father she was hiding, she reached up for a hidden pistol. "It was him or the kids, so I shot him," she says, unflinching. "It was a moment of excitement. I did it! I did it! The kids are safe! Then it was, what do I do with the body?"

Still haunted by the thought of that night, she finds solace that she saved over 150 people, mostly children. The 80-year-old retired psychoanalyst, now living in DC, states, "It was never a question . . . For somebody's life, how could you not?" Pritchard attributes her behavior to her emotionally healthy upbringing. Her father was a judge and mother a homemaker. The household atmosphere was child-oriented and non-punitive. She reflects on her early emotional upbringing. "I got all my questions answered. When you are brought up that way, with complete love, respect, and understanding, that is how you try to treat people when you grow up."

Though many of the neighbors knew what she was doing, they were "good Dutchmen, anti-Nazi, and rescuers in their own way," Pritchard says. They sneaked her milk and vegetables to supplement her meager rations. Pritchard struggled to keep house while finding havens for other outlawed Jews. "I had to go on, to stay strong for the family," she says. "I wish it hadn't been necessary. But it was the better of two evils."

Rescuers are risk-takers and are courageous when they have to be. Perhaps the most daunting would be a rescuer among the Nazis. Major Karl Plagge may have quietly saved the lives of some 250 Lithuanian Jews. An engineer from Darmstadt, he found himself in charge of a camp where military vehicles were repaired. Time after time, he saved Jews from prison, SS death squads, and the ghetto by issuing them work permits as "indispensable" laborers essential to the war effort. Plagge, who died in 1957, rescued because "I thought it was my duty."[36] He was honored by Yad Vashem in 2005. One of the surviving 250 acknowledged, "There are always some people who decide that the horror is not to be."

Pieter Broersma, age 81, grew up in Groningen, Holland, and came of age during the war, working as a scout/interpreter for the Allies, and came from a large family of rescuers.

> My father was an engineer and my mother was a homemaker. It was a fairly average family but then the war came, and I don't remember why, but we started taking in onderduikers on a regular basis. Maybe it was how you say "fuck you" to the Nazis. We'd keep them for a while like a safe house and then get them into the countryside. I am not certain what motivated my father to rescue – maybe it was because the whole family was involved. All my five uncles and their families did the same. Perhaps it was a form of fighting back – we hated the Germans and it was a stick in their eye. And we couldn't understand why they hated the Jews. They were our neighbors and friends at school. Maybe it was that my father was a religious man and he hated things that were unjust. I was about fifteen years old and my sister was nineteen at the time. It never bothered us that we had a house with people in and out at night. Nobody seemed to mind. If the Nazis knocked on my door today, I would do the same thing. I am not nearly as religious as my father so it wouldn't be for religious reasons, it would be for righteous reasons. And I think my kids would do the same. It is just the right thing to do.

LEVELS OF DEVELOPMENT

For psychologists, helping and rescuing is part of a larger concept called moral development. Moral development has to do with complex judgments and decision-making – thinking that incorporates not only individual needs, but takes into account the context (social constraints) and the proverbial higher road.

Developmentalists determine varying levels of moral development by administering and scoring a series of moral dilemmas. The basis of the scoring has to do with moving from black-and-white thinking as immature to seeing the grey or bigger picture: a more mature and sophisticated mental process. For example, when asked if they would ever consider killing their children, most people will answer an emphatic no.

But it is not so simple, and one cannot always go with gut instinct. Princeton postdoctoral fellow Joshua Greene offers several moral dilemmas to subjects in his test lab.

> Enemy soldiers have taken over your village and will kill civilians they find. You are hiding in the cellar of a house with a group of townspeople and you hear the soldiers enter the house. Your baby starts to cry, and the only way to quiet him is to hold your hand over his mouth and, eventually smother him. But if the baby keeps crying, the soldiers will discover your group and kill everyone, the baby included. What should you do?

The respondents are equally divided on whether to kill the baby, but when a functional magnetic resonance image (fMRI) is administered, not only do the emotional parts of the brain light up, but the abstract reasoning sections do as well. This suggests a strong interplay between more complex moral questions. The gut response (to save your child) may be automatic but the behavior may be mediated by other considerations. For instance, Greene suggests that we take into consideration both the personal (emotional reaction, reasoning) and social (empathy, norms) consequences.

He employs the trolley dilemma as well.

> A trolley is hurtling down the tracks toward five people who will be killed if it proceeds on its present course. You can save these five people by diverting the trolley onto a different set of tracks, one that has only one person on it, but if you do this that person will be killed. Is it morally permissible to turn the trolley and thus prevent five deaths at the cost of one?

Greene notes that most people say yes and then he continues with a twist in a slightly different direction.

> Once again, the trolley is headed for five people. You are on a footbridge over the tracks next to a large man. The only way to save the five people is to push this man off the bridge and into the path of the trolley. Is that morally permissible? Most people say no. But what makes it okay to sacrifice one person for the sake of five others in the first case but not in the second case? But there is also a psychological puzzle here: How does everyone know (or "know") that it's okay to turn the trolley but not okay to push the man off the bridge? My collaborators and I have collected brain-imaging data suggesting that emotional responses are an important part of the answer.[37]

Through interpretation of various responses, moral developmentalists have been able to determine levels or stages of maturation. Differences between the types of helping may be highlighted by the declining degrees of cultural conformity as expressed by the following questions: Tier I: What would my boss/clergy/people in authority say? Tier II: What would the neighbors think? Tier III: What can I do to help despite others' opinions? (see Table 5.2).

Level I: preconventional helping
The first level of helping has to do with preconventional morality. Such morality can be thought of as obedience to the culture and societal needs. At this level, people function out of fear – fear of ostracism and fear of recrimination. For example, "I had better help or someone in authority (priest, parents, friends) will disapprove and there will be hell to pay." When preconventional people help, they do so in order to relieve their own discomfort. At this earliest form of development, there is a limited form of exchange of needs and a desire exists for some sort of external reward. There is limited recognition of the other person as anything other than an object of demand and opportunity for reward. Empathy is limited. Helping at

Table 5.2 *Levels of helping and rescue*

Tier	Preconventional	Conventional	Postconventional
	I	II	III
Level	perpetrator	bystander	rescuer
Helping	reward-based	role-based	altruism
Emotional	rigid	conforming	autonomous/open
	least coping	average coping	sophisticated coping
	cognitive simple	moderate	complex
	superstitions/myths	stereotypes	least stereotyped
	tribal/ethnic identified	partial	emotional identity
Relations	self-centered	self + other	other-centered
Experience	survival	culturally meaningful	emotionally meaningful
Play	competitive	role-based	noncompetitive
Friendship	exploitive	role-based	deep feeling states
Self	false	semi-authentic	authentic
Motivation	fear	power	curiosity
Politics	fascist	conservative	liberal/democratic
Religion	fundamental	conventional	universalistic

this level is always self-serving. Those at a preconventional level may help others, but such behavior ceases once the payoff stops.

Level II: conventional helping

This second level of morality has to do with mutuality – "I will help you as you might help me" – but any form of rescue is subject to cultural approval. Conventional helpers act in accordance with their role in the society (e.g. I want to be thought of as a good, charitable person or citizen since those qualities are esteemed by others). Sociologists like the Oliners[38] found in their sample that for most people rescue was norm based (normocentric) (52 percent) – helping behavior that was rewarded by society (empathy accounted for 37 percent and principles 11 percent). Since most adults operate at the conventional level of moral development, who and how much they choose to help can become politically manipulated. Upholding high levels of involvement in church, family, and country may be conventionally right, but morally wrong.

Martin Niemoeller could have stayed at the preconventional or conventional level. He did not. Initially, he did champion the Nazi cause as Nazis fused church–state ties. But he began to move from the conventional toward the postconventional stage as the ugliness of fascism became clearer. Niemoeller spearheaded the anti-Nazi Pastors' Emergency League, and by 1933 he was suspended from preaching. On July 1, 1937, he was arrested for inciting disobedience and was sentenced to Moabit prison. He was offered release on the condition that he preach Nazi ideology but he refused. Niemoeller was then transferred to Sachsenhausen and Dachau concentration camps but eventually he was released. He remained in Germany until his death in 1984, but his now-famous statement demonstrates the increased levels of emotional awareness:

> When Hitler attacked the Jews I was not a Jew; therefore I was not concerned. And when Hitler attacked the Catholics I was not a Catholic and therefore I was not concerned. And when Hitler attacked the unions and industrialists, I was not a member of the

unions and I was not concerned. Then Hitler attacked me and the Protestant church – and there was nobody left to be concerned.

Level III: postconventional helping

Recall the defiance and courage of the lone student in Tiananmen Square (1989) in a standoff with an oncoming tank as he protested against the Chinese government. Now switch to images of 1994 Rwanda and Paul Rusesabagina is lying to Hutu mercenaries about the number of people he has billeted in the Hotel Rwanda, knowing that the slightest indiscretion or revealing of anxiety will result in death for himself and more than a thousand others he has sought to protect. Fast forward to Darfur and the stories we will one day hear of similar feats.

Why do they do it? What makes people rescue when others are too scared or are themselves perpetrating killing? Their acts will not make the society pages, and often no public glory comes of their deeds. They do not boast about themselves or their accomplishments. In terms of humanity, they seem to encompass all that is right and good in the world.

Rescuers ensured safe passage through North America's Underground Railroad. They were the ones who did not believe that South African apartheid was just or that the caste system is fair; they did not heed the call to Hutu Power or Greater Serbia. These are the individuals who, in spite of threat, recrimination, and retaliation have linked courage with wisdom and heart.

It isn't always easy for a rescuer. There are no parades or fanfare. At times they are even shunned by their immediate social group as in the case of the Holocaust, when they were marked as being "Jew lovers." Some left for Israel where they would be accepted, while others had difficulties adjusting to Israel. Sometimes they were killed as in the case of a Lithuanian carpenter who hid twelve Jews, and in 1952 was assassinated by a fellow Lithuanian.[39]

The same people would call Hugh Thompson a traitor. His actions, however, spoke the language of a rescuer. Most of us do not know the name Hugh Thompson. He quietly died in 2006 at the age of 62, after a long bout of cancer. In the middle of the My Lai massacre (1968) Thompson ordered his helicopter crew to fire on the US troops perpetrating the massacre and rescued Vietnamese women and children. He received no honors and became a pariah receiving threatening phone calls and messages. But in 1998, the Pentagon issued him the Soldier's Medal – the highest award for bravery not involving enemy conflict.

Postconventional rescuers have achieved the highest level of morality. They relate to others based on universal needs and democratic and human rights. Postconventional rescuers help because they believe it is the best thing to do for the person in need. Their motivation is, "I'll help where and when I can."

This higher level of moral development is apparent as one examines the life of Dietrich Bonhoeffer. Bonhoeffer was the Lutheran pastor whose participation in the plot to assassinate Hitler led to his arrest, imprisonment, and eventual execution at the age of 39. Nelson Mandela and Martin Luther King Jr. come quickly to mind as other exemplars of altruism and higher functioning. But human development is not an all-or-none phenomenon; rather, there are stepping stones and events that can propel some into the highest levels. Such shifts were apparent in Australian writer Thomas Keneally's portrayal of German Christian rescuer Oskar Schindler.

Conventional morality should have dictated that 28-year-old bank night watchman Christoph Meili do his job and turn his head the other way. But he didn't. He blew the whistle on Swiss banks concealing assets of the Nazi era. One January night in 1997, Meili saw ledgers of Nazi-era survivors being shredded in Union Bank's Zurich head office. He knew if he spoke the truth to superiors, he could get into trouble. Upon informing the police, Meili was fired and charged with violating bank-secrecy laws. Death threats and antisemitic hate mail soon followed: "We will hunt you down in your new home. Even the American Jew-Mafia will not be able to protect you." Today he lives with his wife and two children in a West Orange, NJ, apartment, where he works as a doorman, having received asylum.[40]

There were many other unsung heroes in many other genocides. Immaculée Ilibagiza is one of them. As one who was rescued in Rwanda, she now has become a rescuer. Ilibagiza was a Rwandan college student who survived for three months with seven other women in the bathroom of a local pastor's home as machete-wielding killers searched for them. She highlights her account in *Left to tell*.[41]

Leo Kabalisa has another story. Now a grade school teacher in Toronto, Kabalisa returns to Rwanda every year and helps rebuild the nation. "I can tell you a story of two priests who lived with each other," reports Kabalisa. He continues,

> It is beyond understanding of rational and irrational – one priest took great chances and hid over sixty people and when he was unable to help at times, they said he would cry. His roommate, an educated man, a Catholic and higher up, was part of those who raped women and hurt. The perpetrators let many out with AIDS to rape. Some Hutus died with Tutsis rather than continue to kill.

Most will not know the name of Damas Mutezintare Gisimba,[42] but the 32-year-old Rwandan protected sixty-five orphans, staff, and hundreds of refugees in the middle of the 1994 Rwandan genocide. The Red Cross evacuated the people he saved to safety. One observer offered this admiring assessment of his humanity: during the genocide, Gisimba looked beyond ethnicity. Many more were better placed to help but did not. He was a true hero because even though he knew that he could lose his own life protecting Tutsis, he stuck to his convictions. He was convinced that all human beings are alike. He chose to defend the life of others as he would defend his own.

His more famous colleague (Hotel Rwanda) Paul Rusesabagina divulges,

> Over and over people kept telling me that what I did at the
> Mille Collines was heroic, but I never saw it that way, and I still

don't. I was providing shelter. I was a hotel manager doing his job. That is the best thing anyone can say about me, and all I ever wanted.[43]

The overseer of the Rwandan nightmare was General Roméo Dallaire. He recounts his command of the 2,548-man UN Assistance Mission for Rwanda (UNAMIR) 1993–1994 peacekeeping mission. He tried to warn the UN of the pending Rwandan genocide but was dismissed. On January 11, he wrote to tell Kofi Annan that Hutu extremists (*Interahamwe*) "had been ordered to register all the Tutsi in Kigali" pending extermination.

> If I had done something differently could I have saved my Belgian
> soldiers when they were in the custody of the Rwandan Presidential
> Guard? Should I have ignored the direct orders I received from
> New York – orders not to protect Rwandan civilians and not to use
> force until fired upon? Was I right to remove the bullets from my
> pistol ahead of my meetings with the leaders of the Interahamwe
> militia forces or should I have given in to the compulsions to kill
> men whose shirts were spattered with dried blood? Should I, Roméo
> Dallaire, have shaken hands with the devil?[44]

Dallaire suffered from PTSD for the next decade and was given a medical discharge in April 2000. "My soul is in Rwanda. It has never ever come back and I'm not sure it ever will," he said in a recent interview.

Postconventional rescue goes beyond cultural and ethnic status. Diminished cultural conformity and independence of thought beyond culture's grip seem to hold the key. Rescuers experience people emotionally, not culturally. Although rescuers come from all walks of life, each holds a similar world view that transcends religion, politics, and culture. That mindset is universal, marked by internal principles of democratic justice and an intolerance of injustice culminating in a social contract of protection of the rights of all individuals.

CULTURES OF RESCUE

Sir Martin Gilbert (2004) observed that whole nations at times prevented deportation of Jews or enabled them to escape, as was the case in Italy and Hungary prior to the German military operations of 1943 and 1944 respectively. It was true of Denmark (see interview with Knud Dyby, p. 212), Finland, and Bulgaria.

In March, 1943, 8,500 prominent Jews in Bulgaria were to be the first from that country to be deported to the death camp at Treblinka. Bulgaria was allied with Germany. Yet another European Jewish community – this one inheritors of the distinctive culture of the Jews of medieval Spain – seemed destined for quick annihilation. In that same month, the Bulgarian government had deported the 11,500 Jews of Bulgarian-occupied Thrace and Macedonia to the Nazis. And yet, after waiting several hours at deportation centers, these targeted Bulgarian Jews were simply told to go home. Ultimately, despite Nazi pressure, the entire 50,000-member Jewish community of Bulgaria was spared the Holocaust. Theirs was the only Jewish community to survive intact in Nazi Europe.[45]

During World War II, something unusual occurred as well with Holland's Antirevolutionary Church and Germany's Confessing Church, Italy's Assisi villages and France's Le Mazet, Fay-sur-Lignon, Tence, Chabannes, La Suchère, Montbuzat, and the Protestant enclave of Le Chambon-sur-Lignon. At Le Chambon the entire village became a haven for Jews fleeing from the Nazis and their French collaborators. The Chambonnais hid Jews in their homes, sometimes for as long as four years, provided them with forged ID and ration cards, and helped them over the border to safety in Switzerland. With their history of Huguenot persecution as a religious minority in Catholic France, empathy for Jews as the people of the Old Testament, and the powerful leadership and example of their pastor and his wife, André and Magda Trocmé, the people of Le Chambon helped save lives. Consistent with all other rescuers, the Chambonnais rejected any labeling of their behavior as heroic. They said: "Things had to be done and we happened to be there to do them. It was the most natural thing in the world to help these people." Quakers and other Protestant organizations provided assistance to Le Chambon to set up homes for children whose parents had been deported. A cousin, Daniel Trocmé, headed of one of these homes and in June 1943 he and the children were arrested and interned in Majdanek concentration camp where they perished. To this day, the Trocmés are recognized by Yad Vashem as Righteous among the Nations with trees planted to honor André, Magda, and Daniel's courage in leading a culture of help and rescue.[46]

WHERE ARE THEY IN PEACETIME?

The meaning of life? That's easy, to help others.

Dalai Lama

While the Carnegie Hero Commission names heroes, Yad Vashem honors Righteous Christians. The foundations Pay It Forward and Random Acts of Kindness maintain accounts of deeds most of us will never hear, of altruistic helpers and rescuers who have not asked to be identified. Nor have they built a high-profile life of status. Most die penniless and without fanfare. But you can see and hear them if you look and listen closely. As I worked in a nearby hospital, I noticed a small plaque outside the house-turned-town-library in Monroe, Michigan. It reads with the following inscription:

> Eduard Dorsch (1827–1887), physician, poet exiled from Germany after a failed revolution in 1848 ... his love for freedom led him to make this home a station on the Underground Railway, willing it for use as a Public Library.

I recalled another rescuer named Albert Schweitzer.

> Albert Schweitzer was the eldest son of a Lutheran Pastor. His personal philosophy was based on a "reverence for life" and on a deep commitment to serve humanity through thought and action. By the age of 21, Schweitzer had decided on the course for his life. He studied philosophy and theology at the University of

Strasbourg, where he received a doctor's degree in philosophy in 1899. At that time he also served as a lecturer in philosophy and a preacher at St. Nicholas' Church in Strasbourg. Two years later he obtained a doctorate in theology. He believed that atonement for the wrongs that Christians had done to underdeveloped peoples was in itself a justification for missions. In October 1905 Schweitzer made his intention to study medicine known to family and friends. At 38, Schweitzer received his degree with a specialization in tropical medicine and surgery. In March 1913, Dr. and Mrs. Schweitzer left for Africa and built a hospital at Lambarene in the French Congo, now Gabon. The hospital started out in a chicken coop, and gradually expanded to treat thousands of patients. In the beginning, Schweitzer equipped and maintained the hospital with his own income and energy. Later, gifts from individuals and foundations from all over the world enabled him to expand and continue doing great work in Africa. Not even serious setbacks during and immediately after World War I deterred him from his mission. In 1918 Schweitzer returned to Alsace with his wife, where their daughter Rhena was born on January 14, 1919. They enjoyed several years together before Schweitzer returned to Africa alone in 1927. Helene, to her sorrow, was not well enough to accompany her husband, but maintained frequent correspondence. Rhena saw very little of her father during her childhood, but when her own children were grown, she acquired technical lab skills and left for Africa to serve with her father. Schweitzer had requested that, upon his death, Rhena assume the role of Administrator of the hospital, and when he passed away at the age of 90, she filled that role for many years. In 1953, at the age of 78, Schweitzer was honored for his humanitarian work with the Nobel Peace Prize. He used the $33,000 Nobel Prize to expand the hospital and to build a leper colony. In 1955 Queen Elizabeth II awarded Schweitzer the "Order of Merit," Britain's highest civilian honor. Although retired as a surgeon, Schweitzer continued to oversee the hospital until his death.

I later came across Albert Einstein's biography that held similar themes.

> As a protest, Einstein rejected German citizenship in favor of US nationality and continued his work at Princeton University. Humanitarian, vegetarian, and a steadfast Zionist (one who advocates a Jewish homeland) he was offered the Prime Ministership of Israel but turned it down, citing his own work as a physicist instead of politician. He maintained his focus on humanitarian and scientific causes – ten years on special relativity, eight years on general relativity, and more than three decades on the unified field theory that he hoped would be able to knit together all of physics. Merely concerned with finding universal truths in the "cosmic religious sense," he once insisted to his friend Carl Seelig – "I have no special talents. I am only passionately curious."

Although their numbers are small, I came to understand that rescuers are in every culture in every country. Here is an obituary I recently read.

> Edmond Kaiser authored several books on poetry and music, but was better known as a humanitarian. He recently died and was buried in India. In working with the French Resistance during World War II, he was awarded the Chevalier of the Legion of Honor in 1990 but turned it down citing the following. "Sitting in the middle of dead or suffering Biafran children or with the children of Vietnam whose skin has been peeled away by napalm, it would be as if I found it normal to be honored for their martyrdom."[47]

In Auckland, New Zealand, I discovered another rescuer's legacy.

> Elsie Locke was a veteran peace campaigner and battler for human rights. She edited an early feminist journal, helped found the Family Planning Association, and was a member of the Communist party. She helped found the Campaign for Nuclear Disarmament and published children's books. After being appalled

by the lack of Maori material, she fought to include a Maori perspective.[48]

Another morning, in a Toronto newspaper, I read of another unknown from the Chinese community.

His greatest tribute came when the Chinese Canadian National Congress acknowledged his part in changing racist immigration laws. At a special ceremony in Toronto, Mr. Yip was awarded a certificate to commemorate the 50th anniversary of the repeal of the Chinese Exclusion Act and for helping to create Canada's cultural landscape, as it is known today. Mr. Yip's vision of Canada as a land of equality and opportunity is perhaps best reflected in his response to a friend who asked why he was studying law when Chinese were not allowed to practice law in Canada. "Yes that is true, but I am not Chinese, I am Canadian."[49]

Joe Slovo (1926–1995) is another rescuer. Born to Lithuanian Jewish parents who emigrated to South Africa to escape escalating discrimination, he became an attorney-cum-renegade who, with Nelson Mandela and others, led the African National Congress to end apartheid. Exiled at times in England, Angola, Mozambique, and Zambia he returned to South Africa in 1990 where he served as housing minister in the first government of Nelson Mandela. In 2004 he was voted 47th in the Top 100 Great South Africans and was depicted in Phillip Noyce's film *Catch a Fire* (2006).

Sometimes rescuers need rescuing themselves. In various forms of arrest for nearly two decades, Nobel Laureate Aung San Suu Kyi sits and waits. The Oxford University educated leader of the National League for Democracy (NLD) is currently under house arrest, and though the NLD won national elections in 1990, the Burmese military regime prevented it from taking leadership of the country.

Rescuers do not have to be known heroes and most lives of compassion go unnoticed. There are several older adults in the family I come from, but only one (Herb Willis), at age 85, still picks up baked goods each Saturday from donating bakeries and distributes them to downtown LA missions. Herb is an eternally childlike, playful, and gentle man, as is Morris Paulson.

Paulson is a rescuer. The 81-year-old retired child psychologist spends his retirement days rescuing. I asked him why he rescues instead of spending time on leisurely retirement activities. He replied – with the characteristic response of many rescuers – that he never considered an alternative to helping.

> I've been a bereavement counselor for the Red Cross for almost a
> decade. First in Iowa, then Georgia, Oregon, New York City,
> Washington, Pennsylvania for the floods, and in South Carolina for
> the hurricane and Los Angeles for the earthquake and fires. Then
> there was New York. You remember all of them. One little girl
> that we couldn't save ... [His eyes well up and he changes the
> subject]. There was the tornado in Piedmont Alabama a few years
> ago that hit this little country church on Palm Sunday with 22
> dead and 88 injured. Then came Oklahoma City. Then the TWA
> flight #800 crash. The first week I was in the reception center
> where all the families had gathered to hear word of the rescue
> attempts and if their loved ones had been found. We were to be
> available on a 24-hour basis for the families. After a week of that I
> was transferred down to the Coast Guard Station where the bodies
> were being retrieved by the New York State Police scuba divers
> and Coast Guard. You can't imagine the horror stories these
> fellows had as they came off the dive. It got worse as time went on
> as the bodies began to fall apart. This 85-year-old lady whose
> daughter and granddaughter had died. The granddaughter was
> going over to France to present a DNA paper. In a few months she
> was going to graduate from Michigan State with doctorates in
> microbiology and veterinary medicine.

John Rabe was a Siemens executive working in Nanjing, China when the war broke out. The German national may have helped as many as a quarter of a million Chinese by organizing a safety zone, which the Japanese avoided while the Rape of Nanking was conducted.

As many as a quarter million Jews were rescued during World War II. The rescuer names and nations begin with Holland's Corrie ten Boom, Diet Eman, Jan Zwartendijk; Poland's Jan Karski; Sweden's Raoul Wallenberg and Per Anger; Switzerland's Carl Lutz; England's Nicholas Winton; Italy's Giorgio Perlasca; Portugal's Aristides de Sousa Mendes; Japan's Chiune Sugihara; France's André and Magda Trocmé; Belgium's Henri Reynders aka Father Bruno; but do not end there. British spy Frank Foley may have saved more than 10,000 Jews. Wilhelm Bachner posed as an Aryan and headed a construction crew hiring Jews with false identity papers to take them to safety. Father Pierre-Marie Benoit issued 4,000 false papers. The undermining efforts by Pastor Martin Bonhoeffer and student Sophie Scholl – the list is long.

One 32-year-old journalist named Varian Fry left a safe New York and spent the next thirteen months rescuing 2,000 endangered Jewish artists and intellectuals from Nazism. The eminent included Chagall, Ernst, Arendt, Bretano, and Koestler, who directly owe their lives to Fry's efforts. The thrill of rescue was part of his motivation, but so was his sense of humanity. When asked why he rescued, he replied, "It was my duty to help."[50]

Former Danish police officer Knud Dyby began his rescuing by joining an underground resistance group during World War II. On August 29, 1943, Knud and his cohorts learned of German plans for an imminent raid to round up all Danish Jews for transport to concentration camps. Mr. Dyby took a leading role in mobilizing the commercial fishermen in Copenhagen's North Harbor to transport Danish Jews in small groups to safety in nearby Sweden. First the Jews had to be found and informed of the rescue effort. Knud discovered that going through doctors' offices was one of the most efficient means – everyone had a doctor, and the doctors proved to be entirely cooperative. Getting the Jews to the harbor at the appropriate moment entailed organizing the city's taxi drivers. When that was insufficient, policeman Knud arranged for the use of state police cars. The success of the operation depended on the fishermen being able to avoid German naval patrols as well as the Danish Coast Police (Coast Guard) on the Danish side, and Swedish informers on the Swedish side. The danger of being caught and prosecuted was known to all those involved in the risky operation. Using their small fishing vessels, the fishermen brought nearly every Danish Jew to safety in Sweden within one week, saving about seven thousand people.

At 87 years old, Knud Dyby doesn't hear as well as he did, but still possesses a twinkle in his eye. He now gives lectures to groups on hate and joins panel discussions on the subject throughout California.

> You ask why did I rescue? Well I think the better question is why didn't others rescue more? I tell you, first of all I was 25 years old and not married, so it is more difficult when you are older. Well then, I do not know – perhaps because I was always independent and respected others and never religious, I think that helped. Religion tells people things that are wrong. [Like antisemitism?] Yes. For example, look at Poland, they are very religious and killed most the Jews but they were more [conforming?] Yes. We never considered Danish Jews anything other than Danes with a different religion so it was helping your fellow Dane. It was very unorganized though maybe I was a little more organized because of police training. Hitler found only 256 Jews when he finally got to us.

From previous travels to Germany, 29-year-old London-based stockbroker Nicholas Winton knew about the plight of German Jews. Switching plans from a ski trip to prewar Prague, he saw a Jewish refugee camp and decided to save as many children as he could. He returned to London to plead with governments and all but Sweden and Britain rejected his proposals. With the help of friend Trevor Chadwick, his mother, and a few volunteers, he gathered data on 5,000 children on lists. British newspapers published advertisements for foster parents while he and Chadwick organized rail and ship transportation to England (the Home Office also required US $3.500 per child to cover future repatriation costs). The first children left Prague on March 14, 1939, and this continued to the day war broke out on September 3, 1939, when the Nazis ended all transport of children. In total, some 669 children had been rescued. At 97 years old, "Nicky" is still vibrant. The families of the 669 children saved now number close to 5,000 and include doctors, writers, engineers, and Members of Parliament. He was conferred a knighthood and was granted the Honorary Freedom of the Royal Borough of Windsor and Maidenhead for a lifetime dedicated to humanitarian causes.

From the time of the Dred Scott decision it was another century before civil rights were secured. Segregation laws required that African-Americans not only vacate their seats, but vacate entire rows of seats. When a White man entered the bus on December 1, 1955 in Montgomery, Alabama, the driver called for the first row to vacate. Three people moved and a second call was issued for this last woman to heed. Rosa Parks (1913–2005) refused and was arrested. Her arrest triggered protest after protest and Ms. Parks emerged as a symbol of courage and a role model to all who value human rights and freedom.

> People think it was the arrest – but I didn't have no need to get arrested. People don't really know that I had been working in civil rights years before and no one made no fuss before that.

In the summer of 1961, seven Blacks and six Whites boarded buses in Washington DC bound for New Orleans to protest against segregated train and bus stations in the rural American south. Attacked by mobs, firebombed, jailed, and taunted as communists, the Freedom Riders persisted (a Gallup Poll at the time declared that most (63 percent) Americans disapproved). San Francisco lawyer and Freedom Rider John Dolan recently recounted the times:

> We were taught that Americans were better than the Germans or the Japanese who held one race to be superior over another ... I

wanted to do it [tell the story] before the people who were a part of it are either no longer alive or are alive in such small numbers that we won't know for sure what happened back then.

Writer Czeslaw Milosz reminds us that moral acts proceed not from the functioning of the reasoning mind, but from a revolt of the stomach. Wrestler Sputnik Monroe (Rock Brumbaugh) had plenty of stomach trouble before the civil rights movement and almost single-handedly desegregated sporting events in Memphis. Monroe wanted more of his fans to get into the auditorium, so he bribed a door attendant to miscount the number of African-Americans admitted. Soon, there was no place else to sit but in the White section. Whether fans were Black or White, promoters could see nothing but green, and seating at Ellis Auditorium was now integrated. Monroe tag-teamed with African-American Norvell Austin. It was the first time many fans had seen a Black wrestler. Monroe retired from wrestling at age seventy when his knee gave out. He lived a quiet retirement with his wife and two cats in Houston until he passed away in November 2002 at age 77.

Danny Welch, age 40, knows about revolts of the stomach. He monitors Klanwatch for the national hate-watchdog Southern Poverty Law Center in Montgomery, Alabama.

I was with the Montgomery Police Department for ten years and that was fulfilling. One of the experiences that stands out is when a close friend of mine and fellow police officer was killed in the line of duty. It made me realize how suddenly the light of life can dim and go out. And it made me appreciate God for my own life. Now I'm Director of Klanwatch and when I first came on board I remember the day we were in open court and a member of the Klan had been convicted of hanging a 19-year-old Black man. He then turns to the mother of the victim and asked this elderly woman for forgiveness. And she turned to him and said, "I do forgive you. From the day I found out who y'all was, I asked God to take care of you and he has." I don't need to explain why this mattered. Then last year my mother was diagnosed with terminal cancer and that has been extremely difficult. She has so much faith and such a positive attitude that it affects all of those around her and I think I have a better attitude myself because of it.

The official count of those who rescued Jews during World War II by the Israeli based Yad Vashem is closing in at 25,000. As Yad Vashem is concerned only with authenticating actual lives saved, the actual helping and aiding figure is undoubtedly much higher. The agency does not recognize the work of Rev. Dietrich Bonhoeffer as, though heroic, no direct rescue was made. The agency does not recognize intention. The agency is not concerned with those who briefly assisted. Yad Vashem is concerned with documenting rescue efforts and separating out those whose efforts were exemplary from bogus accounts.

It would seem to be the case that many examples of helping went unrecorded. Perhaps it is wishful thinking but, by these estimates, it would appear that the upper 20 to 30 percent of a general population functions at a higher level with greater emotional wherewithal. If the only thing necessary for the triumph of evil is for good men to do nothing, then these rescuers are beyond good in that they help when and where they can. Their lives reflect: "l'ame ne connait pas la haine" *(The soul has no hate).*

NOTES ON CHAPTER 5

1. K. Brehony (1999) *Ordinary grace.* New York: Riverhead. Binti Jua was one of twenty-five most intriguing "people" of 1996 in *People* magazine. See article in *People* Sept. 2, 1996. For an alternative perspective that focuses more on circumstance, empathy and social network see Jessica Casiro's (2006) Argentine rescuers: a study on the "banality of good." *Journal of Genocide Research,* 8, 437–454. It is not the purpose of this book to enter the altruism vs. egoism debate. But the reader is referred to C. Daniel Batson (1991) *The altruism question.* Hillsdale, NJ: Erlbaum and his empathy–altruism work, demonstrating that empathy promotes an altruistic motivation. For evolutionary factors, the reader is referred to

Richard Dawkins (1976) *The selfish gene.* New York: Oxford University Press; and for reciprocity and altruism to examine Robert Trivers (2002) *Natural selection and social theory.* New York: Oxford University Press. For arguments that say we help those who are similar to us and similar to our group, e.g. kin and kith, see Elliott Sober & David S. Wilson (1999) *Unto others.* Cambridge, MA: Harvard University Press.

2. M. Radke-Yarrow (1981) *New York Times* 5/23/07 P. A21; www.usinfo.state.gov

3. R. Satloff (2006) *Among the righteous.* New York: PublicAffairs, p. 160.

4. Sam Oliner, personal communication, 4/15/02. Rescuer estimates of 10–20 percent are based on Erich Fromm (1974/1986) *For the love of life.* New York: Free Press. Gordon Allport (1954) in *The nature of prejudice.* Garden City, NY: Anchor Doubleday, estimated 20 percent of the population to be nonprejudiced. Historian Christopher Browning, as well, suggests the proportion of Nazis who avoided murdering at 10–20 percent. Most were not fanatical antisemites and only 5–10 percent among SS guards were estimated to be sadists. Of German police units, Browning found less than one third to be enthusiastic killers, another 20–30 percent consistently refusing or evading orders to kill and the rest falling into the middle: C. F. Browning (2000) *Nazi policy, Jewish workers, German killers.* New York: Cambridge University Press, p. 17. Also see an antisemitism–philosemitism study of A. Kovacs (1999) *Antisemitic prejudices in contemporary Hungary.* Jerusalem: SICSA ACTA #16. Estimates of rescuers are between 50,000 and 500,000; see S. P. Oliner & P. M. Oliner (1988) *The altruistic personality.* New York: Free Press.

5. Pierre Sauvage, *Weapons of the Spirit,* 1987 post-film interview with Bill Moyers.

6. M. J. Solomon (1991) The transmission of cultural goals: Social network influences on infant socialization. Unpublished doctoral dissertation. Harvard University, DAI 52, O8B 4495.

7. S. P. Oliner & M. Oliner (1988) *The altruistic personality.* New York: Free Press.

8. E. Fogelman (1995) *Conscience and courage.* New York: Anchor. Also see E. Fogelman (1993) Rescuers of Jews during the Holocaust. *Tikkun, 9,* 61–90. S. P. Oliner & M. Oliner (1988) *The altruistic personality.* New York: Free Press. It should be noted that the Oliners and Staub believe that "a prosocial value orientation" is more important than other traits. But a

basic ethical orientation is unlikely to mean anything unless the rescuer has the emotional wherewithal to help. (It is likely that many bystanders and even perpetrators had been exposed at some point to a basic ethical orientation.) Consequently, traits which explain emotional development provide fuller answers. Also see P. Oliner, J. Wielgus & M. Gruber (1998) Religious culture and outgroup altruism. Presentation at the 106th Annual Convention of the American Psychological Association, San Francisco. Also G. Block & M. Drucker (1992) *Rescuers*. New York: Holmes & Meier.

9. 39 vs. 13 percent: see E. R. Midlarsky & M. I. Midlarsky (2004) Echoes of genocide: Trauma and ethnic identity among European immigrants. *Humbolt Journal of Social Relations*, 28, 38–53.

10. K. R. Monroe (2004) *The hand of compassion*. Princeton: Princeton University Press, p. 204.

11. P. M. Oliner (2004) *Saving the forsaken*. New Haven: Yale University Press, p. 57.

12. S. P. Oliner (2003) *Do unto others*. Boulder: Westview Press.

13. D. K. Huneke (1985) *The Moses of Rovno*. New York: Dodd Mead.

14. M. Klempner (2006) *The heart has reasons*. Cleveland: Pilgrim Press, p. 38.

15. www.miepgies.dk/

16. E. R. Midlarsky and M. I. Midlarsky (2004) Echoes of genocide: Trauma and ethnic identity among European immigrants. *Humbolt Journal of Social Relations*, 28, 38–53.

17. www.maslow.com/

18. Robyn Dawes (2001) *Everyday irrationality*. Boulder: Westview, p. 153.

19. I. W. Charny (2006) *Fascism and democracy in the human mind*. Lincoln, NE: University of Nebraska Press, p. 3.

20. E. L. Deci (1995) *Why we do what we do*. New York: G. P. Putnam's Sons, p. 2.

21. N. Tec (2001) Toward a theory of rescue. In D. Scrase, W. Mieder & K. Q. Johnson (eds.) *Making a difference*. Burlington, VT: Center for Holocaust Studies at the University of Vermont.

22. London 1970 cited in N. Tec (1986) *When light pierced darkness*. New York: Oxford University Press. At one point, he suggested that "the desire to participate in what were inherently exciting activities" separated out rescuers from bystanders.

23. E. Staub (1995) How people learn to care. In P. Schervish, V. A. Hodgkinson, M. Gates & Associates (eds.) *Care and community in modern society*. San Francisco: Independent Sector/Jossey-Bass.

24. T. Kasser (2002) *The high price of materialism*. Cambridge, MA: MIT Press.

25. D. K. Huneke (1985) *The Moses of Rovno*. New York: Dodd Mead.

26. A. Foxman (2004) *Never again*. San Francisco: Harper

27. N. Tec (1986) *When light pierced darkness*. New York: Oxford University Press.

28. H. W. Bierhoff & E. Rohmann (2004). Altruistic personality in the context of the empathy–altruism hypothesis. *European Journal of Personality*, 18, 351–365.

29. S. P. Oliner & M. Oliner (1988) *The altruistic personality*. New York: Free Press.

30. Supported earlier work by Midlarsky & Oliner which found the best predictor is altruistic motivation: see E. Midlarsky & S. P. Oliner (1985) The aged Samaritan: Heroes of the Holocaust forty years later. Paper presented at the 93rd Annual Convention of the American Psychological Association, Los Angeles.

31. B. Duriez (2004) Are religious people nicer people? Taking a closer look at the religion–empathy relationship. *Mental Health, Religion and Culture*, 7, 249–254.

32. N. Tec (2001) Toward a theory of rescue. In D. Scrase, W, Mieder & K. Q. Johnson (eds.) *Making a difference*. Burlington, VT: Center for Holocaust Studies at the University of Vermont.

33. Johtje Vos, cited in E. Fogelman (1995) *Courage and conscience*. New York: Anchor.

34. Tanay, personal communication. Also see K. R. Monroe (2004) *The hand of compassion*. Princeton: Princeton University Press, p. 204. Also see D. P. Gushee (2003) *The righteous gentiles of the holocaust*. St. Paul, MN: Paragon House.

35. N. Tec (2001) Toward a theory of rescue. In D. Scrase, W. Mieder & K. Q. Johnson (eds.) *Making a difference*. Burlington, VT: Center for Holocaust Studies at the University of Vermont.

36. M. Gilbert (2004) *The righteous*. New York: Owl.

37. Greene US News & World Report, February 28, 2005, p. 60. Also see the work of J. Haidt (2006) *The happiness hypothesis*. New York: Basic, and his website www.yourmorals.org

38. S. P. Oliner & M. Oliner (1988) *The altruistic personality.* New York: Free Press.
39. M. Paldiel (2000) *Saving the Jews.* New York: Schreiber.
40. T. Keneally (1993) *Schindler's List.* New York: Touchstone; for Meili see www.cnn.com/US/9705/07/swiss.guard/index.html
41. I. Ilibagiza (2006) *Left to tell.* Carlsbad, CA: Hay House.
42. See Gisimba interview in African Rights (2003) *Tribute to Courage.* London: African Rights.
43. P. Rusesabagina (2006) *An ordinary man.* New York: Viking, p. 190.
44. R. Dallaire (2005) *Shake hands with the devil.* Toronto: Carol and Graf.
45. T. Todorov (2001) *Fragility of goodness.* Princeton: Princeton University Press.
46. M. Gilbert (2004) *The righteous.* New York: Owl.
47. Kaiser obituary 3/5/00, *Toronto Globe and Mail.* See also www. unfoundation.org 3/6/00
48. Elsie Locke, *Otago Daily Times* 4/5/01, p. 1. Also see *New Zealand Herald,* 3/9/01, p. A5.
49. See Yip interview in Toronto *Globe and Mail,* July 27, 2001.
50. For Foley see M. Smith (1999) *Foley.* London: Hodder & Stoughton. For Bachner see S. Oliner & K. Lee (1996) *Who shall live.* Chicago: Academy Publishers; Samuel P. Oliner, Lawrence Baron, Pearl M. Oliner, Lawrence A. Blum, Dennis L. Krebs, M. Zuzanna Smolenska (eds.) (1992) *Embracing the other.* New York: New York University Press. For Varian Fry see S. Isenberg (2001) *A hero of our own.* New York: Random House. For John Rabe see J. Rabe (1998) *The good man of Nanking.* Knoxville: University of Tennessee. For Righteous awards see M. Paldiel (2000) *Saving the Jews.* Rockville, MD: Schreiber. There is also another group of rescuers. During the Holocaust, there were an estimated 30,000 Jews who escaped from the camps and joined hundreds of thousands of non-Jewish partisans. Sometimes resistance took the form of smuggling children out of ghettos, and creating false documents.

6 Towards an emotionally developed world

The individual personality ... is only valid from the moment when it emerges ... It is deeply vulnerable and profoundly dependent on a climate of life and freedom to grow: within family, within community, within nations and within human society as a whole.

Gitta Sereny from Into that Darkness

North Buxton, Ontario, is a quiet, little enclave located fifty miles north of the Michigan border in the center of the Canadian heartland. The expansive farm fields are punctuated by the occasional sound of a pickup or the sight of a drive shed. There are a few farmhouses, a small church and cemetery; a one-room schoolhouse and a log cabin exhibit.

The exhibit is the Buxton National Historic Site and Museum, a stone's throw from the original Uncle Tom's Cabin. The exhibit is a testament to a time that most would like to forget. On display are human chains, bear-trap devices for humans and vestiges of nineteenth-century North American slavery. North Buxton was the northern terminus of the Underground Railroad, the network that aided runaway slaves to freedom. Between 1820 and 1860, some 20,000 African-Americans are said to have escaped to settle here.

Slavery had been abolished in Canada by 1810, but the decendants of the Underground Railroad know that racism still remains. Gwen Robinson is the 81-year-old custodian and resident expert in nearby Chatham, Ontario.

People think there was no slavery for us in Canada, but there was slavery here under the British – they just got rid of it sooner. And my children have had incidents with the townsfolk. I remember when the universities here had admission quotas for minority students. There was racism here but it was typically Canadian – quieter and more polite.

Bryan Prince is her nephew, a boyish 55-year-old farmer and writer who, with his wife Shannon, maintains the exhibit. He touches what looks like a bear trap: "Some of what is in here doesn't seem real, these things were used on people." He poses the question "Where does all the hate come from?" His Aunt Gwen has a ready answer. "People who are thoughtful don't hate," says Gwen, "but," she adds, "most folk aren't thoughtful."

The thoughtlessness that Gwen Robinson is addressing comes from a lack of maturation and a preponderance of social identification.

Social identity is a curious thing. When we were young, it was so essential to developing a sense of ourselves, of who we came from and where we were to go. Moreover, for much of human history, the social group defined "us" – sometimes by region, e.g. Jesus of Nazareth, or by profession, e.g. Willie the Shoemaker, or by heritage, be it race, religion, or ethnic status. Our tribe and group provided us with an identity as in "son of David" or David Jr. or David II, and the group often helped us negotiate life's inevitable passages. Rituals and rites of the community were there for us as we married, bore children, became ill, and died. We repaid the group by staying faithful and never straying too far away. If we left the group it was at the cost of sin and a bit of social death. At one point it was not uncommon for parents to mourn or disown their own when a child dishonored the family or group by converting out or leaving. With more severe violations of norms, group justice was meted out and life went on, as portrayed by the villagers who killed in the Dutch film *Antonia*.

But with social group identity comes social group prejudices. "That's why he [Hitler] fried six million of those guys, you know.

Jews would have owned the goddamned world. And look what they're doing. They're killing people in Arab countries," declared David Ahenakew, leader of the Federation of Saskatchewan Indian Nations.[1]

As long as people feed into their social group identity, as long as they believe they represent their group in the world, as long as they remain unable to distinguish between personal and social identities, then ethnocentrism and xenophobia continues. "Little did I know," says former Nazi Bruno Manz, "that collective pride [was] a narcotic for the mentally homeless."[2]

It is collective group pride caught in a tug-of-war between selves. "Being only your [personal] self is what ethnic nationalism will not allow," observes political scientist Michael Ignatieff analyzing the Serbian conflict. He continues, "when people think of themselves as patriots first, individuals second, they have embarked on a path of ethical abdication."[3]

But it is not a moral issue as much as a psychological one. "To be secure in the knowledge that your common humanity is more important than your most significant differences," responded Bill Clinton when asked how to resolve social group differences.

It is the right answer, but the bigger problem is how to implement it and create a culture where the much-needed shift from social to personal identity begins. The following represents some ideas along the lines of (1) education, (2) community involvement, (3) correcting social wrongs.

EDUCATION

"You want to undo hate? – educate," quips Danish rescuer Knud Dyby. He continues, "more important than the three Rs of schooling, I think are the three Cs – compassion, conscience, consideration." Dyby and indeed all rescuers possess the traits for which we are searching. While the traits appear somewhat natural for rescuers, education may be the only means by which non-rescuers can develop. To that end, the following ideas are proposed.

Teach defiance

"Far more, and far more hideous, crimes have been committed in the name of obedience than ever have been committed in the name of rebellion," noted writer C. P. Snow. The potential is made clear in the Milgram study. Recall that in the original study, Milgram's results suggested that there was 65 percent compliance. But there was another side to the experiment that is rarely addressed. An alternative experiment was performed by Alan C. Elms (Professor Emeritus at the University of California, Davis) in conjunction with Stanley Milgram as they were compiling data from the original study. Elms and Milgram called this experiment the resistance version to their classic shock experiment. The resistance version included a resistance team and consisted of the real subject and two confederates. Partway into the procedure the confederates defied the experimenter and refused to continue – one at 150 volts the other at 210 volts. When this occurred, a full 90 percent of the naive subjects followed their example and dropped out at some point before the end of the shock series. In other words, only 10 percent of the subjects in this experiment were fully obedient. Clearly techniques which encourage and stimulate independent thinking and less compliance may prove worthwhile.

Teach maturation

In seeking a solution to the Palestinian and Israeli conflict, social psychologist Herbert Kelman has called for negotiating social identities.

> The essence of the framework ... is mutual acknowledgment of the identity of the other and willingness to accommodate it. This amounts to some revision in both sides' national narratives – at least to the extent of eliminating from their own identities the negation of the other and the claim of exclusivity.[4]

The acknowledgment of the other's humanity is certainly a place to start, but once in place the next step would be to move toward a similar vision based on emotional development and the shift to personal identity. Yet the intractable conflict may require techniques that promote emotional development. Perhaps we need to examine childhood conflict resolution.

Chicago teacher Vivian Paley thinks so. Like colleague Jane Elliott, Paley tried an experiment at her school. She instituted a rule in her classroom that all children must be included in schoolyard play. At first most children resisted and did not seem to respond. After some discussion, the children gradually began to adjust their behavior and play with each other. A quick aside: the children who were most vehemently opposed to the new rule to including every-one were later identified as the classroom bullies.

Paley is putting Loevinger's concept of emotional development into action. In addition, she is employing and fostering what I. W. Charny has called the democratic mind, a mindset that is expansive, open to new experience and creative. He writes:

> The democratic mind exercises its rights for expressing opinions, for dissenting with authority or with "the way things are done in our organization or government," and for demands for obedience and conformity. It also takes an active stand in situations in which a misguided politeness, courtesy, and traditions of "avoiding conflict" lead people to stand by and let bad things happen.[5]

Teach tolerance

When it comes to knowing about other social groups, there is much misinformation. Most of those from one social group do not know about the history of those from other social groups. Details and class discussion could address such events as the Stonewall Inn (1969) incident sparking the rise of the gay movement, and the African-American pogroms of Tulsa and Greenwood, Oklahoma (June, 1921) and Rosewood, Florida (January, 1923), where hundreds of innocent African-Americans were shot, looted, jailed, and burned by their white neighbors. Information could be dissemination regarding the April 5, 1977 San Francisco sit-in that resulted in the American Disability Act. This could also include explanations of the events of

Greensboro North Carolina, November 3, 1979. There, civil rights protesters tried to organize labor and were shot to death by the KKK and American Nazi Party while local police turned their heads. The five dead included a nurse, two medical doctors, a Cuban immigrant graduate from Duke, and a Harvard divinity school graduate.

The lack of knowledge of injustice has global consequences as well. What of South Africa's Sharpeville Massacre (1960), in which police killed sixty-nine apartheid protesters? What is known of the plight of Thai border refugees, Indonesian ethnic Chinese, the Congolese? What of Tibetan rights? What of the people of Darfur? What of a world held hostage by terrorism?

Teach empathy

Empathy and diversity training are also a good beginning. Poet Maya Angelou made a statement on a television show that incorporates the principle of empathy education.

> The real truth is that the majority of people look at other people, if they can get beyond their superficial fear they can look at other people and say, "That's a mother, I understand mothers. That's a father, I understand fathers. Although I am Jewish or that's a big brother and I understand big brothers even though this kid is a blond and this one is Black." The majority of people in our country I am convinced are really goodhearted. I believe that.[6]

Target perpetrators

While education has been attentive to children who have "special needs," impairments, and disability, it is not as effective at helping would-be bullies and perpetrators. At present, there are no hate rehab programs, but would-be perpetrators could be identified by teachers and sent to special programs not unlike the learning disabled and those with special needs that need more attention. The "an ounce of prevention is worth a pound of cure" approach is employed against later developing fascists and bullies. It is certainly not an unreachable group, by any means. For instance, when social psychologist Raphael Ezekiel interviewed Detroit area skinheads, he found

> The members are pretty ordinary people with more emptiness than most of us – more spiritual emptiness than most of us, and a lot of objective emptiness. They don't have money. They don't have family ... They are pretty hungry lost souls.[7]

Underneath the hate, beyond the machismo, behind the bravado, were throwaway people who did not truly want to have thrown away lives. They did not know where else to turn. Alternatives have to be demonstrated, as former skinheads who have turned around will attest.

COMMUNITY INVOLVEMENT

"Racism is something we created. There are things we can do to fight it," says community activist Diane Bock. Bock is a White suburban housewife who decided to do something about Los Angeles's racial tensions. Knowing that the best way to break down stereotypes is to promote personal contact among people of different groups, she proposed a family matchmaking program. When agencies like the United Way turned down her proposal, she created and bankrolled Community Cousins, a program that paired up ethnically different families. She distributed brochures at the library, the pediatrician's office, markets, and church bulletin boards. 40 "cousins" attended the first "party" and today more than 300 families have participated in the monthly connections. Says one 8-year-old cousin, "I've learned you can never tell what people can do just by looking at them."[8]

There is another success story as well. Tammie Schnitzer and the town of Billings, Montana became a model for many communities to eradicate hate. The Montana homemaker first became involved with hate in 1993. Growing up Lutheran, she had never experienced hatred, but marrying a Jewish man, and being one of 500 Jews living in the state, changed her life. Placing an ad to arrange Jewish social activities in the local paper netted her an initial phone call consisting of the command "Jew-Bitch, die." This was followed up with the back of her van being shot out, a cinder block being hurled through her son's window, and a campaign of hate mailings and supremacist graffiti. The harassment soon extended to Billings's American Indian residents as well. The local paper, the *Billings Gazette*, printed a full-page advertisement depicting a large shining menorah (Jewish candelabrum) and asked people to hang the picture in their windows. In a population of 80,000, about 10,000 pasted the page on their windows. The campaign of hate soon ended. Schnitzer now speaks out against hate, encouraging every city to form bias response teams. A few years later, when vandals smashed a front window of a Jewish home for displaying a menorah during Hanukkah, the Christian neighbors of Newton Township again placed menorahs in their windows as an act of solidarity. An 18-year-old was later charged with ethnic intimidation and two 17-year-olds were released to their parents.[9]

The bias response team developed from Tammy Schnitzer's efforts and other calls to action. It is an important tool in the war on hate. An arm of the Justice Department, the bias response team works in collaboration with local police to monitor hate and its crass expression. A number of bias response teams have been formed in various communities across the nation and in Canada, as well as in parts of Europe. They hold the following objectives:

1) We assume that when people are attracted to the Right there are rational reasons for that. So instead of lecturing how bad they are for buying into the Right's racism, sexism etc. we instead try to talk to their legitimate psychological, ethical, or spiritual concerns and show them that these can't really be fulfilled by the Right's approach.

2) We acknowledge that liberal politics has not understood the frustration people are having living in a society that systematically undermines loving relationships and that frustrates our need for meaning.

3) When people express anger and demean others, we acknowledge that the pain in their lives that leads them to anger must be real, but challenge the idea that the pain is caused by those others.

Correcting social wrongs

Martin Luther King once remarked that though legislation cannot change the heart, it could restrain the heartless. Legal action has been effective in stemming hate's tide. The need is always there. Currently, the battle includes a state's right to regulate or oppose discrimination laws at the cost of contravening federal protection. Currently, there are fifteen state legislature proposals imploring the federal government to exclude itself from immigration policies, social assistance programs, environmental regulation, and civil rights laws.

Morris Dees and the Southern Poverty Law Center,[10] know about the battle for civil rights. Realizing early on that hate groups needed money to operate, he has successfully brought civil suits against several racist organizations. Dees filed suit on behalf of the Vietnamese Fishermen Association when they competed with Texas fishermen and the Klan became involved. Several militia-training camps in Alabama were also shut down. A similar suit against the North Carolina White Patriot Party subsequently led to their disbanding in 1984.

Using legislative efforts to protect minorities has come of age. The James Byrd Jr. Hate Crimes Act, named for the African-American who was dragged to death by racists, passed Senate confirmation on May 5, 2001 and was signed into law by Texas governor Rick Perry. The Act extends rights to those of differing sexual orientation, gender, disability, age, and national origin. The District of Columbia and twenty-three other states have legislation preventing violence against homosexuals. As of June 27, 2003, state sodomy laws criminalizing gay consensual sex were overturned by the Supreme Court.

A major blow to religious hate occurred with the 1965 introduction of Vatican II Nostra Aetate, a declaration that deplored the hatred, persecution, and displays of antisemitism. Similar decrees and apologies followed, issued by French Catholics, American Lutherans, and the Vatican.

But there is more that is needed elsewhere. Australia has a National Sorry Day to apologize to that nation's Aboriginal people. Alabama, Virginia, Maryland, and North Carolina have apologized to those states' African-Americans for slavery. Yet, apologies by Turkey to Armenia, Japan to Korea, America to the American Indians, Germany to the Gypsies are still pending.

The psychological import of reconciliation and trials for the perpetrators of genocide is now understood. With origins in the Nuremberg trials, truth and reconciliation commissions have played a key legal and emotional role in the lives of victims. South African psychologist Brandon Hamber found that permitting the traumatized recipients of apartheid to bear witness and testify and feel heard was healing for the individual as well as the nation. Such symptoms of trauma as PTSD, self blame, anger, and bereavement, were debriefed. The force of reconciliation and accountability was so powerful that the TRC staff needed emotional debriefing from listening to the multiple tales of trauma.[11]

Finally, speech that inspires hateful acts must be restricted, though it is hard to prove, especially when it hides behind religion. One cannot yell fire in a crowded theater, but one can still call for jihad in Western nations without fear of imprisonment. The 5,000 + Arabic web pages calling for jihad operate with impunity – though recently some prosecutions have begun, e.g. Younis Tsouli. One cannot use profanity in a public place, but one can display swastikas without penalty. Sex is not tolerated on commercial television though satellite permits all sorts of exceptions including the addition of multiple Arab network hate stations – several of which were deemed so inciting of hate that transmission signals were blocked by the American and French authorities, e.g. al-Manar.

Trinity Western University (TWU) is a private Christian University, located in suburban Vancouver, British Columbia, Canada, whose core belief is that the Bible is the direct, supreme Word of God and the ultimate Truth. This philosophy is evident in the school's educational goal of creating proselytizing disciples of God by integrating Christian beliefs, doctrines, and values with education, campus life, and student behavior both on and off campus. The latter has arguably made TWU one of the more controversial post-secondary institutions in Canada because students are required to sign a pledge promising to abstain from specific activities deemed by the school to be immoral including premarital sex and homosexuality. This requirement was the focal point of a 1995 court battle between TWU and the British Columbia College of Teachers. The latter denied certification to Trinity Western, stating that the TWU pledge is discriminatory and only teaches future educators that discrimination in certain cases is acceptable. Ultimately, the Supreme Court of Canada ruled in favour of TWU. "The concern that graduates of TWU will act in a detrimental fashion in the classroom is not supported by any evidence," the judge ruled.

But out of the classroom, there is reason to suspect that hate hides behind religion and politics. Rwandan courts understand this first hand. It was in Rwanda where a popular radio station broadcast so many infectious racist ideas that a tribunal held the station's manager and staff responsible for inciting the 1994 genocide which killed 750,000.

The Rwandan courts understand that words can kill. And now we know that cartoons can kill. Recall the global Muslim protests between September 30, 2005 and March 30, 2006. Flemming Rose, the cultural editor at the Danish newspaper, *Jyllands-Posten*, asked twelve illustrators to draw the Prophet for them. While depictions of the Prophet are permitted throughout Iran and Shia-based cultures, all depictions of the Prophet are forbidden under Sunni Islam. Any verbal or written statement that mocks the Prophet is considered blasphemy, punishable in some Islamic sects by death.

The immediate payback for humiliating Islam was 5,000 Muslim immigrants taking to the streets in protest. Within hours, the ambassadors of eleven Muslim countries, including Indonesia, a number of Arab states, Pakistan, Iran, and Bosnia-Herzegovina, complained about the cartoons in a letter to Prime Minister Anders Fogh Rasmussen. Labor strikes began in Pakistan and by January 2006 a boycott of Danish products began. In Damascus, the Norwegian embassy and buildings that housed the Danish, Swedish and Chilean embassies were torched, as was the Danish General Consulate in Beirut. *Jyllands-Posten* was posted on the Al Qaeda website as a possible terrorist target and a second group circulated pictures on the internet which show bombs exploding over pictures of the newspaper and blood flowing over the national flag of Denmark. Protests globally escalated for six months culminating in 139 deaths.

The Muslim world's protest ended as quickly as it began. Perhaps it was the appeasement of the United Nations Human Rights Council resolution to "prohibit the defamation of [Islamic] religion," on March 30, 2006. Perhaps it was a fear of retribution. The reasons for the quick cessation are unknown as are the mechanisms which could organize 1.2 billion Muslims – though transmission over the Internet and satellite television are a likely bet. The non-Muslim world had never seen anything like it and was left collectively scratching its head. Complaints and letters to the editor are understood. Even the threat of a lawsuit. But anger and destruction and death?

This is hate, and the infectious distortions that accompany it should not be protected when it hides behind religion. Recall that Hitler was never excommunicated and to date no fatwas have been issued against Osama bin Laden. In the new world of radical Islam, well-intended ideas such as multiculturalism and freedom of speech have to be vetted and eventually restricted or abuses of free speech will occur.[12]

Hate does nothing good for anyone. Who in the UK is missing Omar Bakri? What did Stalin, Pol Pot, or Milosevic accomplish? How far did the Chinese leap forward? What survives of the Nazi legacy except for 50 million dead and hollow promises of never again? We need a new way of understanding how to develop people's minds.

Personal identity development
"Indeed," continues Fromm, "we should be fully born when we die. Although it is the tragic fate of most individuals to die before they are

born." Social identity undermines the process of developing our-selves emotionally. Hate too often fills in the gaps.

As if to underscore Fromm's perspective, an uncanny juxtapos-ition of CNN news stories were reported a few months before 9/11. The broadcast began by marking the anniversaries of the Oklahoma City bombing and the Columbine High School shooting. The camera then closed in on White South African racist leader Eugene TerreBlanche, whose sentence was upheld for his attack on a Black farm worker with a lead pipe. Next the camera pans towards a former Klansman who denied any wrongdoing for his part in Birmingham's Sixteenth Street Baptist Church fire, though there was tape-recorded evidence of his bragging about it. The story line next shifts to a Reverend Randell Mickler who was attempting to block a pending high school address by Rabbi Steve Lebow. "To have a person who is a nonbeliever of Christ is, in a sense, dishonoring Christ and opens the way for Muslims, Hindu, Buddhist, and Wiccan involvement," explained Rev. Mickler.[13]

The news that same day announced that Prodigy Internet founder Greg Carr bought the twenty-acre former neo-Nazi Aryan Nations compound in Hayden Lake, Idaho. After the Southern Poverty Law Center won its suit to bankrupt them, Carr was going to refurbish the compound as an education center for human rights issues.

Michael Weisser has put emotional development into practice. When the synagogue singer moved into Lincoln Nebraska, the wel-come wagon included hate. "You will be sorry you ever moved into 5810 Randolph St. Jew boy," the caller first told Michael Weisser. Two days later a packet was placed on the family front porch marked: "The KKK is watching you scum." Inside were caricatures of hook-nosed Jews, gorilla-headed Blacks and dead minorities. "The Holohoax was nothing compared to what's going to happen to you," read another note. The cantor knew " 'It's a sickness' ... They don't know better or they wouldn't do it." Subsequently the perpetrator, Larry Trapp, not only stopped the hate, he converted to Judaism in the very synagogue he once planned to blow up. What happened? Why the change of heart?

Weisser discovered that Trapp was wheelchair-bound and phoned him back. "Do you know that the very first laws Hitler's Nazis passed were against people like yourself who had physical deformities or physical handicaps?" he said and he hung up. Not long after, Weisser phoned again, this time asking Trapp if he needed anything from the grocery store. Trapp was taken aback. "That's okay. That's nice of you but I've got that covered." His hate-filled rantings on the television cable access softened and eventually he made a return call to Weisser offering an apology. "I'm sorry I did that. I've been talking like that all my life ... I can't help it." Behind the hatred was an abused, frightened little boy whose father had beat him, called him "queer" and filled him with ethnic slurs. When Trapp was ten years old his father beat him into unconscious states. By the fourth grade, Trapp was an alcoholic with a mission to belittle others as he had been. About his reconciliation with the Weisser family, Julie Weisser gracefully stated, "Larry gave us as much as we gave him."[14]

As the world teeters on destruction from extremist Islamic groups, Western culture has begun to make the shift. Conferences against racism adorn university campuses and genocide studies programs are beginning to take form. Cities are adopting Hate-Free Zones. Anti-hate campaigns are beginning to take hold as well. The United Nations has declared March 21 the International Day for the Elimination of Racial Discrimination, commemorating the 1960 deadly Sharpeville, South Africa anti-apartheid protest. Subway and government billboards reminding people to Stop-the-Hate and that Racism-is-Uncool abound in Canada and Europe. British Columbia offers End-Racism awards to individuals who have performed outstanding work in that province. Universities such as Harvard incorporate an entire week to honor Dr. King's birthday and heighten multicultural awareness.

None of these actions would have occurred a decade or two earlier. We see how far we have come and acknowledge how far we have to go. To paraphrase Dr. King, we may not get there with you, but this and subsequent generations have to try.

A new understanding of hate generates more questions than answers. For instance, about a third of Glendale, California is ethnic Armenian. In deference to the Armenian genocide, the city council asked for the flag to be flown at half-mast on April 24. Veteran groups expressed opposition and cited the lowering of the flag for such a thing as anti-American. Turkish groups were up in arms. But the larger questions of social identity and political rights loom.

There are plenty of ways to stem hate but there are just as many politics involved at times. On February 24, 2005 the EU Justice and Interior ministers shelved proposals to ban the Nazi swastikas and later failed to agree on how such a ban could stem racism. Deluged by requests to ban additional symbols of repression (e.g. hammer and sickle), leaders from Britain, Denmark, Italy, and Hungary decided to drop the proposed ban. They were wrong. To not make forms of hate illegal, makes them legitimate in the eyes of the racist.

The UN Commission on Human Rights and NGO Conference on Racism illustrate other efforts to stem hate although the former currently includes multiple violating nations including Sudan, Syria, Algeria, Libya, and Saudi Arabia while the latter was marked with pro-Palestinian/anti-Israeli/antisemitic protest in September 2001. Democratic principles must be upheld to reverse the current theocratic and political trend.

Though there are some missed opportunities, others have not been missed. The United Nations International Criminal Tribunal for Rwanda sentenced three media executives to jail for broadcasting names and addresses of those who were to be killed. "Without a firearm, machete or any physical weapon, you caused the deaths of thousands of innocent civilians," reported the judge regarding RTML radio's culpability.

Many of the questions raised have to do with politics and policy, as we have seen. Should Americans tell others what to do about hate? What is to be done regarding hate-based madrassas, churches, or mosques? What is to be done about economic slavery, honor killings, and female genital mutilation? Why is it that most

White American adults still think of Martin Luther King's birthday as "those people's holiday" instead of as a day for celebrating civil rights?

Here is how one decides – universal psychological needs and democratic principles should supersede politics. For instance, no one claimed the Nazis were freedom fighters. Neither can we claim, in a postmodern world, that all fighting, including fighting to defend fundamentalism, fascism, or distorted thinking, carries equal weight and is justified.

When society protects rescuers and condemns persecutors, then all people within that society can function at their highest level of emotional development. When a culture supports all that is known to be good and kind and helpful, then no longer will anyone be confused into believing that the killing or persecution of the innocent is acceptable or just.

Some tentative conclusions

"Let me tell you the most important thing I learned about evil," says Paul Rusesabagina, the Hotel Rwanda manager.

> Evil is a big ugly hulking creature. It is a formidable enemy in a frontal attack. But it is not very smart and not very fast. You can beat it if you can slip around its sides. Evil can be frustrated by people you might think are weaklings.[15]

These so-called weaklings are emotionally the most highly developed members of society: the rescuers and the bystanders.

Research on those who are less prejudiced or nonprejudiced shows that such persons hear the same social myths, hateful remarks, and falsities and pay no attention. They see the same differences in people as racist people do but ignore those differences. They feel the same initial immature feelings that others do, but delay acting on them.

The perpetrators and remaining bystanders hate out of ignorance. They hate out of pain. They hate because they are mentally unbalanced and immature. They hate when they are stressed and scared. They hate when their egos aren't filled. They hate when they can get away with it.

And while there are perennial favorite objects of scorn, whom they hate doesn't seem to matter – new enemies are invented every day and old ones are revitalized. Reality rarely seems to matter – social perception does. The Darfurs and 9/11s will continue until we learn to rise above social perceptions.

On the other hand, some cultures appear to hate less. They are less competitive and seem to value cooperation – the exact opposite of perpetrators who honor cultures. They are all around the world. South America's Paori tribes are gentle. Malaysia's Semai are renowned for their peace. The Islamic Sufis dance and hold themselves in direct contrast to their Islamic fanatic brethren. Such cultures of kindness exist. But they are few, noncompetitive, slower moving, and materially impoverished.

Sometimes there are built-in mechanisms which minimize conflict. Ladahkis, Eskimos, Bhutanese, Tibetans, Tahitians, the Amish invoke multiple rules and beliefs to prevent aggression. For instance, the Dogon people of Mali, West Africa are known for their art and peaceful ways. Part of the reason they resolve conflict well is that there are structures for conflict resolution that are part of everyday life. For example, when two parties disagree, they sit with the village elders in a circle underneath a gazebo-like structure. The structure is wide enough to accommodate a fairly large group but is only three feet high. If one of the parties decides to walk off in a huff or stand to make his case, he cannot without bumping his head and forcing himself to sit back down. Once down, the elders continue to negotiate with the hothead until the differences are resolved.

South Africa's Bahemba tribe is reputed to have an even more interesting notion of reducing conflict, one person at a time. When an individual has acted irresponsibly, he or she is placed in the center of the village. All activity ceases as the village community gathers in a large circle around the accused individual. Then each one individually tells of the good things the person has done. The tribal ceremony may last for days, culminating in a joyous celebration as the accused is welcomed back into the tribe.

Psychoanalyst Erich Fromm called such lofty notions humanistic radicalism, but they should not be so lofty or so radical. In an emotionally developed world, kindness equates with strength and all rescuer qualities – compassion, courage and wisdom – would be esteemed. Whether humanitarian awards will ever achieve the same level of appreciation as the Oscars or the Olympics is uncertain though wise men from Fromm to Santayana have wished it so. Until then, we must work on resolving our psychological problems or, as Santayana warned, we are doomed to repeat history.

Programs that accentuate social group differences should be thwarted because of the nature of groups, viz. ethnocentrism, xenophobia, and social dominance. Multicultural programs should be encouraged. A case in point is Amsterdam where the city council proposed a major park to be named after Dr. King, and the decision was applauded. The park is not far from President Kennedy Street and Allende Street, as well as Anne Frank House, the Homo Monument and other symbols of freedom and justice. But multiculturalism cannot coexist with Muslim extremism, which creates a siege mentality and backlash.

There is an old Native American legend, which seems to capture the idea. The tale tells of a Cherokee teaching his grandson about life. "A fight is going on inside me," he says to the boy. "It is a terrible fight and it is between two wolves."

"One is evil – he is anger, envy, sorrow, regret, greed, arrogance, self-pity, guilt, resentment, inferiority, lies, false pride, superiority, and ego." He continued, "The other is good – he is joy, peace, love, hope, serenity, humility, kindness, benevolence, empathy, generosity, truth, compassion, and faith. The same fight is going on inside you – and inside every other person, too." The grandson thought about it for a minute and then asked his grandfather, "Which wolf will win?" The old Cherokee simply replied, "The one you feed."

Which one we feed depends on the willingness to take the emotional higher road. We have to become rescuers and that shift from social identity to personal identity must occur. It is the only direction to move beyond hate's frenzy to end the genocidal mindedness. I don't know if I answered Charlotte's question but she would have liked the direction – which is that the only way out is up.[16]

NOTES ON CHAPTER 6

1. B. Prince (2004) *I came as a stranger*. Markham Ontario Canada: Tundra; Antonia (1995) Antonia's Line. For Ahenakew's comments see www. jewishsf.com/content/2-0-/module/displaystory/story_id/19472/ edition_id/395/format/html/displaystory.html
2. B. Manz (2001) *A mind in prison*. Washington, DC: Potomoc.
3. M. Ignatieff (1998) *The warrior's honor*. New York: Metropolitan/Holt.
4. H.C. Kelman (2007) The Israeli–Palestinian peace process and its vicissitudes. *American Psychologist*, 62, 287–303, quote on p. 301.
5. V. Paley (1993) *You can't say, you can't play*. Cambridge, MA: Harvard University Press; I. W. Charny (2006) *Fascism and democracy in the human mind*. Lincoln, NE: University of Nebraska Press.
6. Maya Angelou on Oprah "People you'd love to have dinner with." Originally broadcast 1/2/96.
7. R. Ezekiel (1995) *The racist mind*. New York: Viking.
8. Diane Bock, see www.cuzz.org/oprah.php
9. Tammie Schnitzer, see www.tolerance.org/teach/magazine/features. jsp?cid=568.
10. www.splcentre.org;
11. B. Hamber (1998) The burdens of truth. *American Imago*, 55, 9–28.
12. For examples of freedom of speech abuses see Adam Sherwin's report on the "distorted" Channel 4 *Dispatches* episode called "Undercover Mosque" where both Muslims and non-Muslims had something to say on the matter. Alleging that the news story painted Muslims in an unflattering light, a preacher at Birmingham UK's Green Land mosque said: "If I were to call homosexuals perverted, dirty, filthy dogs who should be murdered, that is my freedom of speech, isn't it?" See "Muslim outrage at Channel 4 film prompts new inquiry by watchdog." *The Times* August 9, 2007, p. 24.

13. CNN. Original broadcast 4/20/01; Y. Tsouli (2007) A world wide web of terror. *The Economist*, July 14, pp. 28–30.
14. Michael Weisser, www.friendsacrossamerica.com/klansman.html. Also see Kathryn Watterson (1995) *Not by the sword*. New York: Simon & Schuster.
15. P. Rusesabagina (2006) *An ordinary man*. New York: Viking, p. 203.
16. Charlotte Guthmann-Opfermann, died on 22 November, 2004 in Houston and is entombed in her parents-in-law's grave in Mainz, Germany.

Index